Welcome to the EVERYTHING® series!

These handy, accessible books give you all you need to tackle a difficult project, gain a new hobby, comprehend a fascinating topic, prepare for an exam, or even brush up on something you learned back in school but have since forgotten.

FACTS
Important sound bytes
of information

You can read an *EVERYTHING®* book from cover-to-cover or just pick out the information you want from our four useful boxes: e-facts, e-ssentials, e-alerts, and e-questions. We literally give you everything you need to know on the subject, but throw in a lot of fun stuff along the way, too.

ESSENTIALS
Quick handy tips

We now have well over 100 *EVERYTHING®* books in print, spanning such wide-ranging topics as weddings, pregnancy, wine, learning guitar, one-pot cooking, managing people, and so much more. When you're done reading them all, you can finally say you know *EVERYTHING®*!

ALERT
Urgent warnings

QUESTIONS?
Solutions to
common problems

THE EVERYTHING® Series

Dear Reader,

Whether you are hoping to manage stress as a preventive or as a last-ditch effort, *The Everything® Stress Management Book* will show you how to recognize the kind of stress you have, or are likely to have soon. Then, this book will show you how to manage your stress, adjusting it to a level that is productive rather than counterproductive, by employing the stress management tools and techniques that appeal to you.

Believe me, I know about stress. I'm a single mom to two very active young boys and a writer with sporadic paychecks, living in a house that is in constant chaos. I'm always trying to turn in articles, write books, teach classes, go to PTO meetings, exercise, eat right, set a good example, and remain professional in front of colleagues—I look stress squarely in the face on an hourly basis.

But I've also got some powerful tools at my disposal. After coauthoring many books on intensive stress-reduction techniques like yoga, meditation, and some of the healthiest lifestyles in the world, I have embraced stress management as a lifestyle. Not as a hobby, or something to do when I have time, but as a number one priority. Stress management isn't "penciled in." For me, stress management has to come first or I won't be able to be a good parent, a competent worker, or a happy person. Thanks to stress management, I have learned to be all three.

In this book, I share those tools with you, walking you through the different ways you can make stress management work in your life. Of course you aren't exactly like me. You may be completely different. But I bet we both have a lot of stress in our lives. You can make stress management work for you, too.

So take a deep breath (a great stress reduction technique), jump in, and start reading. Know your stress to disarm it. Find your triggers and tendencies, then bit by bit, you can begin shaping and creating the kind of life you always dreamed you could live: a life efficiently managed, sleep that is satisfying, meals that feed your body and soul, relationships that are more fulfilling, better health, a daily sense of ease and well being, and yes, self-satisfaction. Stress management is the key.

May every one of your days be a little bit better, and a little less stressful, than the last.

Sincerely,

Eve Adamson

THE
EVERYTHING®

STRESS
MANAGEMENT
BOOK

Practical ways to relax,
be healthy, and maintain
your sanity

Eve Adamson

Adams Media Corporation
Avon, Massachusetts

EDITORIAL
Publishing Director: Gary M. Krebs
Managing Editor: Kate McBride
Copy Chief: Laura MacLaughlin
Development Editor: Michael Paydos

PRODUCTION
Production Director: Susan Beale
Production Manager: Michelle Roy Kelly
Series Designer: Daria Perreault
Layout and Graphics: Arlene Apone,
Paul Beatrice, Brooke Camfield,
Colleen Cunningham, Daria Perreault,
Frank Rivera

Produced by Amaranth.

An Everything® Series Book.
Everything® is a registered trademark of Adams Media Corporation.

Published by Adams Media Corporation
57 Littlefield Street, Avon, MA 02322. U.S.A.
www.adamsmedia.com

ISBN: 1-58062-578-9
Printed in the United States of America.

J I H G F E D C B A

Library of Congress Cataloging-in-Publication Data
Adamson, Eve.
The everything stress management book / by Eve Adamson.
p.   cm.
Includes bibliographical references and index.
ISBN 1-58062-578-9
1. Stress management–Popular works. I. Title.
RA785 .A335   2001
155.9'042–dc21   2001046318

This publication is designed to provide accurate and authoritative information with regard to the subject matter covered. It is sold with the understanding that the publisher is not engaged in rendering legal, accounting, or other professional advice. If legal advice or other expert assistance is required, the services of a competent professional person should be sought.
—From a *Declaration of Principles* jointly adopted by a Committee of the American Bar Association and a Committee of Publishers and Associations

Illustrations by Barry Littmann.

This book is available at quantity discounts for bulk purchases.
For information, call 1-800-872-5627.

Visit the entire Everything® series at everything.com

Contents

Introduction

So, you think you're stressed? At least you're in good company! Stress has become a national epidemic, but knowing everyone else around you is suffering as much as you are isn't much help when your muscles are tense, your mind is racing, your palms are sweaty, your stomach hurts, and you can't concentrate on any of the many items on your monumental to-do list.

Although you know what the experts say about stress, you don't have time for a bubble bath, you can't justify the expense of a weekly massage, you wouldn't know how to begin meditating, and, as far as a healthy diet and exercise are concerned, if you don't drive through for fast food on the way home, nobody in the family is going to get fed tonight. Is there hope for you?

Sure there is. You just need a little training in stress management, and you've come to the right place. This book will help you to sort through all the information floating around out there about what stress is, what it is doing to your health and happiness, and why you need to do something about it today. You'll find simple descriptions of many stress management techniques, from mindfulness to de-cluttering, from easy exercise suggestions to advice on how to finally get control of your finances.

You'll also find quizzes and prompts to help you explore your own tendencies for accumulating and reacting to stress, and personalized methods for managing the stress you call your own. You can keep track of your stress and of the effectiveness of different stress management techniques by using templates and a tip-filled stress management journal. It's all here.

You can manage your stress, and you don't have to do it alone. With a little guidance, inspiration, and a commitment to help yourself so that you can be your best possible self, you can be feeling better soon. So relax. Take a deep breath. Put your feet up on your desk and crack open this book. Stress doesn't stand a chance.

CHAPTER 1

Stress Unmasked

You know you're under stress when you rear-end the car in front of you on the way to work (oops!), make it to work three hours late and get fired (no!), then have your wallet stolen on the bus ride home (oh, that's just perfect!). But what about when you get engaged to the love of your life? Or, when you finally get the promotion of your dreams? What about when you have hay fever, or move into a new home, or adopt a dog? Is it stressful to graduate from college, or start an exercise program, or binge on chocolate chip cookies? You bet it is.

What Is Stress?

What's so stressful about a few chocolate chip cookies? Nothing, if you eat two chocolate chip cookies every day as part of a well-balanced diet. Plenty, if you deprive yourself of desserts for a month, then eat an entire bag of double fudge chocolate chunk. You aren't used to all those cookies. Your body isn't used to all that sugar. That's stressful. Not stressful like totaling your car or getting transferred to Siberia, but stressful nonetheless.

FACTS

According to the American Institute of Stress in Yonkers, New York, 43 percent of all adults suffer adverse health effects due to stress, and 75 percent to 90 percent of all visits to primary care physicians are for stress-related complaints or disorders.

In the same way, anything out of the ordinary that happens to you is stressful on your body. Some of that stress feels good. Even great. Without any stress at all, life would be a big bore. Stress isn't, by definition, something bad, but it certainly isn't always good, either. In fact, it can cause dramatic health problems if it happens to you too much and for too long.

Stress isn't just out-of-the-ordinary stuff, however. Stress can also be hidden and deeply imbedded in your life. What if you can't stand your job in middle management but continue to go there every day because you're afraid of starting your own business and giving up the regular paycheck? What if your family has serious communication problems, or if you live in a place where you don't feel safe? Maybe everything seems just fine, but nevertheless you feel deeply unhappy. Even when you are accustomed to certain things in your life—dirty dishes in the sink, family members that don't help you out, twelve-hour days at the office—those things can be stressful. You might even get stressed out when something goes right. Maybe someone is nice to you and you become suspicious, or you feel uncomfortable if your house is too clean. You are so used to things being difficult that you don't know how to adjust. Stress is a strange and highly individual phenomena.

Unless you live in a cave without a television (actually, not a bad way to eliminate stress in your life), you've probably heard quite a bit about stress in the media, around the coffee machine at work, or in the magazines and newspapers you read. Most people have a preconceived notion of what stress is in general, as well as what stress is to them. What does stress mean to you?

- Discomfort?
- Pain?
- Worry?
- Anxiety?
- Excitement?
- Fear?
- Uncertainty?

These things cause people stress and are mostly conditions stemming from stress. But what is stress itself? Stress is such a broad term, and there are so many different kinds of stress affecting so many people in so many different ways that the word *stress* may seem to defy definition. What is stressful to one person might be exhilarating to another. So, what exactly is stress?

Stress comes in several guises, some more obvious than others. Some stress is acute, some is episodic, and some is chronic. Let's take a closer look at each kind of stress and how it affects you.

When Life Changes: Acute Stress

Acute stress is the most obvious kind of stress, and it's pretty easy to spot if you associate it with one thing:

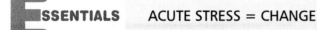

ESSENTIALS   ACUTE STRESS = CHANGE

Yep, that's all it is. Change. Stuff you're not used to. And that can include anything, from a change in your diet to a change in your exercise habits to a change in your job to a change in the people involved in your life, whether you've lost them or gained them.

In other words, acute stress is something that disturbs your body's equilibrium. You get used to things being a certain way, physically, mentally, emotionally, even chemically. Your body clock is set to sleep at certain times, your energy rises and falls at certain times, and your blood sugar changes in response to the meals you eat at certain times each day. As you go along your merry way in life, entrenched in your routines and habits and "normal" way of living, your body and your mind know pretty much what to expect.

ALERT

All of the following are stressful to your mind and body: serious illness (either yours or that of a loved one), divorce, bankruptcy, too much overtime at work, a promotion, the loss of a job, marriage, college graduation, and a winning lottery ticket.

But when something happens to *change* our existence, whether that something is a physical change (like a cold virus or a sprained ankle), a chemical change (like the side effects of a medication or the hormonal fluctuations following childbirth), or an emotional change (like a marriage, a child leaving the nest, or the death of a loved one), our equilibrium is altered. Our life changes. Our bodies and minds are thrown out of the routine they've come to expect. We've experienced change, and with that comes stress.

Acute stress is hard on our bodies and our minds because people tend to be creatures of habit. Even the most spontaneous and schedule resistant among us have our habits, and habits don't just mean enjoying that morning cup of coffee or sleeping on that favorite side of the bed. Habits include minute, complex, intricate interworkings of physical, chemical, and emotional factors on our bodies.

Say you get up and go to work five days each week, rising at 6:00 A.M., downing a bagel and a cup of coffee, then hopping on the subway. Once a year, you go on vacation, and, for two weeks, you sleep until 11:00 A.M., then wake up and eat a staggering brunch. That's stressful, too, because you've changed your habits. You probably enjoy it, and in some ways, a vacation can mediate the chronic stress of sleep deprivation. But if you are suddenly sleeping different hours and eating different things than usual, your body clock will have to readjust, your blood chemistry will have to readjust, and just when you've readjusted, you'll probably have to go back to waking up at 6:00 A.M. and foregoing the daily bacon and cheese omelets for that good old bagel, again.

That's not to say you shouldn't go on vacation. You certainly shouldn't avoid all change. Without change, life wouldn't be much fun. Humans desire and need a certain degree of change. Change makes life exciting and memorable. Change can be fun . . . up to a point.

Here's the tricky part: How much change you can stand before the changes start to have a negative effect on you is a completely individual issue. A certain amount of stress is good, but too much will start to become unhealthy, unsettling, and unbalancing. No single formula will calculate what "too much stress" is for everyone because the level of acute stress you can stand is likely to be completely different than the level of stress your friends and relatives can stand (although a low level of stress tolerance does appear to be inheritable).

ALERT

Pushing yourself to work too hard, staying up too late, eating too much (or too little), or worrying constantly is not only stressful on your mind but also stressful on your body. Many medical professionals believe that stress can contribute to heart disease, cancer, and an increased chance of accidents.

When Life Is a Roller Coaster: Episodic Stress

Episodic stress is like lots of acute stress—in other words, lots of life changes—all at once and over a period of time. People who suffer from episodic stress always seem to be in the throes of some tragedy. They tend to be overwrought, sometimes intense, often irritable, angry, or anxious.

If you've ever been through a week, a month, even a year when you seemed to suffer personal disaster after personal disaster, you know what it's like to be in the throes of episodic stress. First, your furnace breaks down, then you bounce a check, then you get a speeding ticket, then your entire extended family decides to stay with you for four weeks, then your sister-in-law smashes into your garage with her car, and then you get the flu. For some people, episodic stress becomes so drawn out a process that they become used to it; to others, the stress state is obvious. "Oh, that poor woman. She has terrible luck!" "Did you hear what happened to Jerry *this time*?"

Episodic stress, like acute stress, can also come in more positive forms. First, a whirlwind courtship, a huge wedding, a honeymoon in Bali, buying a new home, and moving in with your new spouse for the first time, all in the same year, is an incredibly stressful sequence of events. Fun, sure. Romantic, yes. Even thrilling. But still an excellent example of episodic stress in its sunnier, though no less stressful, manifestation.

Sometimes, episodic stress comes in a more subtle form—such as "worry." Worry is like inventing stress, or change, before it happens, even when it has little chance of happening. Excessive worry could be linked to an anxiety disorder, but even when worry is less chronic than that, it saps the body's energy, usually for no good reason.

Worry doesn't solve problems. Worry is usually just the contemplation of horrible things that are extremely unlikely to happen. Worry puts your body under stress by creating or imagining changes in the equilibrium of life—changes that haven't even happened!

Are you a worrywart? How many of the following describe you?

- You find yourself worrying about things that are extremely unlikely, such as suffering from a freak accident or developing an illness you have no reason to believe you would develop. (Think Woody Allen and his imaginary brain tumor.)
- You often lose sleep worrying about what would happen to you if you lost a loved one, or what would happen to your loved ones if he or she lost you.
- You have trouble falling asleep because you can't slow down your frantic worrying process as you lie still in bed at night.
- When the phone rings or the mail arrives, you immediately imagine what kind of bad news you are about to receive.

- You feel compelled to control the behaviors of others because you worry that they can't take care of themselves.
- You are overly cautious about engaging in any behavior that could possible result in harm or hurt to you or to those around you, even if the risk is small (such as driving a car, flying in an airplane, or visiting a big city).

If even just one of the worrywart characteristics describes you, you probably worry more than you have to. If most or all of these statements apply to you, worry is probably having a distinctly negative effect on you. Worry and the anxiety it can produce can cause specific physical, cognitive, and emotional symptoms, from heart palpitations, dry mouth, hyperventilation, muscle pain, and fatigue to fear, panic, anger, and depression. Worry is stressful.

ESSENTIALS

Like many other behaviors we think we can't control, worry is largely a matter of habit. So, how do you stop worrying? By retraining your brain! The next time you catch yourself worrying, get moving. It's hard to worry when your energy is directed toward following that exercise video or breathing in the fresh air as you run through the park.

When Life Stinks: Chronic Stress

Chronic stress is much different from acute stress, although its long-term effects are much the same. Chronic stress has nothing to do with change. Chronic stress is long-term, constant, unrelenting stress on the body, mind, or spirit. For example, someone living in poverty for years and years is under chronic stress. So is someone with a chronic illness such as arthritis or migraine headaches or other conditions that result in constant pain. Living in a dysfunctional family or working at a job you hate is a source of chronic stress. So is deep-seated self-hatred or low self-esteem.

Some people's chronic stress is obvious. They live in horrible conditions or have to endure terrible abuse. They are in prison, live in a war-torn country, or are a minority in a place where minorities suffer constant discrimination. Other chronic stress is less obvious. The person who despises her job and feels she can never accomplish her dreams is under chronic stress. So is the person who feels stuck in a bad relationship.

Sometimes, chronic stress is the result of acute or episodic stress. An acute illness can evolve into chronic pain. An abused child can grow up to suffer self-loathing or low self-esteem. The problem with chronic stress is that people become so used to it that they often can't begin to see how to get out of the situation. They come to believe life is supposed to be painful, stressful, or miserable.

All forms of stress can result in a downward spiral of illness, depression, anxiety, and breakdown, physical, emotional, mental, and spiritual. Too much stress is dangerous. It saps the joy out of life. It can even kill, whether through a heart attack, a violent act, suicide, a stroke, or, as some research suggests, cancer.

FACTS

According to a January 2001 article in *Time Magazine,* scientists have discovered that a sedentary forty-year-old woman who starts walking briskly for thirty minutes four times per week will have about the same low risk of heart attack as a woman who has exercised regularly for her entire life. It's never too late to start taking care of yourself!

Who Has It?

So, who is affected by all this stress? You? Your partner? Your parents? Your grandparents? Your kids? Your friends? Your enemies? The guy in the next cubicle? The woman in the elevator? The CEO? The people in the mailroom?

Yes.

Almost everyone has experienced some kind of stress, and many people experience chronic stress, or constant, regular stress, every day of their lives. Some people handle stress pretty well, even when it is extreme. Others fall apart under stress that seems negligible to the outside world. What's the difference? Some may have learned better coping mechanisms, but many researchers believe that people have an inherited level of stress tolerance. Some people can take a lot and still feel great and, in fact, do their best work under stress. Other people require very low-stress lives to function productively.

Nevertheless, we all experience stress some of the time, and these days, more and more people experience stress all of the time. The effects aren't just individualized, either. According to the American Institute of Stress in Yonkers, New York:

- An estimated 1 million people in the work force are absent on an average workday because of stress-related complaints.
- Nearly half of all American workers suffer from symptoms of burnout, or severe job-related stress that impairs or impedes functioning.
- Job stress costs U.S. industry $300 billion every year in absenteeism, diminished productivity, employee turnover, and direct medical, legal, and insurance fees.
- Between 60 percent and 80 percent of industrial accidents are probably due to stress.
- Workers' compensation awards for job stress, once rare, have become common. In California alone, employers paid almost $1 billion for medical and legal fees related to workers' compensation awards.
- Nine out of ten job stress suits are successful, with an average payout of more than four times the payout for injury claims.

Stress has become a way of life for many, but that doesn't mean we should sit back and accept the insidious effects of stress on our bodies, minds, and spirits. While you probably can't do much about the stress experienced by others (unless you're the cause of the stress), you can certainly tackle the stress in your own life (and that's a good way to stop being stressful to others!).

Chronic stress can trick our bodies into thinking they are in equilibrium. Even if something becomes part of your daily routine and you think your body has adjusted to, say, working late, eating junk food, or not getting enough sleep, the stress of not giving your body what it requires will eventually catch up with you.

Where Does It Come From?

Stress can come from inside. It can be caused by your perception of events, rather than by the events themselves. A job transfer might be a horrible stress to one person, a magnificent opportunity to another. A lot depends on attitude.

But even when the stress is undeniably external—say, all your money was just embezzled—stress affects a host of changes inside your body. More specifically, stress in all its many forms interferes with the body's production of three very important hormones that help you feel balanced and "normal":

1. *Serotonin* is the hormone that helps you get a good night's sleep. Produced in the pineal gland deep inside your brain, serotonin controls your body clock by converting into melatonin and then converting back into serotonin over the course of a twenty-four-hour day. This process regulates your energy, body temperature, and sleep cycle. The serotonin cycle synchronizes with the cycle of the sun, regulating itself according to exposure to daylight and darkness, which is why some people who are rarely exposed to the sun, such as those in northern climates, experience seasonal depression during the long, dark winter months—their serotonin production gets out of whack. Stress can throw it out of whack, too, and one result is the inability to sleep well. People under stress often experience a disturbed sleep cycle, manifesting itself as insomnia or an excessive need to sleep because the sleep isn't productive.

2. *Noradrenaline* is a hormone produced by your adrenal glands, related to the adrenaline that your body releases in times of stress to give you that extra chance at survival. Noradrenaline is related to your daily cycle of energy. Too much stress can disrupt your body's production of noradrenaline, leaving you with a profound lack of energy and motivation to do anything. It's that feeling you get when you just want to sit and stare at the television, even though you have a long list of things you absolutely have to do. If your noradrenaline production is disrupted, you'll probably just keep sitting there, watching television. You simply won't have the energy to get anything done.

3. *Dopamine* is a hormone linked to the release of endorphin in your brain. Endorphin is that stuff that helps kill pain. Chemically, it is related to opiate substances like morphine and heroin, and, if you are injured, your body releases endorphin to help you function. When stress compromises your body's ability to produce dopamine, it also compromises your body's ability to produce endorphins, so you become more sensitive to pain. Dopamine is responsible for that wonderful feeling you get from doing things you enjoy. It makes you feel happy about life itself. Too much stress, too little dopamine, and nothing seems fun or pleasurable anymore. You feel flat. You feel depressed.

ESSENTIALS

Stress can disrupt your body's production of serotonin, noradrenaline, and dopamine. When the disruption of these chemicals results in depression, a physician may prescribe an antidepressant medication. Many antidepressant medications are designed specifically to regulate the production of serotonin, noradrenaline, and dopamine to re-establish the body's equilibrium. If stress management techniques don't work for you, you may require medication. See your doctor.

So, as you can see, stress comes from the inside as well as the outside. Your perception of events and the influences (such as health habits) on your body and mind actually cause chemical changes within your body. Anybody who ever doubted the intricate connection of the mind and body need only look at what happens when people feel stress and worry. It's all connected. (And therein lies a clue to what you can do about stress!)

When Do You Get It?

Because there are so many forms of stress, stress can happen at any time. Stress is obvious when you experience a major life change, so expect stress when you move, lose someone you love, get married, change jobs, or experience a big change in financial status, diet, exercise habits, or health.

But you can also expect stress when you get a minor cold, have an argument with a friend, go on a diet, join a gym, stay out too late, drink too much, or even stay home with your kids all day when school is cancelled due to that irritating blizzard. Remember, stress often results from any kind of change in your normal routine. It also results from living a life that doesn't make you happy; if that is you, your whole life may be one long stress session. You need stress management now!

FACTS

Americans don't tend to take care of themselves, which results in stress on the body. Nearly 50 million Americans smoke. More than 60 percent are obese or overweight. One in four gets no exercise at all. According to the Center for Disease Control in Atlanta, Georgia, the incidence of adult-onset (Type 2) diabetes has jumped almost 40 percent since 1990.

Why, Why, Why?

Why stress? What's the point? Stress is a relatively complex interaction of external and internal processes caused by something relatively simple: the survival instinct. And that's important, even today!

Life is full of stimuli. We enjoy some of it. We don't enjoy some of it. But our bodies are programmed, through millions of years of learning how to survive, to react in certain ways to stimulus that is extreme. We've evolved so that if you should suddenly find yourself in a dangerous situation—you step in front of a speeding car, you lose your balance and teeter on the edge of a cliff, you call your boss a troglodyte when he is standing right behind you—your body will react in a way that will best ensure your survival. You might move extra fast. You might pitch yourself back to safety. You might think fast and talk your way out of trouble.

Whether you are being chased around the savanna by a hungry lion or around the parking lot by an aggressive car salesman, your body recognizes an alarm and pours stress hormones such as adrenaline and cortisol into your bloodstream. Adrenaline produces what scientists call the "fight or flight" response (which will be discussed further in the next chapter). It gives you an extra boost of strength and energy so that you can turn around and fight that lion, if you think you will win (you're probably better off pitted against the car salesman), or so that you can run like the dickens (also effective against car salesmen).

Adrenaline increases your heart rate and your breathing rate and sends blood straight to your vital organs so that they can work better—faster muscle response, quicker thinking, and so on. It also helps your blood to clot faster and draws blood away from your skin (if you should suffer a swipe of the lion's claw, you won't bleed as much) and also from your digestive tract (so you won't throw up—no, it doesn't always work). And cortisol flows through your body to keep the stress response responding as long as the stress continues.

Even back in the caveman days, people weren't being chased by hungry lions all day long, every day, for weeks on end (or, if they were, they really should have considered moving to a different cave). Such extreme physical reactions aren't meant to occur all the time. They are undeniably helpful during emergencies and other extreme situations, including fun situations like performing in a play or giving the toast at your best friend's wedding. The stress reaction can help you think more quickly, react more accurately, and respond with clever, witty repartee or just the right joke to keep the audience entranced by your sparkling performance.

ALERT

If your life seems stressful even though nothing is different than usual, chances are the culprit is sleep deprivation. Even if your serotonin cycle isn't so disrupted that you *can't* sleep, plenty of people simply *don't* sleep because they stay up late watching television. Most people really do need seven to eight hours of sleep to feel refreshed and to handle normal stress with aplomb.

But if you were to experience the constant release of adrenaline and cortisol every day, eventually the feeling would get tiresome, quite literally. You'd start to experience exhaustion, physical pain, a decrease in your ability to concentrate and remember, frustration, irritability, insomnia, possibly even violent episodes. Your body would become out of balance because we aren't designed to be under stress all the time.

But these days, life moves so quickly, technology allows us to do ten times more in a fraction of the time, and everybody wants everything yesterday, so stress happens. But too much stress will negate the effects of all that great technology—you won't get any work done if you have no energy, no motivation, and keep getting sick.

So, How Do You Get Rid of It?

You may not feel like the stress in your life is quite so bad just yet. You aren't on the verge of a heart attack or a nervous breakdown . . . are you?

But what will happen if you don't begin to manage your stress right now? How long will you allow stress to compromise your quality of life, especially knowing you don't have to let it? That's where stress management comes in, and stress management is the focus of this book.

As pervasive as stress may be in all its forms, stress management techniques that really work are equally pervasive. You *can* manage, even eliminate, the negative stress in your life. All you have to do is find the stress management techniques that work best for you. Learn them and turn your life around.

And that's the point of this book. You'll learn all about stress management in its many forms so that you can design a stress management program that works for you.

CHAPTER 2

What Is Stress Doing to Me?

We have lots of ways to describe the feelings of stress. Keyed up, wound up, geared up, fired up—all those expressions contain the word *up* because the stress response is, indeed, an "up" kind of experience. Muscles are pumped for action, senses are heightened, awareness is sharpened. And these feelings are useful, until they become too frequent. Constant stress exacts a heavy toll on the mind, body, and emotional well-being. Your health and happiness depend on responding to stress appropriately.

Stress on Your Body

You can control some of the stresses on your body; for example, you can determine how much you eat and how much you exercise. These stresses fall into the physiological stressor category. Then, there are environmental stressors, such as environmental pollution and substance addiction.

1. *Environmental stressors.* These are things in your immediate environment that put stress on your physical body. These include air pollution, polluted drinking water, noise pollution, artificial lighting, bad ventilation, or the presence of allergens in the field of ragweed outside your bedroom window or in the dander of the cat who likes to sleep on your pillow.

2. *Physiological stressors.* These are the stressors within your own body that cause stress. For example, hormonal changes that occur during pregnancy or menopause put direct physiological stress on your system, as does premenstrual syndrome (PMS). Hormonal changes may also cause indirect stress because of the emotional changes they cause. Also, bad health habits such as smoking, drinking too much, eating junk food, or being sedentary put physiological stress on your body. So does illness, whether it's the common cold or something more serious like heart disease or cancer. Injury also puts stress on your body—a broken leg, a sprained wrist, and a slipped disk are all stressful.

One of the most common reactions to stress is compulsive eating. The best way to handle your temporary weakness is to find a healthier way to deal with your stressful feelings. A large glass of water, a walk around the block, or a phone call to a friend might be just what you need. Just remember, you can control your life.

Just as potent but less direct are stressors that impact your body by way of your mind. For example, getting caught in heavy traffic may stress your body directly because of the air pollution it creates, but it may also stress your body indirectly because you get so worked up and irritated sitting in your car in the middle of a traffic jam that your blood pressure rises, your muscles tense, and your heart beats faster. If you were to interpret the traffic jam differently—say, as an opportunity to relax and listen to your favorite CD before getting to work—your body might not experience any stress at all. Again, attitude plays a major role.

Pain is another, trickier example of indirect stress. If you have a terrible headache, your body may not experience direct physiological stress, but your emotional reaction to the pain might cause your body significant stress. People tend to be fearful of pain, but pain is an important way to let us know something is wrong. Pain can signal injury or disease. However, sometimes we already know what's wrong. We get migraines, or have arthritis, or experience menstrual cramps, or a bad knee acts up when the weather changes. This kind of "familiar" pain isn't useful in terms of alerting us to something that needs immediate medical attention.

But because we know we are in some form of pain, we still tend to get tense. "Oh no, not another migraine! No, not today!" Our emotional reaction doesn't cause the pain, but it does cause the physiological stress associated with the pain. Pain in itself isn't stressful. Our reaction to pain is what causes stress. So, learning stress management techniques may not stop pain, but it can stop the physiological stress associated with pain.

ESSENTIALS

Therapies designed to help people manage chronic pain counsel patients to explore the difference between pain and the negative interpretation of pain. People living with chronic pain learn meditation techniques for entering and confronting pain apart from the brain's interpretation of the pain as a source of suffering.

When your body is experiencing this stress response, whether caused by direct or indirect physiological stressors, it undergoes some very specific changes. Around the beginning of the twentieth century, physiologist Walter B. Cannon coined the phrase "fight or flight" to describe the biochemical changes stress invokes in the body, preparing it to flee or confront danger more safely and effectively. These are the changes that happen in your body every time you feel stressed, even if running away or fighting aren't relevant or wouldn't help you (for example, if you're about to give a speech, take a test, or confront your mother-in-law about her constant unsolicited advice, neither fight nor flight are very helpful responses).

Here's what happens inside your body when you feel stress:

1. Your cerebral cortex sends an alarm message to your hypothalamus, the part of your brain that releases the chemicals that create the stress response. Anything your brain *perceives* as stress will cause this effect, whether or not you are in any real danger.
2. Your hypothalamus releases chemicals that stimulate your sympathetic nervous system to prepare for danger.
3. Your nervous system reacts by raising your heart rate, respiration rate, and blood pressure. Everything gets turned "up."
4. Your muscles tense, preparing for action. Blood moves away from the extremities and your digestive system, into your muscles and brain. Blood sugars are mobilized to travel to where they will be needed most.
5. Your senses get sharper. You can hear better, see better, smell better, taste better. Even your sense of touch becomes more sensitive.

That sounds like a way to get things done, doesn't it? Imagine the high-powered executive, stunning clients with an on-target presentation and sharp, clever answers to every question. Imagine the basketball player at the championship game, making every shot. Imagine the student acing that final exam, every answer coming immediately to mind, the perfect words pouring from the pen for that A+ essay. Imagine yourself at the next office party, clever and funny, attracting crowds that hang on your every word. Stress can be great! No wonder it's addictive.

ESSENTIALS   You can make yourself relax by associating relaxation with a cue. Get comfortable, breathe deeply, and repeat a word or sound that has positive associations (for example, "love," "yellow," "ahhh") out loud for one minute as you concentrate on relaxing. Do it several times every day for a week. Then, try saying the word whenever you feel stress mounting. Feel your body relax automatically!

But the downside is that stress, while beneficial in moderate amounts, is harmful in excessive amounts, as are most things. More specifically, stress can cause problems in different systems all over your body. Some problems are immediate, like digestive trouble or a racing heartbeat. Other problems are more likely to occur the longer you are under stress. Some of stress's less desirable symptoms, directly related to the increase in adrenaline in the body, include the following:

- Sweating
- Cold extremities
- Nausea, vomiting, diarrhea
- Muscle tension
- Dry mouth
- Confusion
- Nervousness, anxiety
- Irritability, impatience
- Frustration
- Panic
- Hostility, aggression

Long-term effects of stress can be even harder to correct, and include such things as depression, loss or increase of appetite resulting in undesirable weight changes, frequent minor illnesses, increased aches and pains, sexual problems, fatigue, loss of interest in social activities, increased addictive behavior, chronic headaches, acne, chronic backaches, chronic stomachaches, and worsened symptoms associated with medical conditions such as asthma and arthritis.

Brain Stress

We already know that stress causes your cerebral cortex to begin a process that results in the release of chemicals to prepare your body to handle danger. But what else goes on in your brain when you are under too much stress? At first, you think more clearly and respond more quickly. But after you've reached your stress tolerance point, your brain begins to malfunction. You forget things. You lose things. You can't concentrate. You lose your willpower and indulge in bad habits like drinking, smoking, or eating too much.

FACTS

Many people in their forties and fifties begin to experience increased forgetfulness and fear they are developing Alzheimer's disease. In most cases, increased forgetfulness is actually linked to stress, which is often at its peak for those parenting teenagers and experiencing career and relationship changes.

The production of the chemicals from the stress response that make the brain react more quickly and think more sharply are directly related to the depletion of others that, under too much stress, keep you from thinking effectively or reacting quickly. At first, the answers to the test were coming to you without hesitation. However, three hours into the test and you can barely remember which end of the pencil you are supposed to use to fill in those endless little circles. To keep your brain working at its optimal level on a daily basis, you can't allow stress to overwhelm your circuits!

Tummy Trouble

One of the first things that happens when the body undergoes the stress response is that blood is diverted away from your digestive tract to your large muscles. Stomach and intestines may empty their contents, preparing the body for quick action. Many people experiencing stress, anxiety, and nervousness also experience stomach cramps, nausea, vomiting, or diarrhea. (Doctors used to call this "a nervous stomach." Indeed!)

Long-term episodic or chronic stress has been linked to a number of digestive maladies, from irritable bowel syndrome and colitis to ulcers and chronic diarrhea.

Cardiovascular Connection

If your heart races or skips a beat when you are nervous or have enjoyed a few too many cups of coffee or cans of cola, you know what it feels like to have your heart affected by stress. But stress can do much more to inhibit the activity of your entire cardiovascular system. Some scientists believe stress contributes to hypertension (high blood pressure), and, for decades, people have advised the nervous, anxious, irritable, or pessimistic among them that they'll work themselves into a heart attack. In fact, people who are more likely to see events as stressful do seem to have an increased rate of heart disease.

Stress can also contribute to bad health habits that in turn can contribute to heart disease. A high-fat, high-sugar, low-fiber diet (the fast-food, junk-food syndrome) contributes to fat in the blood and, eventually, a clogged, heart-attack-prone heart. Coupled with lack of exercise, the risk factors for heart disease increase. All because you were too stressed out to eat a salad and go for that walk (day after day after day)!

ALERT

Polluting your body with too much saturated fat and highly processed, low-fiber food has a direct effect on health. Just as a polluted river soon cleans itself when the pollution stops, so will your coronary arteries begin to clear out if the body is freed from having to process foods that are damaging to good health.

Stressed-out Skin

Skin problems such as acne are usually related to hormonal fluctuations, which in turn can be exacerbated by stress. Many women in their thirties and forties experience acne during a particular time in their monthly menstrual cycle and despair over the "breakout." Stress can extend the length of time these skin flare-ups occur, and a compromised, stressed-out immune system can result in an increased amount of time to repair the damage.

Men aren't immune, either. Stress can cause chemical imbalances that can cause or worsen adult acne in men. Teenagers, undergoing dramatic hormonal fluctuations just because they are adolescent, are prone to acne anyway, but stressed-out teens may have a much more difficult time getting acne under control. Remember getting that big pimple right before your first date? It's no coincidence. That's stress.

Long-term stress can lead to chronic acne. And it can contribute to psoriasis, hives, and other forms of dermatitis.

Chronic Pain

An impaired immune system and increased sensitivity to pain can worsen conditions that include chronic pain. Migraines, arthritis, fibromyalgia, multiple sclerosis, degenerative bone and joint diseases, and old injuries all feel worse when the body is under stress. Stress management techniques as well as pain management techniques can help ease chronic pain, but they also help the mind deal with pain so the pain doesn't make the stress worse.

Stress and Your Immune System

In what way does stress compromise the immune system's effectiveness? When the body's equilibrium is disturbed due to the long-term release of stress hormones and its associated imbalances, the immune system can't work efficiently. Imagine trying to finish an important proposal during an earthquake!

FACTS

Many studies reveal that self-healing, symptom relief, and a strengthened immune system in patients given a placebo such as a sugar pill, suggesting that the brain has amazing healing powers. And other studies suggest that patients can use this power consciously to help themselves heal.

Under optimal conditions, the immune system is much more able to help the body heal itself. However, when conditions are not optimal, some believe guided meditation or focused inner reflection can help the conscious mind perceive what the immune system requires the body to do to facilitate healing. While some doubt such intra-body experiences, the mind-body interaction is far from understood. Testimonial evidence is widespread that managing stress and listening to the body are essential elements in the promotion of self-healing.

The Stress–Disease Connection

While not every expert agrees on which diseases are linked to stress and which to other factors such as bacteria or genetics, an increasing number of scientists and others believe that the interrelatedness of the body and mind means that stress can contribute to, if not cause, almost any physical problem. Conversely, physical illness and injury can contribute to stress.

The result is a whirlpool of stress–disease–more stress–more disease, which can ultimately cause serious damage to the body, mind, and spirit. The "which came first" question may be irrelevant, and quibbling about which conditions are caused by stress and which are not may be irrelevant as well. Managing stress–whether it caused physical problems or resulted from them–will put the body into a more balanced state, and a body that is more balanced is in a better position to heal itself. It will also help the mind to deal with physical injury or illness, reducing suffering. Stress management may not heal you, but it will make your life more enjoyable. Then again, it may help to heal you, after all.

That being said, please remember that stress management techniques should never be used in place of competent medical care. Stress management is best used as a complement to the care you are already receiving–or should seek–for your physical illness or injury. Follow the advice of your doctor, and give your body's natural healing mechanisms an extra boost by getting debilitating stress out of the way.

Stress on Your Mind

Stress also can cause or be caused by a variety of mental and emotional conditions. Working too hard, pushing yourself too far, spreading yourself too thin, taking on too much, or living in a state of unhappiness or anxiety is incredibly stressful. Like physical stress, mental stress makes life difficult, and the harder things are, the more stress they cause. You are caught in another downward spiral.

Perhaps you are experiencing difficulties in a personal relationship. This is stressful, but rather than deal with the problem (the problem may seem like it has no solution), you throw yourself into your job, working long hours and taking on many additional projects. This new obsession with work adds more stress to your life, as do the long hours, the lost sleep, and the poor dietary habits you've developed. Your body begins to suffer, and so does your mind. At first, you may find you have an extra edge at work because you are channeling the energy from your personal stress into your work. But, eventually, you will reach your stress tolerance point. Your mind will suffer a lack of good judgment. You won't be able to concentrate. You won't be able to pay attention. You'll get extra emotional, or irritable, or both. You'll begin to think badly of your work performance, and of yourself. Frustration, anxiety, panic, or depression will set in.

ALERT

Don't get caught in stress's vicious circle. If you feel stressed by an event that is supposed to be positive, the guilt or confusion you may feel about your stress will make the stress worse. Try to see your stress for what it is—that is, a natural human reaction to change.

Mental stress comes in lots of forms. Social stressors include pressure from work; an impending important event; relationship problems such as with a spouse, child, or parent; or the death of a loved one. Any major change in life can result in mental stress, depending on how the mind interprets the event, and even when an event is positive—a marriage, a graduation, a new job, a Caribbean cruise—the changes it involves, even if temporary, can be overwhelming.

Mental stress can result in low self-esteem, a negative outlook on life, cynicism, or the desire for isolation, as the mind attempts to justify and, in any way possible, stop the stress. If you've ever had an extremely stressful week and want nothing more than to spend the entire weekend alone in bed with a good book and the remote control, you've experienced the mind attempting to regain its equilibrium. Too much activity and change can create a desire for zero activity and reversion to comfortable,

familiar rituals. (After a fight with your best friend, an ice cream sundae just hits the spot.)

If you allow stress to continue for too long, you could suffer burnout, losing all interest in your job as your lack of control increases. You could begin to experience panic attacks, severe depression, or even a nervous breakdown, which is a temporary state of mental illness that could occur suddenly or slowly over a long period of time.

Mental stress can be insidious because you can ignore it more easily than you can ignore a physical illness. Yet, it is just as powerful and just as harmful to the body and to your life. Ferreting out your sources of mental stress is an important key to managing your stress. Life will become more enjoyable when you observe your mental as well as your physical stress tolerance level.

ESSENTIALS Signs of burnout include loss of interest, joy, and motivation in life; an escalating sense of a loss of control; constant negative thinking; detachment from personal or work relationships; and a loss of focus and life purpose.

Stress on Your Spirit

Spiritual stress is more nebulous. It can't be measured directly, but it remains a potent and harmful form of stress that is inextricably linked to physical and mental stress. What is spiritual stress? It is the neglect of and the eventual loss of our spiritual lives, or the part of us that hopes, loves, dreams, plans, and reaches for something greater and better in humanity and in life. It is the noncorporeal in us, the soul. Whether or not you have religious beliefs, you still have a spiritual side. Think of it as the part of you that can't be measured, calculated, or wholly explained—the you that makes you *you*.

When we ignore our spiritual side, we throw our bodies out of balance. When our spiritual lives are further compromised because of the effects of physical and mental stress—low self-esteem, anger, frustration, pessimism, the destruction of relationships, the loss of creativity, hopelessness, fear—we can lose the energy and joy of life.

ESSENTIALS

Signs of a nervous breakdown include personality changes, uncontrolled behavior, irrational thinking, excessive anxiety, obsessive behavior, manic or depressive behavior, severe depression, uncontrolled outbreaks of emotion or violence, severing of relationships, engaging in illegal acts, developing addictions, attempting suicide, or the onset of mental illness like schizophrenia.

Have you ever known someone who when faced with insurmountable obstacles, pain, trauma, tragedy, or loss continues to be happy? Such people have nurtured and nourished their spiritual sides, either through effort or because it comes naturally.

Sure, some people don't buy into the idea that people have a spiritual side or a soul. It's all chemical, they say. Others of us prefer to say it's all related, all intertwined like a dramatic and intricate web. The bottom line? If you manage your stress with the whole you in sight, you'll manage stress fully, effectively, and in a way that really works for your unique self. Preserve, cherish, and nurture every segment of silk in the web of your self; if you do so, you will preserve the miraculous artistry of you, no matter what you happen to label all the different parts.

CHAPTER 3

Stress and Your Self-Esteem

Stress and self-esteem are intricately linked in the same way that stress is linked to your physical and mental health. Not only does low self-esteem make you more vulnerable to stress, but chronic stress of all kinds—physical, emotional, environmental, social, personal, and so on—can profoundly impact your self-esteem.

The Stress/Self-Esteem Cycle

Let's look at how stress can subtly undermine your self-esteem. While it's often hard to pinpoint where the cycle begins, imagine for a moment that you've had a very stressful day. (Maybe you don't have to imagine!) It seems like everything has gone wrong. You smacked your shin on the bottom step. You spilled coffee on your jacket on your way out the door. Your car wouldn't start. And then, at work, your boss dumped a project on you that will make the next two months extremely difficult. You envision many long nights ahead. You have to miss lunch. A colleague tells you that you "look terrible." Then, when you get home at the end of the day, you scrap your plans to go to the gym and you order a pizza and eat the whole thing. Then, you feel guilty. You feel bad about skipping your exercise, about giving in to junk food, about eating way too much. You feel so guilty that you make yourself an ice cream sundae and stay up late watching TV. Forget the dishes.

In the morning, you wake up puffy and lacking energy. A messy kitchen greets you, you go to work exhausted, and you've got all the same stress you had the day before. So, the cycle continues. You keep overeating, undersleeping, and not doing anything about the things that are causing your stress, whatever they are—maybe because you don't have the energy, and maybe because you have no idea what you could possibly do about it. Instead, you begin to feel worse and worse about yourself because you are so tired, so overwhelmed, and so unable to exercise your willpower. The worse you feel about yourself, the more you are likely to continue in the destructive pattern.

QUESTIONS?

What do you see when you look in the mirror?
Most people focus on external features first, but gazing at your reflection in a mirror can be a form of meditation. Gaze into your eyes, deeper and deeper until you no longer recognize your features but the self behind the eyes. This is both an exercise for relieving stress through focus and a technique for pursuing self-knowledge.

Of course, this is just one example. Stress from a chronic condition like arthritis, multiple sclerosis, or chronic fatigue syndrome can take a heavy toll on your self-esteem. You wonder why you can't do all the things other people can do. You get so weary of feeling badly that you don't enjoy yourself anymore. Self-satisfaction seems a distant memory. Likewise, stress that doesn't allow you any personal time makes you feel like you aren't important enough for personal time, or that everyone else is more important than you are. Stress that keeps your mind racing and scattered can make you feel like you aren't capable of focus.

ALERT

The stress cycle works in both directions. Stress can cause low self-esteem, but low self-esteem can be a major contributor to your stress level. If you don't feel good about yourself, lack confidence, or doubt your ability to succeed, you'll be more likely to let stress overwhelm you.

So, what are you supposed to do about this insidious cycle? Solutions are often difficult to come by, especially since the problems don't seem to begin anywhere in particular. How do you jump in and slam on the brakes? By jumping in and slamming on the brakes, that's how!

Build Self-Esteem by Demolishing Excess Stress

The first step in breaking the stress/self-esteem cycle is to isolate something you can do something about. It doesn't have to have anything to do with self-esteem. It's important to start with one thing, since one of the characteristic conditions of stress is a lack of focus. If you have so many things going on in your life that you feel overwhelmed, you probably know what it is like to wander around in a daze, unable to do any of them. Maybe you do a little of one project but then get distracted by the pressing deadline of another project, so you do a little of that one but once again are distracted by something else that needs attention. Before you know it, another day is gone and nothing has been finished.

So, to repeat, the best way to take action to break the cycle is to choose one single thing you can do something about, something you can finish. Yes, lots of other things need finishing, but they aren't going to get finished anyway as long as you are feeling the way you are feeling. You know it's true! The only way to make a difference is to focus.

The way you choose to focus is up to you. It might require getting one thing accomplished on your to-do list—accomplished *all the way*. Or, it might involve some enforced personal time. Meditation might be what it takes to stop that horrible incessant buzzing in your head that is interfering with your productivity and making you feel so rotten about yourself.

What you choose to do also depends on the kind of stress that is overwhelming you. Let's look at some of your options for conquering stress in a way that at the same time specifically helps you to fortify your self-esteem. Let's also look at how each strategy might be used most effectively.

FACTS

Think of all the ways you could waste thirty minutes each day. Watching television. Waiting in line at the drive-through. Surfing the Internet. Throwing a ball against the wall. Eating something you know you shouldn't be eating. Worrying. Talking on the phone. Being irritated at somebody who cut you off in traffic. Thinking about how much you have to do. Just think how much better thirty minutes could be spent doing any of the things listed in this chapter!

Your Self-Esteem–Building Strategies: Point A to Point B

The act of eliminating excess stress in your life builds self-esteem simply by virtue of the fact that the elimination of stress makes you feel better. Thus, all of the stress management strategies in this book have the potential to build self-esteem. And working through those strategies with the specific purpose of building self-esteem can make them work even faster. And remember, you have to finish. You have to start at point A and work all the way to point B without stopping or getting distracted.

None of these strategies take more than thirty minutes, so you don't have any excuse not to do them. Anybody can spare thirty minutes out of a busy day in the name of feeling better and becoming more efficient. Isn't feeling better about who you are and how you are spending your life worth at least thirty minutes of your day?

Take a Reflection Walk

This strategy is for people who (a) don't get enough exercise on most days and (b) tend to worry too much or mentally obsess about negative things in their lives. You know who you are! A reflection walk is a way to proactively take control of your physical and your mental state, at the same time, for one short, thirty-minute period. If you worry all day, sit at a desk all day, or feel rotten all day, then you need a daily reflection walk, and you need it badly. Even you can pretend to be an active optimist for thirty minutes. You may have to pretend at first, but eventually, subtly, the effects of your reflection walk will begin to take hold.

ESSENTIALS

If you don't have a good (pleasant, safe) place to walk in your neighborhood or if the weather is rotten, have a walking backup plan, such as the track, the gym, or the mall.

Although, as you know, exercise helps relieve stress, a reflection walk can help relieve stress and make you feel better about yourself at the same time. This is what you do: First, put on comfortable walking shoes and comfortable clothes that will "work" for moderate exercise and also make you feel good about yourself. In other words, let your criteria be to dress so that if you happen to meet someone you know, you won't feel self-conscious about what you are wearing. Brush or comb your hair. Wash your face, put on some sunscreen, and, if it makes you feel more human, put on some makeup. Go to the front door and take five deep, full breaths. Then, out loud, say: "I'm ready to reflect upon all the good things in my life."

Then, out the door you go! Walk for thirty minutes at a moderate pace—just fast enough to feel as though you are getting some exercise but not enough to wear you out or make you frustrated or your muscles sore. As you walk, continue to take deep breaths and, most importantly, begin your mental list of all the things that are good about your life. Here are some questions you might consider:

- What is working?
- What parts of your life make you feel great?
- Who are the people in your life that make your life better?
- Whom do you love?
- What do you like about yourself?
- What are some of your fondest memories?
- Where do you love to go?
- What are your favorite things to do?
- What foods make you feel really good?
- What is your favorite book?
- What is it that you love about your home, your pets, your car, and your job?
- In what areas of your life are you successful?

E̲SSENTIALS

Don't undermine your own efforts at building up your self-esteem by telling yourself that any accomplishment isn't worth celebrating. If you, say, finally balanced the checkbook, or vacuumed, or turned off the TV last night earlier than you normally would have, that's great! Or, maybe you didn't eat that bag of cookies or spend that $50 on stuff you don't need. You can and should feel good about things like that!

You can get as general as "I love my kids" or as specific as "I set up a system for paying my bills on time that works really well." If you are having trouble focusing or thinking of things, set a goal, such as adding one item to your mental list for every twenty-five steps or for every five breaths. If you get stuck, stop until you think of something, then move on.

The challenge of the reflection walk is to put aside for the thirty minutes all the things that aren't working, the negativity, the things you think you should be doing. After the walk is over, you can get back to work, but put all your stressful thoughts aside for now. They'll still be there when you get back, but they may not seem quite so overwhelming, once you've put them in perspective. After a reflection walk, your life will probably look a lot better, and you'll feel a lot better about yourself, too.

Clean Your Kitchen Sink

② If you are housecleaning-challenged, and if the state of messiness in your house is often directly related to your level of stress, then I have the Web site for you. This Web site can transform the life of anyone who feels they are incapable of getting their housecleaning under control—which is something that can severely undermine your self-esteem but which is a condition of life for thousands of people. If you are one of them, you must go to *www.flylady.net*. Read everything on there, and keep reading. Sign up for the daily reminders and read them until, suddenly, they begin to work.

This Web site contains a complete system for getting your house—and, by association, your life—in order, even if you've never been able to do it before. Flylady has a few ground rules and allows no whining about them. One of the most important Flylady rules is to keep your kitchen sink empty, clean, and sparkling.

ESSENTIALS   Another Flylady golden rule is that every single morning you must learn to get up, make your bed, and get dressed all the way to your shoes. Many resist at first, but once they try it, they discover the miraculous effects. It's amazing. (I'm here to tell ya'!)

A clean sink has incredible stress-relieving power. As Flylady says, "As the kitchen goes, so goes the rest of the house." I would add, "As the kitchen goes, so goes the rest of your life!" The kitchen is the heart and soul of the house, and if one's house is symbolic of one's life (as it is in *feng shui),* then keeping the heart and soul in perfect order will resonate all over your life.

If you aren't one of those people who has a hard time keeping things clean, this step isn't for you. But, if you are like me, you may discover that the kitchen is a clear and direct reflection of how your life is going. When it sparkles, you feel great about yourself and everything in your life is working. When it gets to that point where you won't let anybody in there unless they live in your house and insist on being fed, then chances are, your life is in disarray, too.

The kitchen is a ready-made jumping-in spot in that stress cycle I mentioned earlier in this chapter. No matter how busy you are, no matter how behind or overwhelmed, if you take just thirty minutes—or even fifteen—to go into your kitchen, put all the clean dishes in the dishwasher away, load up the dishwasher with dirty ones, fill the sink with hot soapy water, wash the rest of the dishes that are sitting around (or, if you don't have time, just set them aside on another counter for now), then drain the sink and scrub it down with cleanser, a scrubbing pad, and a spritz of glass cleaner for shine at the end, you won't believe the impact it will have on your self-esteem.

Do this every day, especially every evening, and the effect of waking up and walking into the kitchen to face a bright, shiny sink—as opposed to a sink piled high with dirty dishes, making it impossible even to fill up the teapot—will astound you. Really! This works. And if you need help from there, check out Flylady's Web site.

ESSENTIALS   The best part about getting into the habit of keeping your sink clean is that the rest of the kitchen will soon follow. And once you are in the habit of keeping your kitchen clean, it only takes a few minutes a day to keep it that way.

Seeing Green

When it comes to natural beauty—meaning forests, mountains, flower gardens, and other such scenery—some people can take it or leave it. Other people find that being in or even just looking at natural beauty has a profound effect on how they feel about their lives, the world, and themselves. If you are interested in Ayurveda and have discovered that you are a Pitta type, you are probably one of these people. But even if you don't know anything about Ayurveda, you probably know whether natural beauty has a deep effect on you.

Even if you live in the city, you can use natural beauty to help you relieve stress and feel better about yourself. Surrounding yourselves with images of natural beauty can give you little lifts all day long. Here are some ways to accomplish this:

- Use a computer wallpaper and/or screensaver that shows rotating images of stunning scenery. Sign up at Webshots, at *www.webshots.com*, for free daily photos to use as computer wallpaper and screensavers, hundreds of which are of beautiful scenery, animals, and natural phenomena such as storms and unusual cloud formations. Picking out your photo choice each morning can be like going on a mini vacation—okay, not quite, but it can be revitalizing just to look at them.
- Tonight, instead of your usual sitcoms or drama lineup, watch the Discovery channel, Animal Planet, or a nature show on public television. It's good for your brain, food for your soul, and you just might learn something!
- Spend thirty minutes puttering around your own microenvironment. Even if your yard or the area around your apartment building is small, it probably contains some green stuff. Meander, examining each tree, flower, patch of grass, or planted bed. Don't think about anything else. Just see how much you can observe.
- Get to know the trees on your property. Some cultures believe the trees are spirit guardians. Look at and think about the trees surrounding your home. If the spirit moves you, you might even ask for their protection. Who knows?
- If you have no microenvironment on your property worth examining (although even a single flower can be worth examining), walk or drive somewhere close by, for example, a park or a nicely landscaped neighborhood. Walk around and look, look, look. Fill up your brain with natural beauty, and there won't be room for anxiety, at least not during that thirty minutes you've reserved for this purpose.
- Grow an herb garden or a small flower garden, either from seeds or by transplanting purchased plants in a large planter. Put the planter

on your patio, deck, front step, or back step, or in a sunny window. Check and tend it daily. It's like taking vitamins for your soul!

- Go to your local library or bookstore and browse through a book that contains large color photographs of natural beauty. Maybe you'll feel transported by a photo essay on Hawaii, or maybe the Rocky Mountains are more your style. Or Europe? Africa? The Central American rain forests? Let your imagination whisk you away for thirty minutes.

- Plan your next vacation around a natural wonder, such as the Grand Canyon, or take a cruise to the Caribbean, or camp in a national park or forest, or go to a beach in a neighboring town. Okay, this takes more than thirty minutes, but not if you average it out over the year.

Do One Thing All the Way

④ This one's for all of you who feel like all the little things in your life are out of control. If you have so many things to do that you can't seem to finish any of them, take thirty minutes and complete just one of the short chores listed below. You'll get a feeling of accomplishment you could never get from half-finishing twenty different chores. None of these chores takes very long, but they are all things that a lot of people have a hard time getting around to. When they remain undone, they weigh on your mind and add to your stress and the sense that you aren't able to keep things under control.

Doing just one thing on this list each day can make a huge difference in how you feel about yourself. Try it for a week. You'll see.

- Clean out your car. Throw out all the trash, return the recyclables, put everything back in the house that belongs in the house, and attack those floor mats with the hand vac. Then, wipe down the windows with glass cleaner.

- Clean out your purse or wallet. Throw away all the junk you don't need. File the receipts. Put everything in the right place. Flatten out your money and stack it so that all the bills face the right way. Clean out all the loose change and put it in a jar somewhere. (If you do this every day, you may soon have enough change in that jar to cover college tuition!)

ESSENTIALS Spend some quality time with your pet. Pets relieve stress. And because they seem to love us unconditionally, they can make us feel pretty good about ourselves, too.

- Clean out the coat closet. Take out all the things that don't belong in there and put them away properly. Hang up all the coats that have fallen or have half fallen off the hangers. Store all the scarves, hats, mittens, and earmuffs in a bin. Give away all the stuff that doesn't fit anymore or that nobody wants. Wow! Who knew you had all that space in there?
- Balance your checkbook. Quit griping or dreading it. Just go do it.
- Call the dentist and make that appointment. And keep the appointment!
- Go to your desk and take one manageable stack from your many stacks of things that need to be filed or put away, and file or put away everything in that one pile.
- Drink a really big glass of water, all the way. Finish the whole thing.
- Dust all the flat surfaces in your living room. This should take only five minutes, but it makes a perceptible difference.
- Make your bed. Just do it.
- Take a bath or a shower, then put moisturizer on every square inch of your skin. Put on a bathrobe and relax for fifteen minutes.
- Read one full chapter of that book you've been trying to get to.
- Sweep the garage. Don't worry about the other stuff in there; just sweep out all the dirt you can get to.
- Remember that call you've been meaning to make to work out that problem with that company? Make the call.
- Groom the dog. Just do it.
- You know that thing you've been meaning to tell that person but keep forgetting or putting off? Tell him.
- Set aside fifteen minutes—just fifteen minutes!—to start, experience, and finish your own personal time. Go to a quiet room after instructing others you are not to be disturbed, set a timer, and do something all on your own that you really want to do, and do it for

fifteen minutes solid. Read, listen to music, sew, whittle, whistle, whatever. Don't gyp yourself. Do the whole fifteen minutes, start to finish. Voilà! You're ready to continue with your day.

Was that so hard? I bet you feel better already.

ESSENTIALS

Take a water day. Don't drink anything but water all day long. Just for one day. (If you are addicted to caffeine, you might need just one cup of black coffee or tea in the morning to avoid the inevitable headache.) If you drink about eight cups of water during the day, you'll feel lighter, airier, and you'll have more energy.

Commit to Yourself

It's all well and good to manage your stress for the sake of the others in your life, but you have to commit to yourself, too. Self-esteem, at its very basic level, is about recognizing that you are worth self-care. And, of course, that means you'll be better able to care for others. As the Buddha once said, "Be a light unto yourself." Seek self-knowledge, treat yourself well, care for yourself, and you'll learn to love, appreciate, and esteem yourself.

Then, when stress happens, which it will, you'll understand that the stress that happens outside of you doesn't change who you are, what you are worth, how precious and individual and worthy of self-love you are. No one understands you like you do, and, if you don't try to understand yourself, you can't expect others to. So, make it a point to understand, study, nurture, and honor yourself. The rest—including all those things that cause the stress in your life—will fall right into place.

CHAPTER 4

Your Personal Stress Profile

You've probably tried stress manage-ment techniques before. Part of the problem may be that you didn't learn the technique in a way that worked for you personally. Another part of the problem may be that you just haven't found a stress management technique that fits your unique life. Your personality, the kind of stress you are trying to relieve, and the way you tend to handle stress all factor into your stress management success. So, how do you know which techniques to try? First, you determine your Personal Stress Profile.

The Many Faces of Stress

Stress itself is a pretty simple concept—it's the body's reaction to a certain degree of stimulation. But how stress applies to you is likely to be completely different from how stress applies to your best friend. Your bodies are both releasing adrenaline and cortisol in response to stress, but, while your stress might come from having a demanding boss, supervising ten difficult employees, and being required to meet impossible deadlines, your friend's stress might come from staying home alone with four young children and trying to stick to a demanding budget. While one person might deal with the stress of chronic osteoarthritis, another might feel incredibly stressed by chronic relationship problems.

QUESTIONS?

What should I do when I am feeling stressed?
Doodle! When something is worrying you and you find yourself obsessively trying to work out a logical solution, give your left brain a break and let your right brain exercise for a while. Doodling taps your creative side, balancing out an overworked brain. Your creative side just might come up with the solution you've been scrambling for!

Because the word *stress* can mean so many things to so many different people, it's logical that before any one individual—that means you—can put an effective stress management plan into practice, a Personal Stress Profile is essential. By determining the unique stressors you experience in your life, your personality's stress-related tendencies, and how you personally tend to cope with stress, you can design a Stress Management Portfolio that really works for you.

For example, someone who is physically drained by too much interaction with people may not be helped by strategies that encourage increased social activities with friends. Someone else who is stressed by the lack of a support system might find profound benefit in increased social activity. Some people are deeply calmed by meditation; others find it excruciating. Some people find assertiveness training a relief, but a naturally assertive type might benefit more from learning to sit back and let other people handle things.

You can think of your Personal Stress Profile, or PSP, as something like a business proposal. You are the business, and the business isn't operating at peak efficiency. Your PSP is a picture of the business as a whole and the specific nature of all the factors that are keeping the business from performing as well as it could. With PSP in hand, you can effectively create your own Stress Management Portfolio. Before you know it, you'll be running smoothly, efficiently, and productively (not to mention happily).

ALERT

Drinking two to three cups of coffee will dose you with approximately 400 milligrams of caffeine. This chemical can cause your body to release adrenaline, exacerbating the effects of stress.

So, how do you organize the huge, unwieldy list of details that comprise the stress in your life and your response to it? You will be able to develop your PSP as the result of the information you will discover about yourself through the tests and prompts in this chapter.

Your PSP has four parts:

1. Your Stress Tolerance Point
2. Your Stress Triggers
3. Your Stress Vulnerability Factor
4. Your Stress Response Tendencies

Once you understand how much stress you can handle, what things trigger stress for *you* (even if they don't trigger stress in a friend, a spouse, a sibling), where your personal stress vulnerability lies, and how you tend to respond to stress, you'll be able to build your Personal Stress Management Portfolio. This is the business plan. Once you've mapped out the trouble, you can strategize. You can develop a plan for improving your life by managing your stress.

Your Stress Tolerance Point

Notice I say *managing* your stress, not eliminating it, because eliminating all stress is impossible. As I mentioned earlier, some stress is actually good for you. It can get you charged up just when you need a boost. It makes life more fun, more interesting, more exciting. Don't we all crave some stress? We get bored with the daily routine and long for an exciting vacation. We desire that feeling of falling in love, the excitement of meeting someone new, the challenge of a promotion, the spark generated by learning a new subject, visiting a new place, even getting lost (for just a little while) in a new city or even an unfamiliar part of town.

In other words, while too much stress is bad, some stress is good. Therefore, it doesn't make sense to eliminate all stress from your life. Good stress can be great, as long as it doesn't last and last and last. Eventually, most of us like to get back to an equilibrium, whether that is a routine, an earlier bedtime, or a home-cooked meal.

Maybe you've noticed that some people thrive on constant change, stimulation, and a high-stress kind of life. Think about roving reporters, traveling network administrators, or people who can make the most mundane life events into great dramas. Others prefer a highly regular, even ritualistic kind of existence. Think of the people who have rarely left their hometowns and are perfectly happy that way, thank you. Most of us are somewhere in the middle. We like to travel, to experience the occasional thrilling life event, but are usually pretty glad to get back home or have things settle back to normal (normal being the equilibrium where we function best).

Whichever type of person you are, the changes in your body that make you react more quickly, think more sharply, and give you a kind of "high" feeling of super accomplishment only last up to a point. The point when the stress response turns from productive to counterproductive is different for each person, but, in general, stress feels great and actually increases your performance until it reaches a certain turning point—your Stress Tolerance Point. If stress continues or increases after that point, your performance will decrease, and the effects on your body will start to have a negative rather than a positive effect.

FACTS

According to a recent study conducted by the Higher Education Research Institute at the University of California–Los Angeles, over 30 percent of college students described feeling "frequently overwhelmed," a 16 percent increase from 1985.

Your Stress Triggers

The way you get to that turning point is highly individual. Every person's life is different and is filled with different kinds of Stress Triggers. Someone who has just been in a car accident will experience a completely different stress trigger than someone about to take a college entrance exam, but both may experience equal stress, depending on the severity of the accident and the perceived importance of the test. Of course, since both people probably have a different Stress Tolerance Point, high stress to the test taker may be moderate stress to the car accident victim, and both people may have a higher stress tolerance than the person about to experience the third migraine in a week.

Your Stress Triggers, in other words, are simply the things that cause you stress, and your Stress Tolerance Point is what determines how many and what degree of stress triggers you can take and still remain productive. Your combination of stress triggers is unique to you.

Your Stress Vulnerability Factor

The Stress Vulnerability Factor further complicates the picture. Some people have a high stress tolerance, *except* when it comes to their families. Some can ignore criticism and other forms of personal stress unless it relates to job performance. Some people can take all the criticism their friends and coworkers have to offer but will wail in anguish at a pulled groin muscle.

Every individual, due to personality, past experiences, probably genetics, and a host of other factors, will tend to be particularly vulnerable or sensitive to certain stress categories while remaining impervious to others. The Stress Vulnerability Factor can determine which events in your life will tend to affect you, personally, in a stressful way, and which life events may not stress you out, even if they would be stressful to someone else.

ESSENTIALS   Finding the stress management techniques that work best for you is essential for success. If keeping a stress journal or meditating cause you more stress, those techniques aren't working for you. A stress management technique should feel relaxing and be a positive experience. You should look forward to it. Don't force yourself to do things you don't want to do, or you'll likely make your situation worse.

Your Stress Response Tendencies

Add to this already complex picture your Stress Response Tendencies, or the way you, as an individual, tend to react to stress. Do you reach for food or nicotine or alcohol whenever life gets difficult, or are you more likely to withdraw, sleep too much, or lash out in irritation at friends? Maybe you seek out friends to talk to, or perhaps you practice relaxation or meditation. Maybe you react in one way when it comes to your areas of greatest vulnerability, another for the kind of stress you find easier to handle.

Through stress awareness, conscious tracking of stress triggers, commitment to managing the stress in your life in a personalized manner, experimenting with stress management techniques to find those that work for you, and creating and implementing your Personal Stress Profile, you can handle the stress that is sapping your energy and draining your brain power.

Let's begin by determining some things about you, the stressors in your life, and the way you tend to cope with them. The following quiz will help you to uncover the details of the stress in your life. From this quiz, you'll develop your Personal Stress Profile.

FOOT NOTES   Feb. 26/02

Stress – Tolerance Point

1. (B) or D? B
2. B
3. B
4. C
5. D

Stress Triggers

6. B
7. C
8. C
9. B
10. Stress Vulnerability factors

Stress Vulnerability factors

11. A. & D   15. C
12. C
13. A. & B. & C. & D
14. C or N/A

Stress Response Tendancies

16) B
17) D
18) C
19) C
20) B

} REACT to it

ALERT

Exceeding your stress tolerance point on a regular basis can result in the following:

- Poor performance
- Lack of concentration
- Debilitating anxiety or depression
- A less effective immune system
- Illness

Your Personal Stress Test

Now, don't let this "test" stress you out. It isn't graded! Instead of stressing, use this test as an opportunity to reflect on yourself, your life, and your personal tendencies. Take your time! Also, keep in mind that your answers and your entire stress profile will probably tend to change over time. This year, this month, or this week might be particularly stressful, but next year, next month, or next week might be easier. You can take this test again, later in time, to assess how well you've implemented your Stress Management Portfolio. For now, answer the questions as they apply to you today.

Part I: Your Stress Tolerance Point

Circle the answers that best apply to you:

1. Which of the following best describes your average day?

   A. *Comfortingly regular*—I get up, eat, work, and play at about the same time each day. I like my routines and orderly life.
   B. *Maddeningly regular*—I get up, eat, work, and play at about the same time each day, and the boredom is killing me.
   C. *Regular in essence but not in order*—I get up, eat, work, and play most days, but I never know when I'll do which thing, and if something new happens, then hey, great! I like to go with the flow.
   D. *Highly irregular and stressful*—every day, something throws off my schedule. I long for routine, but life keeps foiling my efforts.

2. What happens when you don't eat or exercise regularly?

   A. I get a cold, the flu, or an allergy attack, bloat, feel fatigued, or there is some other little signal that my good habits have lapsed.
   B. I don't pay much attention to my diet or exercise regimen but seem to feel fine most of the time.
   C. Eat well? Exercise? One of these days, maybe I'll try that, if I ever have the time or energy to work it into my packed schedule.
   D. I feel thrilled and emotionally heightened. I enjoy changing the routine and throwing myself into a different physical state.

3. When criticized by someone or reprimanded by an authority figure, how do you tend to feel?

   A. I feel panicky, hopeless, anxious, or depressed, as if something terrible and beyond my control has just happened.
   B. I feel angry and vengeful. I obsess over all the ways I could have or should have responded. I plan elaborate revenge scenarios, even if I don't intend to carry them out.
   C. I feel irritated or hurt for a little while, but not for long. I focus on how I could avoid another situation like this.
   D. I feel misunderstood by the masses. I know I was right, but, ah, that's the price of genius!

4. When preparing to perform in front of people for any reason (a concert, a speech, a presentation, a lecture), how do you tend to feel?

   A. I feel like throwing up.
   B. I feel stimulated, thrilled, a little nervous, but full of energy.
   C. I avoid situations where I have to perform because I don't like it.
   D. I feel aggressive or boastful.

5. When in the middle of a crowd, how do you feel?

   A. Exhilaration!
   B. Panic!
   C. I feel like causing trouble. Wouldn't it be funny to pull the fire alarm?
   D. I feel okay for a while, but then I'm ready to go home.

FACTS

According to a 1996 survey conducted by *Prevention* magazine, 73 percent of Americans experience "great stress" on a weekly basis.

Part II: Your Stress Triggers

Circle the answers that best apply to you. If none apply (for instance, if you are perfectly satisfied with your work life and it doesn't cause you stress), don't circle any of the answers under a given question:

6. When it comes to where you live, by what do you feel the most stressed?

    A. I feel stressed by city pollution/indoor allergens.
    B. I feel stressed by frequent quarreling with someone in my home.
    C. I feel stressed by sleep deprivation. My living conditions (new baby, noisy roommates) don't ever allow me to sleep as much as I need.
    D. I feel stressed by a sudden change in the people that live in my home, either due to absence (someone moved out, passed away) or presence (someone moved in, a new baby).

7. What habits should you change?

    A. I shouldn't stay inside too much. I know I should get some fresh air once in a while.
    B. I shouldn't constantly put myself down.
    C. I shouldn't smoke, drink, or eat too much.
    D. I shouldn't be too concerned with what other people think of me.

8. What could make your life so much better?

    A. If only I could move out of the city/rural area/small town/ suburbs/this country!
    B. If only I felt better about who I am.
    C. If only I were healthier and had more energy.
    D. If only I had more power, prestige, and money.

9. What do you truly dread?

    A. I dread the holidays. All that holiday cheer everywhere gets me down.
    B. I dread failure.
    C. I dread illness and/or pain.
    D. I dread having to speak in front of people.

10. How do you feel about your life's work or career?

    A. I feel I would be happier in a completely different work environment.
    B. I feel dissatisfied. My personal skills aren't being fully utilized.
    C. I feel stressed. I've already used up all my sick days due to minor illnesses.
    D. I feel pressure to conform to the works habits of my coworkers or the expectations of my supervisor, even though I'm not comfortable working in that way.

Lighten up—it just might save your health! According to a University of Maryland Medical Center study presented at the American Heart Association's 2000 annual meeting, people with heart disease were 40 percent less likely to laugh than those without cardiovascular problems.

Part III: Your Stress Vulnerability Factors

Circle the answers that best apply to you:

11. How do you describe yourself?

    A. I'm an extrovert, energized by social contact.
    B. I'm an introvert, energized by alone time.
    C. I'm a workaholic.
    D. I'm a caretaker.

12. What makes you tense?

    A. I feel tense when I think about my financial situation.
    B. I feel tense when I think about my family.
    C. I feel tense when I think about the safety of my loved ones.
    D. I feel tense when I think about what people think of me.

13. While plenty of areas of your life are under control, where do you suddenly lose control?

    A. I consume too much food and/or alcohol and/or spend too much money.
    B. I worry obsessively.
    C. I clean the house and/or organize constantly.
    D. I just can't keep my mouth shut! I often unintentionally anger and/or offend someone.

14. When it comes to the work, how do you describe yourself?

    A. I'm highly motivated and ambitious.
    B. I'm a drone. Work is boring and unfulfilling.
    C. I'm satisfied but glad I've got a life outside my job.
    D. I'm deeply dissatisfied. I know I could accomplish something so much better than this if only I had the opportunity to try!

15. How are you in your personal relationships?

    A. I'm usually the one in control.
    B. I'm a follower.
    C. I'm always looking for something I don't have.
    D. I'm somewhat distant.

SSENTIALS

A passive attitude can drastically lower your stress level. Letting things go or deciding they don't matter may seem cold or unfeeling in certain circumstances, but often a passive attitude can combat the feeling that things are out of control. If you can't control it, let it go. If you can't change it, accept it for what it is.

Part IV: Your Stress Response Tendencies

Circle the answer that best describes how you would most likely react to each of the following stress scenarios:

16. What would you do if your life were really busy and you had too many social obligations and too much work, and it seemed as though your days consisted of nothing but frantic rushing around to complete your to-do list?

    A. I'd feel overwhelmed, anxious, and out of control.
    B. I'd gain five pounds.
    C. I'd construct an elaborate and detailed system for keeping every aspect of my life in order, which I'd stick to for a few weeks before abandoning it.
    D. I'd cut back on current obligations and say "no" to new ones.

17. What would you do if you awoke with a nasty cold—a scratchy throat, a stuffy nose, chills, and an allover ache?

    A. I'd call in sick and spend the day resting and drinking tea with honey.
    B. I'd pop some cold medicine, go to work, and try to pretend I wasn't sick.
    C. I'd go to the gym and try to sweat it out by going full power in a kickboxing class or by running a few miles on the treadmill.
    D. I'd wonder how this could happen to me when I had so many important things to do. I'd worry about how many things in my life will be disrupted by my getting sick.

18. How would you handle a problem with a personal relationship?

    A. I'd pretend there wasn't a problem.
    B. I'd demand that we talk about it, and talk about it now.
    C. I'd get depressed and think that it must be my fault and wonder why I always ruin relationships.
    D. I'd spend some time reflecting on exactly what I would like to say so as not to sound accusatory, then approach the person about discussing some specific problems. If it didn't work, at least I could say I tried.

19. If your supervisor told you that a client complained about you, then advised you not to worry about it, but suggested you be more careful of what you say to clients in the future, how would you feel?

    A. I'd feel extremely offended and obsess for days about who the client might have been and how I might be able to get revenge for being made to look bad in front of my boss.
    B. I'd feel indifferent. Some people are overly sensitive.
    C. I'd feel aghast if I offended someone and wonder how it could have happened. I'd then act overly polite and accommodating to everyone but my confidence would definitely be deflated.
    D. I'd feel hurt or maybe a little angry but would probably decide to take my supervisor's advice and not worry about it. I would then make a point to notice how I spoke to clients.

20. If you had a big test or presentation in the morning and a lot depended on the result, how would you feel as you tried to get to sleep?

    A. I'd feel a little nervous but excited because I'd be prepared. I'd plan to get a really good night's sleep so that I'd be at my best.
    B. I'd feel so nervous that I probably would throw up. I'd have a few drinks or cookies or cigarettes to calm myself down, even though that usually doesn't work very well. I'd sleep restlessly.
    C. I'd stay up all night going over my notes, even after I knew them by heart. My feeling would be that it can't hurt to look at them again . . . and again.
    D. Thinking about the test or presentation would make me nervous, so I'd pretend nothing was going on and do my best to not think about it.

That's it! You're done. Now, for each section, tally up your answers as follows.

Section One: Your Stress Tolerance Point Analysis

Circle your answers in the following chart, then determine in which column you had the most answers:

	JUST RIGHT LOW	JUST RIGHT HIGH	TOO LOW	TOO HIGH
1.	A	C	B	D
2.	A	B	D	C
3.	C	D	B	A
4.	C	B	D	A
5.	D	A	C	B

Your Stress Tolerance Point indicates how much stress you can take. Which category had the most answers for you? If your answers fell about equally in more than one category, that probably means you can take lots of stress when it comes to certain things and less when it comes to other things, or that some parts of your life are too high in stress and others are just right or even too low. Here's what your Stress Tolerance Point score indicates:

If you scored the most points under **JUST RIGHT LOW,** you don't tolerate too much stress, but you already know that and are good at taking measures to limit the stress in your life. You perform best and feel happiest when the comfortable routine you've created for yourself runs smoothly and nothing too unexpected happens. You can deal with stressful situations for short periods of time, but you are always thrilled to get home after a vacation—no matter how wonderful it was—and you are very attached to your rituals, whether daily (your morning workout, the evening news with dinner), weekly (your every-Friday coffeehouse date with your best friend), or annually (preparing the same Thanksgiving recipes each year, the annual Valentine's Day party, your systematic spring cleaning).

You've crafted a routine that works for you, and when events throw off your routine, you tend to experience stress. Having recognized your low stress tolerance, however, you've already got the tools in place for keeping your life low key and systematic whenever possible. Maybe you are good at saying "no" to things you don't have room for in your life. Maybe you will go on vacation during the Independence Day weekend but refuse to leave home over the winter holidays because that is tradition.

The coping skills you need to cultivate are those that will help you deal with those inevitable times when life changes dramatically or when you aren't able to stick to your routine due to circumstances beyond your control. If you or a family member becomes ill, if you are forced to change jobs or move to another city, if you start or end school, things will, inevitably, change, whether you like it or not. Long-term or permanent changes will require you to make your routine flexible enough to accommodate new circumstances, either temporarily or permanently. Short-term changes may require a temporary suspension of your beloved routine.

Stress management techniques can help you to bend when you feel like breaking so that you can more effectively cope with change.

If you scored the most points under **JUST RIGHT HIGH,** you can take a fairly high level of stress, and you actually like life a bit more exciting. You perform better and feel happier when life isn't *too* routine. You are probably an easygoing person who enjoys seeing what lies around the next bend in life, and strict schedules bore you. Sure, you like traditions and rituals in some areas of your life. You may cherish your morning cup of tea, but you might be just as likely to drink it watching cartoons as reading the *New York Times* financial section. You might sip it at the kitchen table one day, out on the patio the next day, or you might take it in your travel mug on the subway because you decided to sleep in an extra forty-five minutes.

You probably don't always eat regular meals or exercise at regular times, but that's how you like it. You've designed your life—whether consciously or not—around keeping yourself happily stimulated. You know you like things to be interesting, so you resist routines and let just enough stress into your life to keep you humming along efficiently. You may not always look efficient in your whirlwind of activity, but if stress makes you happy, then stress makes you happy. There is a peak point at which a certain amount of stress is satisfying. Your peak point may be higher than someone else's. Maybe you enjoy a little more stress than your friends. But at some point, even for you, the stress will get to be too much and you'll start to compromise your own mental, physical, and spiritual health and happiness.

Of course, not all change is pleasant, and the stress management techniques you can successfully master are those that help you deal with the less pleasant changes life sometimes has to offer—for example, illness, injury, loss of a loved one. Even you can't go with the flow *all* the time. You may also find it difficult to sit still and concentrate. Meditation and other techniques that cultivate inner as well as outer stillness can be of great benefit to you; they can teach you self-discipline and the skill of slowing down (because once in a while, we all need to slow down, like it or not!). You can also benefit from learning *how* to live within a routine, even if you don't always choose to do so. When you are sick, have small children, or live with people who have a lower stress tolerance point than you do, knowing how to work with routines can be helpful. You are already a flexible person. Learning stress management techniques of all kinds (not just the kinds that amuse you in the moment) will make you even more flexible, disciplined, and able to cope with all kinds of situations.

ESSENTIALS

When your mind is overburdened, do something with your hands. Many people find relief in baking bread, painting, gardening, home repairs, or amateur carpentry. Building or creating something helps the mind to focus. When you are hammering a birdhouse together or decorating a birthday cake, you don't have room in your brain to worry.

If you scored the most points under **TOO LOW,** you probably have a very high stress tolerance point and you are operating well below it. Or, maybe, your stress tolerance is relatively low, but you are *still* operating below it. Who knows, since you haven't found your optimal operating level? Your peak of functioning and happiness is best reached under more stimulation than you are currently experiencing. Maybe your life is necessarily highly routine and you can't stand it. You long for excitement, change, anything, anything at all, even if it's just moving the furniture in your living room into different positions.

Not meeting your stress tolerance point can result in frustration, irritation, aggression, and depression. You aren't meeting your potential. But you can do something about it! Afraid to change jobs? Make saving a nest egg an active and systematized goal, then take the plunge. Learn a new subject. Join some new groups. Add social activities to your life in areas that interest you. If you feel your marriage is stagnating, for heaven's sake, don't go out and have an affair but find a counselor who can help you add excitement and vigor to your relationship. Are you a caregiver tied to the home? Master the Internet and you'll find a world out there waiting for you from your personal computer. Call old friends. Take up painting or write that novel you know is inside you.

And, believe it or not, stress management techniques can help you, too. Ironically, not having enough stress to meet your own stress tolerance point is *stressful*. Meet your needs with interesting, positive changes and handle your frustration, aggression, or depression with stress management techniques. Stress management itself can be an exciting learning endeavor. Educating yourself about the various meditation techniques, for example, can be an active and interesting pursuit all on its own.

If you scored **TOO HIGH,** you probably know all too well that you are operating well above a healthy Stress Tolerance Level. You are probably also suffering from some of the ill effects of stress, such as frequent minor illness, inability to concentrate, anxiety, depression, or self-neglect. You may often feel like your life is out of control or your situation is hopeless. Stay with this book! You can learn a lot from the stress management techniques described in these chapters. You can improve your life and feel better. It's never too late to start making gradual improvements in your life. You can do it! Take a deep breath and keep reading.

FACTS

A recent study conducted at the Rush Presbyterian St. Luke's Medical Center in Chicago suggests that a daily dosage of 300 IUs of vitamin E may significantly decrease the chance that mental functioning will decline after age sixty-five.

Section Two: Your Stress Trigger Analysis

Tally up how many *A*s, *B*s, *C*s, and *D*s you marked for this section. Read the sections below for each letter that you checked more than once:

Two or more *A*s: You suffer from *environmental stress*. This is the stress that comes from the world around you. Whether you live in a polluted area, such as near a busy street or in a house with a smoker (or if you are a smoker), or are allergic to something in your surroundings, you'll be exposed to environmental stress. Environmental stress is also the stress you feel when your environment changes. Maybe your neighborhood has changed a lot in the last few years. Maybe you are remodeling your home, or moving to a new home, or a new city. Changes in the household, such as the loss or gain of a family member or even a pet, are considered environmental stress. So is a marriage or a separation. These are also sources of personal and social stress, but they are environmental stress because they change the makeup of your household.

Some people are sensitive to the weather. A blizzard, a big thunderstorm, a hurricane, or just days and days of rain are all sources of stress to some. Do you get anxious and panicky every time you hear a rumble of thunder? Do you watch the weather report in fear of a storm?

Environmental stressors are largely unavoidable, but there are techniques that can help you to turn them from stressors into nothing more than events. Here are some stress management techniques to try if you are particularly bothered by environmental stressors (read more about these techniques in future chapters):

- *Meditation* (for perspective, distance from situation): Chapter 8
- *Breathing exercises* (for calming): Chapter 6
- *Exercise/nutrition* (strengthen physiological resources to combat environmental stress): Chapter 7
- *Vitamin/mineral therapy, herbal medicine, homeopathy* (to strengthen the immune system): Chapter 6
- *Feng shui* (to balance and promote the energy in your environment): Chapter 10

Two or more *B*s: You suffer from *personal stress.* Personal stress is the stress that comes from your personal life. This broad category covers everything from your personal perception of relationships to your self-esteem and feelings of self-worth. If you are unhappy with your personal appearance; have a bad body image; feel inadequate, unfulfilled, fearful, shy, lacking in willpower or self control; have an eating disorder or addiction (also sources of physiological stress); or are in any way personally unhappy, you are suffering from personal stress. Even personal happiness in extremes can cause stress. If you are madly in love, just got married, were recently promoted, came into lots of money, or just started the business of your dreams, you'll also experience personal stress. Under these situations, it's common to feel self-doubt, insecurity, or even overconfidence that can undermine success.

In other words, personal stress happens in your own head. That doesn't make it any less real than environmental or physiological stress. If anything, it feels even more real. The most effective techniques for dealing with personal stress are those that help you to manage your own thoughts and emotions about yourself. Here are some techniques to try:

- *Meditation:* Chapter 8
- *Massage therapy:* Chapter 7
- *Habit reshaping:* Chapter 6
- *Relaxation techniques:* Chapter 6
- *Visualization:* Chapter 8
- *Optimism therapy:* Chapter 9
- *Self-hypnosis:* Chapter 9
- *Exercise (e.g., yoga, weight lifting):* Chapter 7
- *Creativity therapy:* Chapter 9
- *Dream journaling:* Chapter 9
- *Friend therapy:* Chapter 9

Two or more *C*s: You suffer from *physiological stress.* Physiological stress is the kind of stress that happens to your body. While all forms of stress result in a stress response in your body, some stress comes from physiological problems like illness and pain. You catch a cold or the flu and experience stress due to the illness. You break your wrist or sprain your ankle; that stresses your body, too. Arthritis, migraine headaches, cancer, heart attack, stroke—all of these physiological ailments, some mild, some serious, are forms of physiological stress.

Physiological stress also covers hormonal changes in the body, from PMS to pregnancy to menopause, as well as other changes or imbalances such as insomnia, chronic fatigue, depression, bipolar disorder, sexual dysfunction, eating disorders, and addictions. Addictions to substances that harm the body are a source of physiological stress. Misuse of alcohol, nicotine, and other drugs is stressful. Even prescription drugs can be a source of physiological stress. While relieving one condition, they may cause side effects that are stressful.

ESSENTIALS

You can control the stress cycle in your life. Illness and pain can cause stress, and many experts believe stress can cause illness and pain, but managing your stress can help stop the cycle. Take care of your body when you are sick; take care of your mind when you are worried or anxious. If you put a stop to one, it won't lead to the other.

While many kinds of physiological stress are beyond your control, bad health habits are also an important and common form of physiological stress you can control. Sleep deprivation due to the habit of staying up too late, poor dietary habits including overeating or undereating, too little or too much exercise, and general lack of good self-care all cause direct stress on the body.

The best way to relieve physiological stress is to get to the source. Many stress management techniques directly address physiological stress. Here are some to try:

- *Habit reshaping:* Chapter 6
- *Nutrition/exercise balancing:* Chapter 7
- *Massage therapy:* Chapter 7
- *Visualization:* Chapter 8
- *Relaxation techniques:* Chapter 6
- *Mindfulness meditation:* Chapter 8
- *Vitamin/herbal/homeopathic therapy:* Chapter 6
- *Ayurveda:* Chapter 9

Two or more *D*s: You suffer from *social stress*. People who say they don't care what anybody thinks about them are probably not being completely honest with themselves. Humans are social creatures, and we live in a complex, interactive society that is becoming increasingly global. Of course we care what people think. We have to care, or we won't be able to live within the system. Sure, it's healthy not to care too much, but like anything else, the ideal is a balance.

Social stress, therefore, is stress related to your appearance in the world. How do people see you? How do they react to what you do and the things that happen to you? Getting engaged, married, separated, or divorced, for example, while all sources of personal stress, are also sources of social stress because of the societal opinions and reactions to the forming and breaking up of the marital relationship. The same goes for becoming a parent, a grandparent, getting a promotion, losing a job, having an extramarital affair, coming into a lot of money, or losing a lot of money. Society has a lot to say about these events, which are bound to affect the opinion other people have of you, right or wrong, warranted or not. Depending on how vulnerable you are to public (or family) opinion, you may or may not suffer too much from social stress. If social stress is a concern in your life, some good techniques for helping to equalize social stress include the following:

- *Exercise:* Chapter 7
- *Attitude adjustment:* Chapter 9
- *Visualization:* Chapter 8
- *Creativity therapy:* Chapter 9
- *Friend therapy:* Chapter 9
- *Habit reshaping:* Chapter 6

ALERT

Too much stress can result in burnout, a condition characterized by complete loss of motivation, interest, energy, and engagement with work, family, or even personal hygiene. If you feel yourself heading toward burnout, seek stress management immediately! Start by taking a really long nap to catch up on your sleep.

Section Three: Your Stress Vulnerability Factor Analysis

Unlike stress triggers, stress vulnerabilities have to do with your personal tendencies. Everyone's stress triggers are different, but, in addition, everyone's personality and personal vulnerabilities to certain areas of stress are also different. You and a friend might both have stressful jobs, but you might be particularly sensitive to job stress, obsessing over work to the point that your stress is much more than it could be. Your friend may be better able to approach job stress in a healthy way. You both might have two children, but your friend may be particularly vulnerable to obsessive worrying about her children, while you feel more in control of your dependent-related stress.

For this section, each answer reveals different areas in which you are particularly vulnerable to stress. Your vulnerabilities lie in the following areas if you checked the noted answers:

Spending too much time alone, or lack of satisfying social contact: 11.A, 13.D

An extrovert is someone who may relish time alone but who feels drained of energy after too much time away from other people. Extroverts require plenty of social contact to keep their energy high. They work best in groups and may find working alone virtually impossible because they can't get motivated. Personal relationships are extremely important to extroverts, who often feel incomplete without a partner. Extroverts tend to have lots of friends and to rely on their friends for energy, support, and satisfaction.

Extroverts often don't know what they think until they say it. They often think things through out loud. Friend therapy, journaling, group therapy, meditation classes, exercises classes, and massage therapy are particularly effective for extroverts.

Spending too much time around others: 11.B, 15.D

An introvert is someone who may enjoy other people but who feels drained of energy after too much social contact. Introverts require time alone to recharge after spending time with people and find it difficult to accomplish anything productive with lots of people around. Introverts are good at working alone in a home office or at a remote location. While introverts aren't necessarily shy and can benefit immensely from rewarding personal relationships, they also need time alone. Introverts tend to think about what they say before they speak. Sometimes, introverts can seem, and feel, distant, as if a gulf exists between the self and the outside world. That may be a sign that it is time for some alone time. Your body is telling you it needs to be re-energized. In some cases, however, it may be a sign that you are spending too much time alone. Seek balance! Introspective techniques and solitary techniques like meditation, visualization, and chakra centering are great for introverts.

The caretaker conundrum: 11.D

One area worrywarts tend to specialize in is worry about their dependents. If you are a parent, grandparent, or the caretaker to an aging parent or grandparent, you have a focus for your worries right there in front of you, and that focus is dependent on you for his or her health and welfare. That's a big burden, and even if it is one you have readily accepted, it is still a stressful position to be in. Sure, you're a parent, you adore your children, and the burden is fully worth it. But having dependents makes worry a lot easier, and worry makes the stress of being a caretaker a lot harder.

Learning to deal with the stress of caretaking means admitting, first, that the stress is there, then taking measures to care for yourself as well as you care for your dependents. It isn't selfish. You can't be a good caretaker if you neglect your own physical, emotional, and mental well-being. Self-care stress management in its many forms is exceptionally important for caretakers, and that includes making room for your own creativity and self-expression. Don't be afraid to admit the whole complex slew of feelings you have about your caretaking responsibilities—intense love, anger, joy, resentment, appreciation, sadness, irritation, and happiness. Being a caretaker sounds a lot like being a human being, doesn't it? Some might say it's being human with the volume turned up.

**SSENTIALS**

If you are responsible for someone else's care, whether a child or an aging parent, meeting your own needs is essential if you are to be an effective caretaker. Make time every day for yourself, even if it's only fifteen minutes of quiet time spent soaking in a warm bath or reading a really good book before bed every night. Devoting all your energy to someone else will eventually deplete your reserves, and you won't be any good to anyone.

Financial pressure: 12.A

No matter how much money some people make, it always seems to slip through their fingers—or that proverbial hole that's been burnt into their pockets. Money is a huge source of stress for many people and a common area of stress vulnerability. Do you think that enough money really would solve all your problems? Do you spend time every single day worrying about having enough money for what you need or want? Do you obsess about where you put your money, whether your money is working for you, how you might be able to make money? Do you put a lot of importance on a person's financial status?

If money is an area of vulnerability for you, focus on stress management techniques that both help you to take responsibility for your financial situation (if that's the problem) and put finances in a whole-life perspective. Money really can't buy happiness, but freedom from financial stress can certainly help push you in that direction!

**ALERT**

Not knowing how much money you have or where it all is can be a major source of financial stress. Face the truth, no matter how grim, and know exactly how much money you have at all times. The knowledge is liberating, and then you can begin to take control over your finances.

Family dynamics: 12.B

You love 'em. You hate 'em. They see your best side and your worst side. Like it or not, you're pretty much stuck with them, even if you choose never to speak to them again. Yes, I'm talking about your family, another big area of stress for many people. Our families have an intimate knowledge of who we are, or who we used to be, and that can be stressful, especially if we're trying to escape who we used to be (or who we think we used to be). Family members are notoriously knowledgeable about how to push our buttons. Who can anger you more than your brother or sister? Who can embarrass you more than your parents, even when you are all grown up?

All families are stressful to some extent, but for some people, families are particularly stressful because of a dysfunctional aspect or because of past events that are painful. If your family is an area of stress for you, you may benefit by making amends, or by deciding to move on. You may be estranged from your family or fully in their clutches on a daily basis. Either way, recognizing family stress is the first step to managing it. How you manage it depends on your individual situation. You might consider techniques that bolster your people skills or techniques that strengthen the foundation of your own self-esteem. Journaling and other creativity techniques can be highly effective for dealing with family stress, and don't forget friend therapy. One of the great things about friends is that they aren't part of your family!

For many people, family is a sacred and highly cherished part of life. Yet, it's still fraught with stress. That's fine. You can love your family dearly, feel fondly and intimately attached to your family members, and still admit to family as a major cause of stress in your life. Who said life was simple? In any case, recognizing the positive elements of family, the wonderful ways your family has impacted your life, is a great way to help mitigate family stress.

Obsessive worrying: 12.C, 13.B

You know perfectly well if this is you. You worry about everything, and you just can't help it. Or, you have a few choice areas of life in which you are a "worry specialist." Maybe it's your body shape, or the impression you make on others, or your children or grandchildren. Whatever it is, you worry. You worry about the weather. You worry about your family. You worry about your pets. You worry about school, or work, or your social group, or your friends, who probably tend to roll their eyes at you and make exasperated comments like, "Will you *please* stop worrying?"

But it's not so easy to stop, is it? Yet, being a worrywart is really just a bad habit (in some cases, a compulsion) that is immensely stressful. Learning how to stop worrying can be an empowering life skill that will change your daily existence more dramatically than you ever imagined (not that you ever had time to imagine, since you were too busy worrying). Thought control and worry stopping are great techniques to learn. Exercise also provides a great break from worry, especially when it's challenging. You can't worry if your mind is immersed in those yoga moves or that kickboxing routine. There's nothing wrong with quitting the daily news habit. You have enough to worry about, and, if anything really important happens, you'll hear about it sooner or later. Most importantly, focus on relearning how to worry effectively. Worry about things you can change, as a means to figure out how to change them. If you can't change something, worrying about it is just a big waste of time, and life is too short to waste time that way.

The need for constant validation by others: 12.D, 15.B, 15.C

Some people could go their whole lives without knowing or caring about how "cool" they are. Others live by the building and sustaining of their personal image. If your image is more important to you than what's behind it—or even if it just feels that way sometimes—you are probably vulnerable to image stress. It's hard not to be image conscious these days. Appearance, charisma, the whole "cool factor"—it's hard to resist. But being too cool conscious has a price. Going through life constantly on the lookout for how you appear to others can obliterate the real you. Do you sometimes wonder who you are apart from the "you" that you choose to show to the people in the world? Image obsession is stressful, and, even if a certain amount of "cool" is important for your career or even your personal satisfaction, keeping image in perspective is as important as keeping any other aspect of your life in perspective.

Image stress is a big problem for adolescents, but even adults can fall prey. Look for stress management techniques that help you to get in touch with the inner you. The better you know the *you* inside, the more superficial and uninteresting the outer *you* will become. Know yourself and, ironically, your image will improve, anyway. Maybe you've noticed:

People who are unique have inner tranquility and have found a high comfort level with who they are, and they tend to be pretty cool.

Lack of self-control, motivation, organization: 13.A, 13.B, 13.C, 13.D

You cause yourself more stress than is necessary because you haven't taken control of your personal habits, thoughts, or life. No, you can't control *everything*, and, if you try to control *everything*, you'll be vulnerable to control issues on the other side. However, to a large extent, you can control what you do, how you react, even how you think and perceive the world. That's a powerful arsenal of control, and it's all the control you ever really need. Lots of us let all that go, however, making the excuse that our lives are completely subject to fate or the actions of others.

So, what are some of the things in our lives that we could more easily gain control over? We can control our dietary habits, our exercise schedules, our impulse to say unkind things, our road rage, our tendency to bite our fingernails or chew on pencil erasers or never put away our things when we are finished using them. These are simply habits, and, if a habit is causing you stress, then why not change it? Is breaking a habit difficult? Just for a little while. Living with chronic stress is a lot more difficult. Look for stress management techniques that help you to get control: Get organized, get healthy, get responsible, and even (oh, say it isn't true!) act like a grownup. (Being a grownup can be fun. Really!)

In the case of addiction, engaging in certain behaviors is not a matter of self-control. If you are addicted to something—whether it is nicotine, drugs, alcohol, food, gambling, or sex—you can't just decide to quit. The struggle is immense, and you will probably need help. Don't be afraid to ask for help! It isn't a sign of weakness.

Need to control: 14.A, 15.A

You've got control issues on the other side of the fence. You know the best way to do things, and nobody better cross you. You like to have control because you really believe you know best, and you probably do much of the time. The problem is that getting everyone to listen (dare I say, "obey"?) can be pretty stressful. How dare that guy cut you off on the freeway. *You had the right of way!* How dare your colleague not take you up on your excellent suggestion for improving the efficiency of her team. *She'll be sorry!* You may also admit to requiring a certain amount of ego stroking. People should show you the proper respect for your authority, shouldn't they? Is it so wrong to want the reverence so properly due?

No, it's not. We all want to be recognized for our accomplishments, and one of your strengths is a healthy self-esteem. But like anything else, self-esteem can be carried too far. Remember, seek balance! Knowing you are right (in a flexible way) is one thing. Demanding everyone else admit it, too, is quite another. You can benefit by stress management techniques that help you to (pick your metaphor) let go of the reins, coast on neutral, go with the flow. You don't need to be told to "just do it." You "just do it" all the time, unlike the rest of those slackers! The trick for you is to "just let it be." Now, there's a challenge. And you're always up for a challenge, aren't you? We know you can do it. You know you can do it. Just check your ego at the door of self-awareness, and you'll have a lot less to carry. Life is more fun with a lighter load.

Your job/career: 11.C, 14.A, 14.B, 14.D

You may love your job or hate it, but one thing is certain: Your job stresses you out! People who are vulnerable to job stress may have particularly stressful jobs, such as those driven by deadlines, those fraught with difficult people, or those that include high pressure to succeed. Even jobs that wouldn't be stressful to some are stressful to others, however. While one person can easily say, "Hey, I'll get it done when I get it done," another might be thrown into a frenzy of anxiety at the mere mention of an impending deadline.

If your job is an area of stress for you, concentrate on practicing stress management techniques that work in the office (even if it's a home office) and those that target the kind of stress you are likely to encounter on the job, such as techniques for dealing with difficult people, techniques to help stretch and relieve the strain of sitting for long periods, deep breathing and relaxation techniques for combating ultra-high-stress moments, or whatever else is relevant to your particular job.

FACTS

According to the WHO, the Japanese have the longest healthy life expectancy, or years they can expect to live in "full health" (estimated for babies born in 1999). The Japanese healthy life expectancy is 74.5 years. The United States didn't make the top ten, coming in at twenty-fourth out of 191 countries with a healthy life expectancy of seventy years.

In addition, make a special commitment to keep sacred your prework preparation time and your postwork decompression time. Spend fifteen to thirty minutes before and after work each day practicing the stress-relieving technique of your choice to create a cushion around your workday. This will allow the rest of your life to be completely separate from work (wherever possible) so that you don't feel that your stressful work life has swallowed whole the rest of your life. Even if you work at home, set work-time boundaries (even something as simple as "absolutely no work on Friday night"), then leave it behind when it's time. Seek balance!

Low self-esteem: 13.D, 14.D

While you may handle work stress with aplomb, you become vulnerable to attacks on your self-esteem. Maybe a comment about your weight or age throws you into a tailspin. Maybe you see yourself in a shop window while walking down the street and the negative impression you get deflates your confidence for the rest of the day.

Self-esteem isn't just about appearance. If you believe someone is questioning your competency, do you become unreasonably defensive or suddenly insecure? Do you require constant reassurance, compliments, or other self-esteem boosters from the people around you in order to feel good about yourself? Many stress management techniques focus on bolstering self-esteem. The most important thing to remember is that self-esteem, just like your body, requires maintenance. Work on it. Take care of yourself. Keep reminding yourself how special you are, even when you don't really believe it.

Neglecting yourself may help you to ignore self-esteem issues, but it certainly won't address or "fix" them. Seek out sources for affirmations and positive self-talk to keep feeling good about yourself. Assertiveness training may help you to put less stock in the careless comments of others. You can be your own best friend (find out more in Chapter 13). It takes some practice, but believe me, no one is better suited for the job. You are worth knowing, so get to know yourself. You are an endless source of mystery. You are fascinating. You are lovable. And no one will appreciate you until you appreciate yourself. Cliché, perhaps, but also ultimately true.

QUESTIONS?

What is a perfection meditation?
Sit or lie comfortably and close your eyes. Relax and focus on your breathing. Then, every time you exhale, imagine breathing out all the negativity inside you. And every time you inhale, imagine breathing in pure, white light that fills you with positive energy. As you breathe, repeat the word *perfection* out loud or to yourself. As you say the word, know that it describes you. No matter what your so-called faults by worldly standards, or by your own standards, you are a perfect spirit inside.

Section Four: Your Stress Response Tendencies Analysis

This last section determines the ways in which you tend to respond to stress. Keep track of how many times you marked an answer under each of the following columns:

	IGNORE	REACT	ATTACK	MANAGE
16.	A	B	C	D
17.	B	D	C	A
18.	A	C	B	D
19.	B	C	A	D
20.	D	B	C	A

The category you chose most often indicates your stress response style. Here's what each category is about:

Ignore It: If you chose mostly answers in the Ignore category, you tend to ignore the stress in your life. Sometimes, ignoring stress can be an excellent coping strategy. Other times, however, ignoring stress compounds it. Something that could have been easily corrected early on can become a source of greater and greater stress because it was never addressed. Be aware of your tendency to ignore stress so that you can use this strategy consciously. Ignoring stress without realizing it is less productive and can result in burying feelings that are better acknowledged and dispatched. The key to ignoring stress productively is to learn how to be fully aware of the stress in your life. Then, you can choose when to ignore it and when to manage it.

React to It: If you chose mostly answers in the React category, you tend to react to stress with behaviors that can be unhelpful at best and destructive at worst. Maybe you raid the freezer for the ice cream every time stress gets out of hand in your life. Maybe you get depressed or angry or irritable or anxious or panicky. Maybe you worry obsessively. Maybe you smoke, or drink, or try to forget your stress by using other drugs. In any case, reacting to stress makes you the victim and sends your psyche the message that the stress is in control and you are its hapless pawn. Don't be a pawn. Reacting to stress with occasional self-indulgence can be enjoyable in a wallowing, self-pitying kind of way. It can even be a kind of self-care, but only up to a point. Managing stress is much more effective.

Attack It: If you chose mostly answers in the Attack category, you don't just handle stress, you manhandle it, and with a full throttle jab to the solar plexus. You refuse to let stress get the best of you, but, in your exuberance, you sometimes go overboard. Sometimes, the key to managing stress is letting it go, but you don't like to let things go until you've attacked them from every possible angle and pounded them into the dust. Sure, this can be a highly effective technique. A stubborn work problem or a failing business or even a weight problem might respond well to a full-speed, vigorous, full frontal attack. That kind of energy can be highly effective for eliminating certain sources of stress. For other types of stress, however, attack mode may not be ideal. Learning a variety of stress management techniques for different types of stress can add to your coping repertoire. Put relaxation at the top of the list.

Manage It: If you chose mostly answers in the Manage category, you do a pretty good job of managing the stress in your life. You tend to react to stressful stimuli with a moderate rather than an extreme response. You give yourself time to size up a situation before acting on it and don't worry inordinately about things you can't control. Sure, sometimes things happen to make you feel bad, but you've also learned that not everything everyone does is about you. (Most of the time, it probably isn't.) Good job! Of course, doing a good job at managing stress doesn't preclude room for improvement. Learning more and better ways to manage stress will help you prepare for future possible stressors on life—because every life's got 'em.

Your Stress Management Profile

In a special place, like your journal or a notebook you set aside for stress management work, record the results from your personal stress test. Date it, then try the test again in a few months, after you've worked with some of the stress management techniques I'll show you in this book.

Look over your results and write a few paragraphs about your overall impression. How much stress can you take before you start to feel bad? What triggers stress for you? What are your vulnerable areas? How do you respond to stress?

This is your stress management profile. An awareness of your stress profile will help you to choose the stress management techniques that will work best for you, and to schedule your stress management in a way that makes sense in your life.

CHAPTER 5

Your Stress Management Portfolio

Y ou've collected a lot of important information about the stress in your life. Now, you have the knowledge you need to create a plan that will meet your individual needs. In this chapter, you'll lay the groundwork for that plan by mapping out your Stress Management Portfolio.

The Big Picture: Building Your Personal Stress Management Portfolio

You'll write most of this chapter yourself, and you won't do it all in one day. As you work through the rest of this book, reading about the many different approaches to stress management, you can continue to flip back to this chapter and write down your ideas and, after you've tried them, how they worked for you.

Your Stress Management Portfolio, as you may have guessed, isn't set. You write things down, try them out, adjust your approach, try something else, find something that works for part of your life, then continue to experiment in other areas. Your Stress Management Portfolio is a lot like an investment portfolio. If you watch the market and trade your stocks according to changes in the market, it doesn't stay the same. As your life changes, your Stress Management Portfolio will change, too. As you build it, customize it, and implement it, you'll also keep a careful watch on the stress in your life. As it changes, so will your stress management strategy.

As you work your way through this chapter, keep a bookmark in Chapter 4 so that you can easily flip back to your Personal Stress Profile. You'll refer to it often and use it as you build your Stress Management Portfolio. The more personalized you make your strategy, the more effective it will be.

FACTS

A recent British study showed that twenty men and women with high blood pressure took thirty-seven minutes to complete a math test. The men and women without high blood pressure took only ten minutes to complete the same test.

Your Stress Management Portfolio is an in-progress action plan based on both the details and the overall knowledge gained from your Personal Stress Profile. Think about your general impression after completing your PSP. This general impression will form the outline or silhouette of your portfolio. Each section of the PSP will help to determine your stress management strategy.

Stress Management Journals

Besides keeping track of your stress in this book, one of the simplest but most potent stress management strategies you can employ is to keep a stress journal. In your stress journal, you can record the results of your stress test, write about your Personal Stress Profile, and keep track of your stress management strategies, including what you tried, when you tried it, and how well it worked.

A stress journal is also a place for you to record your sources of stress each day, as well as the ways you choose to manage your stress. You can record where stress management strategies succeed and fail, examine why you did or didn't deal with stress in an effective way, even rant about your stress (which is a stress management technique in and of itself). Writing down your stressors and the way you deal with them is helpful in several ways:

• Writing down your sources of stress each day helps you to tune in to the stress in your life. You become aware of stress sources and stress patterns you might not have recognized.

• Writing about your stress and the way you actually handle it helps you to figure out when your stress management strategies are working and when they fall flat. You'll also discover how you feel about the stress in your life and your stress management efforts. Writing can be the very mode of discovery.

• If you are the type who tends to ignore stress, you'll have to acknowledge it when you write it down. If you tend to attack stress, attacking it with the pen is a lot healthier than saying or doing things you'll later regret. If you tend to react to stress, reacting on the page is a lot healthier than reacting by falling into destructive habits.

Your stress journal can take any format—a legal pad, a beautiful bound book of blank pages, even your computer. Whichever you choose, it should be something you enjoy using. You can list your stressors or write paragraphs describing how you felt and what you did about it. Find a way to write in your stress journal that feels right for you.

The most difficult part of keeping a stress journal is getting in the habit of writing in it every day. Like any other habit, writing in a stress journal is something you can learn, and with a little discipline, you can keep it up. You'll be glad you did. The discipline of writing in your stress journal every day is a kind of stress management victory all its own. The additional benefits you'll gain from cultivating your personal stress awareness make the effort easily worthwhile.

ESSENTIALS Organizing just one thing in your life can ease stress considerably. Instead of watching television tonight, why not tackle that sock drawer, that kitchen junk drawer, or that coat closet that's been driving you crazy? Don't expect to do anything beyond the single area you've chosen. You'll be surprised how much better you'll feel with a single drawer or closet put in order.

Putting Your Stress Journal to Work

Once you've found a notebook for your stress journal, you can immediately begin to record your stress management plan. After completing the test and analyzing your results in the last chapter, what was your overall impression of the effect stress has on your life? Think about your overall impression and write it down in your journal. Having these thoughts here will allow you to check back frequently to see if your overall impression is changing. In your journal, you can title the page "My Overall Stress Profile Impressions."

Then, you can begin to focus more specifically on what you've discovered about the stress in your life.

What Works

After completing the questions in the last chapter, you probably noticed patterns and trends emerging as you worked your way through the test. If you didn't, look back and try to determine some trends now. You may have also recognized as you completed the test that you have areas of life you handle pretty well. Some things are actually working!

If this didn't occur to you, think about it now. Recognizing what works in your life will help you see what kind of systems and attitudes you might apply to other areas of your life that aren't working as well.

What things in your life are working pretty well? What parts of your life do you generally feel good about? What are your stress management successes? Where are your productive and efficient systems? What are your best, most supportive relationships? Which of your positive qualities are able to manifest themselves in your life? Spend some time considering what's working, and record it in your journal under "What's Working Well in My Life."

ALERT

Estrogen protects young women from heart disease, but stress can cause estrogen levels to drop, allowing plaque to build up. A 1999 autopsy study revealed that by age thirty-five, most women already had substantial plaque buildup in their coronary arteries. Researchers suspect stress is to blame.

What Doesn't Work

Now, think of the areas of your life that could use some improvement. Do you need more time in your day? More romance in your relationship? Better health habits? A more organized household? A better rapport with your kids? More open communication with your friends?

List the things you would like to improve in your life—the things you'll be better able to improve and focus on once you've got the excess stress in your life under control. You can record this in your journal under "Things I Would Like to Improve."

Targeting Your Strategy

Flip back to the last chapter and record the results of your Personal Stress Profile in your journal. Throughout the chapters in the rest of this book, you'll read about many different stress management techniques. As your read about them, keep in mind the results of your Personal Stress Profile. Each aspect can be targeted with stress management techniques. As you learn about different techniques, experiment with how they can apply to the different areas of your Personal Stress Profile.

Recording Your Test Results

To record your test results and reflect on them at the same time in your journal, you might want to use a template something like the one that follows. You can also make several copies of this template to keep in your notebook or binder.

My Stress Management Profile

Date: _____

My Stress Tolerance Point is (check one):
☐ JUST RIGHT HIGH   ☐ TOO HIGH
☐ JUST RIGHT LOW   ☐ TOO LOW

I believe I am operating (check one):
☐ ABOVE
☐ AT   my Stress Tolerance Point.
☐ BELOW

Here's how I feel about my efforts or lack of efforts to operate at or near my Stress Tolerance Point:

_____

_____

_____

My Stress Triggers are, in general:

_____

_____

_____

ENVIRONMENTAL, specifically:

_____

_____

_____

_____

_____

PHYSIOLOGICAL, specifically:

_____

_____

_____

_____

_____

PERSONAL, specifically:

_____

_____

_____

_____

SOCIAL, specifically:

_____

_____

_____

_____

Some of the techniques I think sound interesting for dealing with my stress triggers are:

_____

_____

_____

_____

_____

_____

_____

In assessing my Stress Vulnerability, I believe I am:

An (check one):
☐ INTROVERT
☐ EXTROVERT

I want to remember to try stress techniques, such as

_____, _____, and

_____, that work with my above tendency.

I am particularly likely to be subject to stress when it is related to (check all that apply):

☐ WORK
☐ SELF-ESTEEM
☐ SELF-CONTROL
☐ MONEY
☐ IMAGE
☐ FAMILY
☐ COMPETITION/CONTROL/EGO
☐ WORRY
☐ MY DEPENDENTS

I plan to focus my stress management techniques on these areas.

Here are my personal observations about my stress vulnerability:

_____

_____

_____

_____

My stress response tendency is to (check one):

☐ IGNORE IT
☐ REACT TO IT
☐ ATTACK IT
☐ MANAGE IT

Here are my thoughts on the way I tend to respond to stress:

_____

_____

_____

_____

Now, you can easily refer to your test results. Use this template again any time you retake the test.

The following sections will give you some ideas for how to target your stress management strategies according to the results of your Personal Stress Profile.

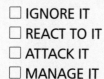
ESSENTIALS

Before you pop a pill to help you ease into dreamland, try counting back slowly from 100 to 1. Imagine each number and visualize how it looks. In your mind, make it look beautiful, in a tranquil color, perhaps drawn in fancy script, or formed by clouds in a beautiful blue sky. Breathe slowly, allowing long inhale and exhale breaths for each number.

Your Stress Tolerance Level Management Strategies

Whether your Stress Tolerance Level was **JUST RIGHT LOW** or **TOO HIGH** or a combination of several levels for different areas of your life, your key to managing your stress is to keep it right around a healthy Stress Tolerance Level. If your level was **JUST RIGHT LOW,** you need to keep making a conscious effort to eliminate excess stress from your life so that you can continue to enjoy your low level of stress. Remember what is working. How are you already able to keep stress low? Then, plan for those times when stress will surely increase. Be prepared!

If your stress level is **JUST RIGHT HIGH,** you also need to continue to make a conscious effort to keep stress at the level that works for you. While you may be able to handle more stress than some other people, you can still get overstressed. Techniques that help you cultivate mind-body awareness will signal you to when stress is getting out of control in your life. People who can take more stress than average tend to neglect their stress level awareness, thinking they can take anything, but we all have our limits.

If your stress level is **TOO HIGH** or **TOO LOW,** you also need a plan. How can you begin to effectively eliminate stress so that you can achieve a healthy Stress Tolerance Level? Or, how can you begin to add stimulation to your life in healthy and productive ways so that you can achieve a healthy Stress Tolerance Level? Remember, too much stress is hard on your body, but not enough stress (not enough for your own personal needs) makes for a pretty dull and unfulfilling life.

Record your Stress Tolerance Level in your journal as a reminder. Then, as you read through the rest of this book, list possible strategies that sound interesting to you. After you've tried them, describe how they work. Finally, record "keeper" strategies to add to your stress management repertoire and daily or weekly routine.

Keeping track of the effectiveness of various techniques is important. While you may remember in the short term that, say, a certain herbal remedy worked well or that a certain relaxation technique was tedious, a month later, you may forget—and you'll be glad you wrote down your experience.

You can format this section in your journal based on the following template, or you can make several copies of these blank templates to keep in a binder.

My Stress Tolerance Level is:_____

Stress management strategy to try	How often tried/ over what period of time? (e.g., daily for two weeks)	How effective was this technique in helping me to achieve a healthy Stress Tolerance Level? (on a scale of 1–10)	Keep (K), or not for me (N)?

ESSENTIALS   Indigestion is a common reaction to stress because the stress response signals the body to channel blood away from the digestive system. The next time you suffer from an attack of indigestion, rather than popping antacids on the run, try sitting still for five minutes, breathing deeply, and savoring a cup of yogurt. The "friendly" bacteria in yogurt may help to promote healthy digestion.

Your Stress Trigger Management Strategies

Whether you get a new roommate, the flu, married, a failing grade, pregnant, or a speeding ticket, stress triggers add to the stress in your life. Managing your Stress Triggers is key to working with your Stress Tolerance Level. Remember, Stress Triggers can come in four categories: Environmental, Personal, Physiological, and Social. The categories in which your Stress Triggers tend to fall can be the key to the stress management strategies you should try.

In your journal, record the categories into which your Stress Triggers tend to fall (see your Personal Stress Profile in the last chapter). Then, you can plan which stress management techniques to try in order to manage (eliminate or ease the stress of) each one of your Stress Triggers.

As you read through the rest of this book, turn back to this section and record Stress Management Techniques that you think might address the Stress Triggers in certain categories. For instance, improving your dietary habits and increasing your daily exercise might address your frequent minor illnesses in the Physiological Stress category. Social anxiety might be effectively addressed by friend therapy or regular self-esteem maintenance. Don't worry about trying to figure out which stress management techniques address which categories. I'll be sure to cue you in each section. You just record the techniques that sound interesting.

Many Stress Triggers are best handled individually, no matter what category they happen to fall into. List your individual Stress Triggers in this section, and the way you decide to tackle each one. Again, you'll be glad to have this record. Not only will you be able to remember later on what worked and what didn't, but you'll be able to see, right here in black and white, how you are proactively managing your own stress rather than letting your Stress Triggers manage you.

ALERT

Watch the way you hold the phone. Many people hunch up their shoulders and bend their necks to hold phones against their ears, keeping their hands free. This posture can contribute to significant muscle tension and misalignment in your spine. If you spend a lot of time on the phone, invest in a headset. They work great for cellular phones, too.

As you tackle your Stress Triggers one at a time, keep track of what you tried and how well it worked in your journal. You can use the following template as a guideline:

My Stress Trigger	This is what I tried	Here's how it worked

Your Stress Vulnerability Adjustment Strategies

Knowing your Stress Vulnerability Factors, or the specific areas of your life in which you are particularly vulnerable to stress, is a great opportunity to use specific stress management techniques to target these areas. Whether you are vulnerable when it comes to your job, your family, or your self-esteem, you can find techniques individually suited to you. Keep track of them in your journal.

As you read through the rest of this book, keep track of the strategies that interest you as they apply to your Stress Vulnerability Factor. I'll cue you when a certain strategy is particularly effective for a certain area of life. For example, debt management strategies can be highly effective in managing financial stress. That's an obvious one. Not so obvious is the effectiveness of visualization for boosting self-esteem, or the power of prayer and spiritual development for boosting the immune system. Here is a template you can use to keep track of your stress vulnerabilities in your journal:

My Vulnerable Area	Here's what I tried	Here's how it worked	Keep it (K) or not for me (N)

ESSENTIALS A warm cup of chamomile tea can help you to unwind before bedtime. Chamomile is thought to have relaxing properties, but how you drink it can be a relaxing experience, too. Focus on the taste, aroma, warmth, steam, the teacup, and how it feels to swallow the tea. This meditation will calm your mind after a busy day and prepare you for sleep.

Your Stress Response Tendency Adjustment Schedule

Here's where you can monitor your natural tendencies to respond to stress. Keep track of the things you tend to do that work and the things you tend to do that are less effective or are destructive to your physical, emotional, or mental health.

In the previous chapter, you grouped your Stress Response Tendencies into four categories: You react to stress, attack it, ignore it, or manage it. You probably respond to stress differently depending on what kind of stress it is. In your journal, you can periodically monitor your stress responses, which will allow you to see your progress. As mentioned previously, you'll be glad you kept track.

You can use the following template in your journal to check your Stress Response Tendencies every week for six weeks. During each week, you'll probably respond to stress in a variety of ways. List them all and describe the kind of stress you were responding to. Staying aware of the ways in which you respond to stress is one of the best ways to help yourself respond to stress in healthy and productive ways. In the second column, for each item, describe the ways you could respond more productively. (If you responded well, congratulate yourself! Who says grownups can't get gold stars?)

My Stress Responses

	This Week	My Plan for Next Week
Week 1	1._____	1._____
Dates:	2._____	2._____
_____	3._____	3._____
to	4._____	4._____
_____	5._____	5._____
Week 2	1._____	1._____
Dates:	2._____	2._____
_____	3._____	3._____
to	4._____	4._____
_____	5._____	5._____
Week 3	1._____	1._____
Dates:	2._____	2._____
_____	3._____	3._____
to	4._____	4._____
_____	5._____	5._____

My Stress Responses

	This Week	**My Plan for Next Week**
Week 4	1._____	1._____
Dates:	2._____	2._____
_____	3._____	3._____
to	4._____	4._____
_____	5._____	5._____
Week 5	1._____	1._____
Dates:	2._____	2._____
_____	3._____	3._____
to	4._____	4._____
_____	5._____	5._____
Week 6	1._____	1._____
Dates:	2._____	2._____
_____	3._____	3._____
to	4._____	4._____
_____	5._____	5._____

Back pain is most often experienced in the lower back. Lower back pain can be a signal from your body that you have too much stress in your life. Listen to your body and let your back pain tell you when it's time to slow down. If back pain is persistent or severe, please see your health care practitioner.

Map Out Your Stress Fault Lines

Some people just aren't writers. If writing doesn't come easily to you or if you just don't enjoy it, keeping a stress journal won't be productive. It will just become a source of more stress, one more thing lingering perpetually on your to-do list. If this sounds like you, you might be more comfortable drawing a map of your stress. Mapping your stress is like writing in a stress journal, but instead of using words, you'll use pictures, symbols, and signs.

Draw your stress map as if it were a map of a city. Each building is a stressor. Each region is an area of vulnerability. Each street is a link between stressors, such as the link between your lack of exercise and your joint pain, or the link between your financial problems and your lack of willpower when it comes to spending. One-way streets represent direct cause-and-effect stressors (insomnia → sleep deprivation, knee injury → chronic pain).

Don't worry if you aren't much of an artist. Your map can be a simple picture of basic labeled shapes. Or, if you so desire, it can be a work of art. The point is to find a mode of expression with which you feel comfortable, and that will best help you discover or visualize the way the stress in your life is interconnected, where individual stressors originate, and how some stressors are merely the effect of other stressors. By eliminating or effectively managing a single stressor, you may find you can eliminate several other stressors, too.

Set Your Stress Management Goals

We've spent a lot of time cultivating stress awareness because recognizing your stress is incredibly important. It is only one step in the stress management process, however. It's also important to define your goals. Do you want to be able to concentrate better? Get sick less often? Stop screaming at your kids? Be more productive at work? Manage your chronic pain? Alleviate your depression? All of the above?

Think about your stress management goals. What do you want to accomplish? Why did you choose this book in the first place? You probably had some goal in mind, even if it was just to stop feeling so stressed all the time. After giving your goals some thought, record them here. This important part of your Stress Management Portfolio will evolve just as other parts of your stress profile and portfolio will evolve. As you accomplish certain stress management goals, you'll certainly define new ones. For now, make a list of your current stress management goals. Don't worry about getting every one down now. You can record new goals as they come along and check off old ones as they are accomplished.

ESSENTIALS

When you are feeling stressed, stop for a moment and notice your expression. Is your face all scrunched up with stress? Is your forehead wrinkled? Are your brows lowered? Is your mouth frowning? Make a conscious effort to relax your forehead, lift your chin, and smile. Simply adjusting your face can make you feel a lot better (and look a lot better, too!).

Implement Your Stress Management Plan of Action

You've analyzed your sources of stress, discovered what is working and what isn't in your life, and thought about all the things you'd like to try to help alleviate your stress. What's left? Jumping in and alleviating that stress!

At first, figuring out exactly where to start may seem difficult. You may feel at a loss or even frustrated by all the information and the ideas that you have. You might think that you could never possibly manage all that stress.

But remember, if you don't recognize all your sources of stress, you'll never be able to deal with them. You've accomplished that important first step, and you've even begun to think about what to do about it. You'll continue to discover new stress management techniques and should continue to add them to your lists. But for now, you need an orderly doable list so that you know where to start.

To implement your stress management plan of action, prepare a numbered list. Decide where you want to start by picking a stressor you think will be fairly easy to deal with. For example, maybe you know you need to get more sleep. That's an excellent place to start because you'll have a hard time handling, let alone managing, any stress at all if you aren't getting enough sleep.

ALERT

Have you heard that certain stressors, such as early childhood trauma or self-esteem issues, show up as pain or tension in certain body parts? While there might be something to these theories, chances are the way stress affects a body is highly individual. Your intuition is probably the most reliable source for information about where in your body your stress is "settling." Or, perhaps some individual counseling may be in order.

Keep your stress management plan goals daily for a while so that you'll feel like you can manage the tasks you set out for yourself. It will also be easier to decide, for example, to go to bed at 10:00 P.M. *just for today*. The thought of going to bed that early every day for the rest of your life may sound impossible, even depressing. You *like* staying up late. That's fine. But if you know it's *just for today,* it will be easy. The same goes for deciding to eliminate junk food from your diet *just for today*, or to go to the gym *just for today*.

As you get into healthier habits, you'll be able to set out your goals for a week, then a month at a time. As you try different approaches, you'll be able to adjust your goals in ways that work for you.

Perhaps your stress management plan of action will look something like this:

My Stress Management Plan of Action for Today

Reasons for stressor	Action today
Sleep deprivation:	1. No TV tonight
Watching television late	2. Tape my shows
	3. Bedtime at 10:00 P.M.

Begin with the stressors you have ideas about handling. The more you learn, the more ideas you'll get on how to handle the areas of stress in your life that seem more challenging.

Stress Management Maintenance

Learning a new system for anything is always fun, even exciting. When you first spend time with the beginning chapters of this book, you may be inspired to banish every iota of unpleasant stress from your life. But after the novelty wears off, stress management must become, like anything else you stick to, a habit. If you don't make a commitment to stress management and pace your efforts so that you don't burn out on too much change all at once, you won't stick to it. You know how it goes. You've probably tried all kinds of new ways of living—healthier eating, that step aerobics class, throwing out half your stuff in an effort to simplify— and as soon as the novelty wears off, the practice gets tiresome, and you don't stick with it.

But stress management is so important to your happiness, health, and well-being that making it a habit and an integral part of your daily existence is worth a serious commitment. So, don't try to do it all at once. Make realistic goals and take gradual steps. Change your life a little at a time, and you'll find you're able to settle comfortably into the changes. Bit by bit, you'll tweak your life until you are operating right at a healthy Stress Tolerance Level. And when that happens, you'll feel great!

After you've worked on your stress management plan for ninety days, take the Stress Test in the previous chapter again and record the results in your journal. Then, if it seems appropriate, you can rework your plan, adjusting your stress management strategies as you gradually get different areas of your life under control. Next, fill out your Personal Stress Profile again, recording the results in your stress journal. Then, you can re-establish your plan, adjusting your management strategies as your stress profile changes.

A nasty tension headache can ruin your whole day and make everything you do more stressful. As soon as you feel a tension headache coming on, try running hot water (not uncomfortably hot) over your hands for ten minutes. This process will draw blood away from your head and into your hands, which could stop a tension headache in its tracks.

CHAPTER 6

Building a Stress-Proof Body

I t's time to start learning about stress management strategies. The more you learn about different stress management techniques, the more options you'll have available when you really need them. In this chapter, we'll cover some of the most basic things you can do to start relieving your stress *today*. This chapter will cover some easy strategies that will set the groundwork for a body and a mind that can handle the necessary stresses of life.

Sleep Away Your Stress

One of the first and most important things to do to build a stress-proof body is to get enough sleep on a regular basis. According to the 2000 Omnibus Sleep in America Poll, conducted by the National Sleep Foundation *(www.sleepfoundation.org),* 43 percent of adults surveyed said that for a few days every month, they are so sleepy during the day that it interferes with their daily activities, and one out of five (20 percent) adults experienced this level of daytime sleepiness at least a few days or more per week.

ESSENTIALS

Having trouble getting your ZZZs? That cliché about drinking a cup of warm milk is backed by science. Milk contains tryptophan and calcium, both of which boost serotonin levels. Serotonin is the chemical released in your body to induce sleep. It also puts you in a good mood. If you have trouble digesting milk, however, this remedy could keep you awake instead of soothing you to sleep.

If you need more convincing that sleep deprivation interferes with life, consider these results from the National Sleep Foundation's survey:

- Over half of the American work force (51 percent) reports that sleepiness on the job interferes with the amount of work they complete.
- Forty percent of adults admit that the quality of their work suffers when they're sleepy.
- At least two thirds of adults (68 percent) say that sleepiness interferes with their concentration, and 66 percent say sleepiness makes handling stress on the job more difficult.
- Nearly one out of five adults (19 percent) reports making occasional or frequent work errors due to sleepiness.
- Overall, employees estimate that the quality and quantity of their work is diminished by about 30 percent when they are sleepy.
- More than two thirds (68 percent) of shift workers report experiencing problems sleeping.

- Nearly one out of four adults (24 percent) has difficulty getting up for work two or more workdays per week.
- A third of adults would nap at work if it were allowed. (Only 16 percent of employees surveyed reported that their employers allow naps.)

Furthermore, over 30 percent of American drivers admit they have fallen asleep at the wheel at least once. According to the National Sleep Foundation, approximately 100,000 traffic accidents and 1,500 traffic-related fatalities are caused by a driver falling asleep at the wheel. Yikes!

The numbers are even more frightening for the younger generation, or those between the ages of eighteen and twenty-nine. According to the poll, over 50 percent of young adults surveyed said they woke up feeling "unrefreshed," and 33 percent suffer from significant daytime sleepiness, a percentage slightly higher than that of notoriously sleepy shift workers!

FACTS

Herbs are a more natural, less harsh method than prescription or over-the-counter sleep aids for treating occasional insomnia. One British study showed that lavender oil released through a diffuser worked as well as prescription medication to treat insomniacs.

Many young people admit staying awake too late to watch television or use the Internet, and 53 percent admit to sleeping less in order to accomplish more. Young adults also suffer aggravated on-the-job stress due to sleep deprivation:

- Over 35 percent of people 18 to 29 years old reported having difficulty getting up for work (compared with 20 percent of those 30 to 64 years old and 9 percent of those 65 and older).
- Nearly 25 percent of young adults reported being occasionally or frequently late to work due to sleepiness (compared to 11 percent of people 30 to 64 years old and 5 percent of workers over 65).
- Forty percent of younger adults are sleepy at work at least two or more days a week (compared to 23 percent of those 30 to 64 years old and 19 percent of those over 65).
- Sixty percent of young adults admit to having driven while drowsy in the past year, and 24 percent report having fallen asleep at the wheel.

Sleep deprivation has a specific and dramatic physical effect on the body. The average adult requires eight hours of sleep per night, and teenagers require 8.5 to 9.25 hours. If you don't get enough sleep, you could experience the following:

- Increased irritability
- Depression
- Anxiety
- Decreased ability to concentrate and understand information
- Increased likelihood of making mistakes and having accident
- Increased clumsiness and slower reaction times (dangerous behind the wheel)
- A suppressed immune system
- Undesirable weight gain

Unfortunately, sleep disorders often disturb our sleep even if we go to bed on time. These sleep disorders include insomnia, snoring (either by you or the person next to you who is keeping you awake), sleep apnea (breathing disturbances during sleep), sleep walking and talking (parasomnia), and restless leg syndrome (a condition in which your legs are uncomfortable and you feel compelled to move them). Also, jet lag or working the night shift can cause sleep disturbances.

Making sure you get enough sleep may require a two-pronged approach:

1. Make the time for sleep.
2. Treat the sleep disorder.

However, if you do not have a sleep disorder but need to make time for sleep, or if you have plenty of time to sleep but have a sleep disorder, you obviously require only a single approach. In any case, if you aren't getting enough sleep, you are increasing your stress, compromising your health, and probably operating well below your potential. Getting enough sleep is so important that it should be your number one item on your stress management to-do list.

Whichever your situation, the following Stress Management Strategies will have you snoozing soon.

ALERT

Restless leg syndrome is a disorder than can affect sleep. According to the National Sleep Foundation, its symptoms are an urge to move the legs, often accompanied by uncomfortable sensations such as a creeping or crawling feeling, tingling, cramping, burning, or pain. Some patients only experience the need to move. Symptoms worsen when the person tries to lie or sit still. There are various treatments available, from relaxation techniques to medication.

Stress Management Strategies: Sleep

If you commit to getting a good night's sleep, you'll find your stress management reserves growing. Here are some tips to get you started on the road to eight quality hours of sleep each night:

- Figure out why you aren't getting enough sleep, then commit to changing your routine. Where are you wasting time during the day? How could you rearrange your schedule to get some things done earlier, allowing for an earlier bedtime? Could you rearrange your schedule to allow a later wake-up time? If you are staying up late to watch TV or surf the Internet, try skipping the media blitz for a few nights to see how the extra sleep changes your mood and energy level.
- Create a bedtime ritual for yourself. Parents are often advised to give their sleep-resistant children a routine, but the technique works for grownups, too. Your routine should include a series of steps that are conducive to relaxation—for example, a bath or shower, then perhaps a few minutes of deep breathing or other relaxation technique; a cup of herbal tea; a good book instead of the television or computer; swapping back rubs, neck rubs, or foot rubs with a partner; writing in your journal. Then, it's lights out.
- Try not to get into the habit of falling asleep in front of the TV. Once in the habit, falling asleep without the TV will probably take longer, and you may not sleep as well. If this happens, try some relaxation techniques.

- If you feel you are wasting precious time by sleeping when you should be getting things done, keep reminding yourself that sleep *is* getting things done. While you sleep, your body is busy healing, recharging by conserving energy, growing and regenerating cells, and consolidating memory and discharging emotions through dreams. You're actually being pretty productive when you sleep, and you'll be even more productive after you've had a good sleep.

- Don't get all stressed out about not being able to get to sleep. An occasional night of too-few ZZZs won't hurt you as long as you usually get enough sleep. Rather than lying in the dark, tossing and turning in frustration, turn on the light and find something to read. Get comfortable. Sip some warm milk or chamomile tea. Meditate. Steer your mind away from worries and think about pleasant things—not sleep, just pleasant things. Breathe. Even if you don't get to sleep, at least you'll get to relax. And you'll probably feel drowsy soon.

FACTS

To treat insomnia, one technique recommended in *The Breathing Book,* by Donna Farhi (Henry Holt, 1996), is to lightly wind a soft cotton bandage around the forehead, eyes, and temples just before sleep. The pressure against the muscles in the face quickly induces a relaxed state.

If you are having trouble sleeping, try these suggestions:

- Don't drink or eat anything with caffeine after lunch if you are having problems getting to sleep. That includes coffee, tea, cola, and many other sodas (check the label); certain over-the-counter pain medications and cold medications (check the label); stimulants designed to keep you awake; and even cocoa and chocolate.

- Eat a healthy, light, low-fat, low-carbohydrate dinner. Fresh fruits and vegetables, whole grains instead of refined grains, and low-fat protein like fish, chicken, beans, and tofu will help your body to be in a calmer, more balanced state come bedtime. Avoid high-fat, overly processed foods in the evening. You'll be more likely to suffer digestive problems that can keep you from sleeping. (You know the feeling—getting up at 3:00 A.M. in a desperate attempt to find those Tums . . .)

- Eat a light dinner. Late, large dinners are upsetting to your digestive system. For a peaceful night's sleep, make dinner your lightest meal.

- For an evening snack, eat foods high in tryptophan, an amino acid that encourages the body to produce serotonin, a chemical that helps you to sleep. Serotonin also regulates your moods, helping you to feel good. Foods high in tryptophan include milk, turkey, peanut butter, rice, tuna, dates, figs, and yogurt. A light snack about thirty to sixty minutes before bedtime that includes any of these foods can help promote restful sleep.

- Don't drink alcohol in the evening. While many people have a drink thinking it will help them get to sleep, alcohol actually disrupts sleep patterns, making your sleep less restful. Alcohol may also increase snoring and sleep apnea.

- Get enough exercise during the day. A well-exercised body will fall asleep faster, sleep longer, and sleep more productively.

- If you are still having problems sleeping, talk to your doctor about it. Studies show that two thirds of Americans have never been asked by their doctors how well they sleep, but 80 percent have never brought up the subject with their doctors, either. Tell your doctor you are concerned about your sleep problems. He or she may have a simple solution.

ESSENTIALS

If you are too stressed to sleep, help yourself relax with a cup of herbal tea. Herbal tea helps you to relax in three ways. Herbs such as lemon balm, chamomile, and mixes designed to promote relaxation and sleep can help to calm the body. The slow process of boiling water and steeping the tea in the steamy cup slows you down and helps you to relax and focus. Then, the process of drinking the tea requires sitting still and slowly sipping. Let yourself relax and enjoy the process as a nighttime ritual. You'll be resting soon!

Stress Management Strategies: Hydration

Sometimes, one of the most helpful things you can do for your body when you're feeling anxious is to have a drink of water. Human bodies are about two-thirds water, but many people are mildly dehydrated (3 percent to 5 percent below their body weight due to fluid loss) and don't know it.

While severe dehydration (10 percent or more fluid loss) has dramatic symptoms and can even result in death, mild dehydration may go unnoticed and is more likely to occur after intense exercise, in extreme heat, while dieting, and after vomiting or diarrhea, either from illness or as a result of food poisoning or drinking too much alcohol.

When you are walking around without enough water in your body, your body will experience stress, and you'll be less equipped to handle stress from other sources.

Are you dehydrated? Symptoms of dehydration include the following:

* Dry mouth
* Dizziness
* Light-headedness
* Dark urine (should be pale yellow)
* Inability to concentrate
* Confusion

ALERT

Dehydration is very dangerous for infants and small children and is a real danger during periods of gastrointestinal illness. If your child has a dry mouth, sunken eyes, dark urine, seems listless, or has a sunken fontanel (the opening between the plates of the skull in infants), seek medical treatment immediately. Dehydration can also be dangerous for seniors, who may not recognize the symptoms and may not be inclined to drink a lot of water.

One reason people tend to be so often dehydrated is that caffeinated beverages are so popular and widely available. While you feel like your thirst is being quenched when you drink a can of cola, the caffeine is actually acting as a diuretic to flush water out of your system.

The other reason for dehydration is simple: People don't drink much water anymore. While water used to be the main and only practical drink of choice for most people, today it's much easier and, many feel, more pleasant to get a can or bottle of soda, a sugary fruit drink, or a cup of hot or iced coffee or tea. While bottled water is also widely available (and is often safer than the tap water in many areas), some people rarely if ever drink water in its plain, unadorned form.

Yet, water can offer your body many benefits, not the least of which is a stronger defense against stress. If you are dehydrated—according to the statistics, you very well may be—your body can't rally its energy in the cause of stress management because it is too busy trying to compensate for its lack of water.

Drinking more water is one of the easiest changes you can make to help manage your stress. With a well-hydrated body, you'll feel better. Your skin will look better. You'll have more energy. So, drink up!

Like anything else, drinking water is a habit. If you don't get into the habit, you'll drink water for a few days then go back to your five-cans-of-diet-soda-per-day habit. Here are some tips to get into this healthful habit:

- If you really don't like the taste of plain water, try a few brands of mineral-added bottled water. The minerals give the water more flavor. Or, add a wedge of lemon, lime, or orange to your water. If you just have to have those bubbles, try club soda instead of soda. Still not charmed? Dilute real fruit juice (not the sugar-added stuff) with half water or half club soda.
- Ideally, you should drink sixty-four ounces, or eight cups, of water each day. That sounds like a lot, but if you space it throughout the day, it's not so much. Have sixteen ounces first thing in the morning, sixteen ounces with lunch, sixteen ounces with dinner, and sixteen ounces in the evening. Add another sixteen ounces or more if you've been sweating or getting a lot of exercise.
- We have become so removed from our natural sensations of hunger that we often mistake thirst for hunger and eat when all we really need is a tall cool glass of H_2O. A glass of water before each meal and whenever hunger pangs strike between meals should satisfy your body's need for water and help to curb excessive eating.

Get a Handle on Bad Habits

Bad habits can be irritating, to ourselves or others, but they can also be stressful. Many bad habits undermine physical health, emotional well-being, and mental acuity. To begin building a body capable of managing the stresses that life necessarily entails, get control over your bad habits; they are the stresses that aren't necessary.

Habits are stressful in three ways:

1. **Direct.** Many habits have a direct, negative effect on the body. Smoking, drinking too much alcohol, and taking certain drugs (legal or illegal) can introduce toxic or harmful substances into the body that can compromise the body's ability to function properly, lead to addiction, even encourage disease processes. Habits can also directly impact our emotional or mental functioning. Becoming intoxicated, overly distracted, or otherwise impaired can make one more prone to accidents, rages, and mistakes. When your body and/or mind are directly affected in a negative way by a habit, your stress level will increase.

2. **Indirect.** Habits also have an indirect effect on your stress level. Knowing you drank too much, stayed up too late, and ate too much the night before can add to your frustration and low self-esteem in your work life the next morning. Your stress will be higher than it would have been had you not spent the evening before being controlled by a bad habit. Maybe someone will comment on your ragged nails and make you feel embarrassed and angry at yourself. Later, you might snap at a friend because you feel bad about your lack of control. Habits can make us feel helpless when they control us, causing stress because we worry about our lack of self-control, the effect our habit may have on others, and the deleterious health effects of whatever the habit may be.

3. **Combination.** Some habits can have both direct and indirect negative effects. Probably most bad habits fall into this category. After all, anything that affects us negatively and that we could have controlled but didn't will tend to undermine our emotional state and self-esteem, leading to related stress. Compulsive overeating, for example, is

dangerous to the body because the body isn't designed to take in huge amounts of food at one time. It can also create negative emotional states such as frustration, depression, and anxiety. Even less dramatic bad habits like habitual messiness can have a combination effect. If you can never keep things clean, for example, you might suffer frustration over never being able to find things, financial loss because of disorganization, and low self-esteem because it seems like everyone else is able to keep things neat but you (which, of course, is not true).

ESSENTIALS

Attitudes and personality determine behavior, but behavior can also determine attitude and personality. Rather than succumbing to the notion that you'll always smoke, overeat, or interrupt people because "that's just the way you are," pretend for a single day that you aren't "that way." Pretend you don't have that bad habit. It may be easier than you think, and soon you may find that you can be that person all the time—that that person was you all along!

Some habits, of course, are good. If you always clean up your own messes, have a habit of being polite, or are devoted to your daily bowl of fresh salad, you probably already know that those habits are keepers.

Some habits are neutral. For example, you always eat a favorite cereal, or you prefer a certain gas station, or you have a habit of humming while you wash the dishes. If they don't bother anybody, no problem.

Other habits aren't so good. What makes a habit bad? A bad habit is a habit that makes you less healthy or less happy. Even if you *feel* good while indulging your habit, you probably know when it's just a temporary high, like when you go to the mall and spend $400 on stuff you don't really need. You get a rush, but as soon as you get home and put the things away, you begin to feel guilt, regret, or even anger at yourself. The habit was controlling you rather than the other way around.

You may feel helpless in the throes of your nail biting, hair twirling, chip munching, TV watching, or procrastinating habit. But as helpless as you feel, rest assured that it's a habit, and habits can be broken. How do you break a bad habit? First, determine if your habit really is bad. If, for example, you drink a cup of coffee every morning because you really enjoy it, that's probably fine. If your habit controls you—if you gulp down java by the quart all day long and feel panicky or nonfunctional without it, you've got a bad habit.

Once you've determined that you do, indeed, have a bad habit (most of us have several), the next step is to identify your bad habit and make sure you understand, logically, why it is, indeed, a bad habit. Once you've recognized and admitted your habit, you can work on getting control over it. Let's look at some common bad habits and the ways they can cause you stress. See where you recognize yourself.

ALERT

When your bad habit is also an addiction, typical habit-control methods may not work. Addictions such as to cigarettes, drugs, alcohol, gambling, or even sex are more complex than simple habits and can be life threatening or life destroying. When your body chemistry or a complex psychological process is involved, you may need additional help, whether it be a nicotine patch, counseling, or a stint in rehab. Talk to your health care provider or counselor about the best way to handle your addiction.

Personal Habits

Personal habits are those things you do that probably drive somebody crazy, or that you never do in front of other people because you know it *would* drive them crazy. Personal habits include nail biting, hair twirling, knuckle cracking, spitting, whining, habitual coughing or throat clearing, habitual cursing, and gum snapping. You can probably think of plenty of others. A personal habit is worth getting rid of if it annoys you, annoys people around you (at least those that you'd rather not annoy), makes you feel bad about yourself, or is bad for you.

Drugs: The Legal Ones and the Other Ones

Drugs can be important tools for maintaining or regaining good health. When used for purposes other than for correcting a health problem, however, drugs can cause imbalances in the body that contribute to health problems. There are people who use legal drugs, which include alcohol, nicotine, caffeine, and prescription drugs. And there are people who use the illegal ones. People use illegal (and sometimes legal) drugs because these drugs make them feel good, increase their energy, or have a calming effect.

Some substances used occasionally in moderation (such as alcohol or caffeine) probably aren't harmful for some people, but other drugs—especially "hard" drugs such as cocaine and heroin—can be very harmful to the body. A glass of wine with dinner is probably fine for someone who isn't addicted to alcohol, isn't prone to alcohol addiction, and really enjoys it. One marijuana cigarette could be dangerous to somebody with asthma and has immediate short-term stressful physical effects on anyone (even if you think it makes you feel relaxed). Illegal drugs pose multiple risks, not the least of which is the potential for getting in trouble with the law. If you want to talk stressful, consider a jail term.

But any substance that artificially alters your mental state taken too often or in large amounts will, at best, keep you from dealing with your stress and, at worst, add significantly to your stress. Legal though it is, few would dispute the dangers of overconsumption of alcohol. Sure, it's easier when you're feeling stressed or don't like your life the way it is to use a drug to help distract you or to help you forget about how things are. But working to improve the way things are—to manage your stress rather than bury it under a temporary euphoria—is a lot more productive in the long term. If you use mind-altering substances to avoid the issues in your life, it's time to rethink this destructive habit.

Overeating

Eating too much weighs down your body and makes you feel sluggish. Overeating at night keeps your digestive system working overtime and can disturb your quality of sleep. Eating too many simple sugars can raise your insulin level and promote bingeing, which perpetuates the cycle of overeating. Eating too much can also lead to overweight; unfortunately, it has already done so in over half the population of the United States.

Eating disorders are the culprit in many cases. Well-known disorders such as bulimia and anorexia, as well as lesser-known but quite common disorders such as binge eating disorder, often have complex psychological causes as well as physical causes. Please seek help from your doctor, counselor, or other health care professional if you think you or someone you love has an eating disorder. Left untreated, both bulimia and anorexia can be fatal.

In some cases, overeating is simply a habit, encouraged by a culture that is obsessed with food (and also with being thin, ironically). Eating a lot of food that tastes good is enjoyable. Good food is everywhere and often doesn't cost much. Watch television for an hour and you'll see many commercials for mouth-watering food. Plus, when life is stressful, it's easy to convince yourself that you deserve that candy bar or that double pepperoni pizza at midnight. You work hard. Don't you deserve a treat?

In the next chapter, you'll learn more about eating right to maximize your stress management potential. But for now, if your overeating is a bad habit, you can help to retrain yourself using the stress management strategies for breaking bad habits at the end of this section.

Overworking

Working hard may seem to you more like a necessity than a habit, and for some people, that's certainly the case. For others, however, overworking really is a habit. Maybe you work to forget that you don't have a social life. Maybe you work because you are obsessed with getting that promotion. Maybe your coworkers and work life have become a surrogate family that you really depend on for your sense of well-being—which may be just fine, up to a point, as long as you aren't depending on your coworkers to provide something they aren't going to provide.

Whatever the case, if you are in the habit of overworking and your work is impinging on your life—that is, you feel you have no personal time, no time to just relax without thinking about work, no privacy because people from work call you at home at all hours—then overworking has become a habit; one, however, that you can gradually reshape.

Too Much Media

Digital cable, satellite dishes, premium movie channels, video rental stores on every corner, radio on the Internet, CD players in the car, high-speed Internet connections, DVD—ours is a technological world, and it can be pretty seductive. Some people can't resist the pleasure of watching a movie on DVD on their laptop while curled in bed, or having the highest of high-end stereo equipment, or exploring the world through the Internet for hours at a time. If you have a media habit, you certainly aren't alone. According to statistics compiled by a group called TV Free America, 98 percent of American households have at least one television, and 40 percent have three or more TVs! The television is turned on in the average American home for seven hours and twelve minutes every day, and 66 percent of Americans eat dinner while watching TV. Eighty-four percent of us have at least one VCR, and we rent 6 million videos every day, compared to 3 million public library items checked out. Almost half of Americans (49 percent) admit they watch too much TV.

Like anything else, technology and media are fine . . . in moderation. But also, like anything else, too much of a good thing soon becomes a bad thing. If your media habit is taking up more than its fair share of your time and you are sacrificing other, equally important or more important parts of your life because of your media fixation, then it's a *bad* habit.

Consider the daily news. People depend on the news to be informed about world events, to hear the next day's weather, and to keep up on local happenings. But obsessive news watching can result in preoccupation with events far removed from your own life, anxiety about the state of the world (justified in many cases, sure, when you can do something about it, but not worth lying awake at night), even depression as a result of focusing too much on all the bad things that happen. Unfortunately, news often focuses on tragedy. Seek balance in your media habits. Set boundaries. Don't let Internet surfing or channel surfing keep you from sleeping enough, eating right, or getting up out of your chair and getting some exercise.

FACTS

According to the A. C. Nielsen Co. (1998), the average American watches three hours and forty-six minutes of television every day, which comes to a total of more than fifty-two days of nonstop TV each year. By age sixty-five, the average American will have spent a total of nine years watching television!

The Noise Habit

The noise habit is related to the media habit. If you always have to have the television or the radio on, whether you are watching it or not, if you can't get yourself to work or do your homework without music or television in the background (or foreground), if you've tried to meditate but absolutely can't stand the silence, if you always fall asleep to the television or to music, then you've probably got a noise habit.

Silence can be not only therapeutic but also remarkably energizing. Finding a space each day for silence and stillness allows the body to recharge. There is nothing wrong with noise, but constant noise keeps your mind from focusing completely on anything and encourages fragmentation. You may be able to get your work or your homework done in front of the television, but it will probably take you longer and you probably won't do as good a job.

QUESTIONS?

Feeling overwhelmed?
Take a vow of silence. Choosing not to speak for an entire day, or just an hour. The experience can be constraining in some ways but liberating in others. Let yourself appreciate the beauty of silence, and teach yourself how to listen well. Taking a vow of silence can be a spiritual discipline, but it also happens to be an excellent technique for slowing down the thought process and focusing on the sounds of the world that aren't being made by you.

People who live alone often like to keep noise in the background. Noise can temporarily mask your loneliness or nervousness. It can calm an anxious mind or distract a troubled mind. Constant noise can provide a welcome relief from oneself, but if it is compromising your ability to think and perform as well as you could, if it is keeping you from confronting your stress and yourself, then it's time to make some space for silence in your life. Too much noise is stressful on the body and the mind. Give yourself a break and let yourself experience silence at least once each day for at least ten minutes. Don't be afraid of silence. To quote Martha Stewart, "It's a good thing."

Shopping

One person's cake is another person's trip to the mall. Some people get a fantastic high from shopping, and shopping can, indeed, become a bad habit (and even an addiction). If you head to the store when you are feeling frustrated, depressed, anxious, or worried about something—even not having enough money to pay the bills—and if the feeling you get from buying a bunch of stuff really makes you feel better, you can be assured you are shopping for the wrong reason.

We are a consumeristic society, and we are encouraged from many different directions to buy things. But we should buy things only for good reasons, such as because we need something or really want something. Just wanting to buy "anything at all," no matter what it is, is not a good reason to go shopping. You work hard for the money you make. Is the time you put in worth the pile of junk you just brought home, junk that you probably won't ever wear, use, eat, or look at again?

The shopping habit can be redirected, just like the overeating habit can be redirected. If you think you shop for the wrong reasons (it's a very common habit), work on finding something else fun to do whenever you feel the shopping impulse. How about something that doesn't cost any money? It may not feel as good at first, but once you get *out of the habit*, you'll wonder how you could possibly have spent so much money on so much junk. To quote a bumper sticker I saw the other day: "The best things in life aren't things."

Procrastinating

Who doesn't procrastinate once in a while? But if you can't ever get anything done on time, no matter how much preparation time you have, no matter how easy the task, then you probably have a procrastination habit. Some procrastination stems from a basic lack of organization, in the home, personal life, office, or wherever. But for some, procrastination exists as a habit all on its own. It doesn't matter how organized you are. You still have a mental block about getting anywhere or doing anything on time.

ESSENTIALS

Procrastination is all in your head—but that means it has a lot of power! When the thought of doing something is so overwhelming that it keeps you from taking action, one way to overcome the paralysis is to meditate on the *thought itself.* Sit quietly, get comfortable, and focus on your dread. Whatever it is, focus on it. Immerse yourself in the dread. Then, imagine enclosing the dread in a bubble. There it is, just a thought, made of nothing. Watch it float away. What's left? A thing that simply needs doing. So, do it!

Chronic procrastinators sometimes despair that procrastination is an ingrained part of their personality and impossible to change. Not true! Procrastination, too, is a habit, and it can be reshaped just like anything else. It will certainly take some doing. Although breaking any bad habit is challenging, it certainly is not impossible. Just remember, you don't have to stop procrastinating all at once. Choose areas to tackle first, like getting to work on time. How can you reorganize your morning and inspire yourself to get up in the first place? Maybe paying bills on time will be your first focus, or retraining yourself to pick up clutter or wash every dish before bedtime. You can do it!

The Top Bad Habits

According to *The Complete Idiot's Guide to Breaking Bad Habits,* by Suzanne LeVert and Gary McClain, Ph.D. (Alpha Books, 1998), these are the top ten bad habits:

1. Lying
2. Being late
3. "Forgetting" and other acts of carelessness
4. Knuckle cracking
5. Belching and passing gas
6. Obsessing over orderliness
7. Being unable to make a commitment
8. Being a skinflint (cheapskate)
9. Procrastinating
10. Cigarette smoking

How many are you guilty of? The fact that a bad habit is common doesn't mean it's okay. Let's look at some tips for curing those first three: lying, being late, and "forgetting," as well as other acts of carelessness.

1. Lying is a habit, not necessarily a character flaw. Some people find themselves bending the truth habitually, even if they don't have a good reason to do so. Do you slant situations or pad the facts so that they are just a little more dramatic? Do you say what you think people want to hear instead of what is really so? Truth telling is a habit, too, and the best way to start is to always pause and think before you say something. Ask yourself, "What am I about to say?" And if your answer is something other than what you know to be the truth, ask yourself, "Is there really a good reason for bending the truth? What would happen if I simply said what is so?" Becoming aware of your habit as you do it will help you to slowly alter it.

2. Why are you always late? Are you perpetually disorganized? Do you like the power that comes from making people wait for you? Being late is inconsiderate, even rude. It makes you look bad, and it sets a bad example for the people who look up to you (people such as your children). The best way to handle disorganization is to tackle problems one at a time. Let your tardiness be your first goal. Planning is key. Start getting ready for anything you have to do about an hour ahead of time and make sure you have everything you need well

before you need it. And if you are late because you like to make them late, keep reading.

3. "Forgetting" and other acts of carelessness, including being late all the time, show a blatant disregard for other people. You may have plenty of excuses. You were "running behind." You have "too much on your plate." You "didn't think." But these are only excuses. The way you treat other human beings is a direct reflection on your character, but it is also something over which you have control. Take control of your people skills and work on doing something thoughtful for someone every day. Try to imagine yourself as the recipient of your actions. How would you feel if a friend said that or did this or forgot you or failed to show up? As with any habit, once again, awareness is the key.

Stress Management Strategies: Reshaping Bad Habits

Knowing you need to change things can be overwhelming, but having some specific strategies can help you to set goals and work on things one step at a time. Use the following list as a guideline to help you set goals. Try one strategy each week, and don't get frustrated. You've had that habit for a long time, and it may take awhile to retrain yourself, but you can do it!

- Practice the *pause*. Know your habit, and when you are about to fall into your habitual behavior, learn to pause, just for a moment, and think. Ask yourself these questions: Will this nourish my body? Will this nourish my spirit? Is this good for me? Will I feel good about doing this later? Or, will I feel guilty about it later? Is it worth the momentary pleasure? Is it *really* worth the momentary pleasure?

- Don't have habit triggers in your house. If sugar sets you off on a binge, don't keep sugary snacks around. If you can't resist shopping, don't keep your credit card in your wallet when you know you have to go to the mall, or better yet, leave your credit card at home. Bring just enough cash to make your purchase, and no more. Don't keep alcohol in the house if that's your weakness. If nighttime television is your weakness, get that TV out of your bedroom. Put it in the kitchen to make cleaning more interesting, or even (gulp) pack it away.

- If you use your bad habit to soothe your stress, replace your habit (food, cigarettes, excessive Internet surfing) with another kind of "treat" that is just as good or better. Make that "treat" easily accessible in situations where you know you'll be tempted to lapse into your habit. For example, if you automatically turn on the television as soon as you get home from work, allow yourself twenty minutes of quiet time instead. Don't let anyone disturb you! Put on relaxing music and breathe, meditate, have some tea, read a book, peruse a magazine, or just take a catnap. You'll be recharged far beyond what that hour of soap operas or tell-all talk shows could have done.

- Turn your habit into your specialty by becoming a connoisseur! Let food become a genuine pleasure. Focus on quality, not quantity. If you want food, eat a small amount of something really good. Savor every bite. Never waste your time, energy, or health on large amounts of substandard food. The same goes for alcohol. Rather than drinking as much as you can of whatever is available, settle for only small amounts of the very best. And the same goes for shopping. Don't just buy whatever you see. Collect something valuable and learn all about it. For example, learn about early American ceramics or antique train sets or Victorian hat pins or dog statues from around the world—whatever strikes you as interesting.

If you love to watch television, watch only quality television. Become an expert on classic movies or independent films. Watch and learn from nature shows, or science shows, or shows about art, cooking, whatever you like. You might even learn how to make your own movies. If you can't do without noise, learn all about classical music, or jazz, or classic rock, or whatever you like. Life's too short *not* to live well.

Becoming a connoisseur doesn't work for every habit, of course. One can't really become a connoisseur of procrastination, for example. But a little creativity can still transform any habit into a hobby or even a specialty. If procrastination is your bad habit, become an expert on simplicity; that way, you'll have less to do (less to do late) and fewer places to go (fewer places to arrive late).

Or, you can throw yourself into the reverse of your habit. A nail biter? Learn how to do manicures and pedicures. A slob? Become an expert at organizing your household and routines in a way that minimizes cleaning. Many self-professed slobs have reformed and created successful careers for themselves as professional organizers.

Habit Attack Chart: Your Bad Habit Summary

It's time to pull out that trusty stress management journal again! Copy this chart into your journal and use it to list your habits, describe what you think triggers them, and then write down how each habit causes you stress. For example, you might write "nail biting" in the first column, "feeling nervous or bored" in the second column, and "social embarrassment, feeling unattractive, annoyance at myself" in the third column.

Even if you aren't quite ready to give up a habit—perhaps you know you are addicted to television but you aren't ready to quit watching your twelve favorite shows just yet. If that is the case, record your habit in the chart anyway. You can deal with it when you are ready, even if you won't be ready any time soon. At least you'll have all your bad habits officially identified in one place.

When you've filled out the chart and covered the bad habits you think are causing you the most stress, keep reading to see how to manage your habits, one at a time, as you think you can handle them.

HABIT	TRIGGERS	STRESS EFFECTS

HABIT	TRIGGERS	STRESS EFFECTS

Vitamins, Minerals, and More

Another way to build a healthy body that is best able to combat excessive stress is to make sure you aren't suffering from any basic deficiencies in vitamins, minerals, and phytochemicals (substances in plants thought to improve health and strengthen the immune system). While not everyone agrees that supplements are important, most of us don't get a chance to eat a completely balanced, well-rounded diet every single day. So, think of a supplement as an insurance policy.

FOR YOUR BEST NUTRITIONAL DEFENSE AGAINST STRESS, FOLLOW THESE GUIDELINES:

- Eat a balanced diet.
- Take a multivitamin/multimineral tablet every day to strengthen your reserves and cover your nutritional bases.
- Vitamins C, E, beta carotene (a form of vitamin A), selenium, and zinc are antioxidants. Studies suggest extra antioxidants in the diet can reduce the risk of heart attack, stroke, and cataracts and can slow the aging process. (Note: Antioxidant supplements have been shown to increase the risk of cancer in smokers.) Antioxidants from citrus fruits; broccoli; tomatoes; leafy greens; dark orange, yellow, and red vegetables; nuts; seeds; and vegetable oils are always good for you.
- The B vitamins are great in many ways. Many of them are thought to boost immunity, improve skin quality, protect against cancer, help arthritis symptoms, help the body to metabolize food and produce energy, and even help to reduce the effects of stress in the body.

- Calcium is a mineral that is essential for maintaining bone mass, preventing cancer and heart disease, reducing blood pressure, treating arthritis, promoting sleep, metabolizing iron, and reducing PMS symptoms.
- Many other trace minerals keep the body healthy and working correctly, from copper and chromium to iron and iodine to selenium, vanadium, and zinc.
- Amino acids and essential fatty acids are also necessary for a healthy functioning body.
- Much is made of other "supplement-of-the-week" substances. There may be something to some of these claims. Others may later prove false. Read about supplements if it interests you. But remember, the most important thing is to eat a healthy, balanced, varied diet.

ALERT

Supplementation isn't something to get obsessed about, and if it complicates your life or stresses you out to imagine swallowing a handful of vitamins every morning, just eat well and stick to your single multivitamin-mineral supplement. You'll be fine.

Preventative Vitamin Regimen

Some studies point to an increase in certain vitamins and minerals as helpful for boosting the body's ability to heal certain maladies. An extra boost of vitamin C (500 to 1,000 milligrams per day) and a few zinc lozenges may help to shorten the length and lessen the severity of a cold. Many people swear by these remedies. Extra calcium has been shown to lessen the severity of PMS symptoms in women. Some studies suggest that vitamins C and E as well as other antioxidants can protect against certain cancers and heart disease.

This chart will show you what vitamins are found in abundance in which foods. I will help you to target your stress with a nutrient attack.

Vitamin/Mineral	What It Does	Where to Find It
A	Promotes good vision Aids in bone growth Aids in proper cell division May help prevent certain cancers	Liver, eggs, milk Orange and green vegetables Fortified cereal
B_1	Maintains nervous system May protect against heart disease Helps anemia	Pork Milk Eggs Whole grains
B_2	Aids metabolism Aids vision Protects against stress Promotes healthy skin	Milk, eggs Fortified bread and cereal Leafy vegetables
B_3	Promotes a healthy nervous system May lower cholesterol Reduces blood pressure	Meat Fish Eggs Wholegrain cereals
B_5	Aids energy production Promotes healing Protects against stress Governs metabolism of fat	Eggs, yeast Brown rice Wholegrain cereals Organ meats

B_6	Boosts immune system
	May protect against
	   certain cancers
	Relieves PMS and
	   menopausal symptoms
		Fish
		Meat
		Milk
		Wholegrain cereals
		Vegetables

B_9 (folic acid)	Prevents certain birth defects
	May protect against
	   heart disease
	May protect against
	   certain cancers
		Leafy greens
		Wheat germ
		Eggs
		Bananas
		Nuts, oranges

B_{12}	Maintains nervous system Boosts memory Increases energy and healthy growth May protect against certain cancers	Pork, beef Liver Fish Eggs, milk

Vitamin/Mineral	What It Does	Where to Find It

C	Boosts immune system
	May protect against
	  certain cancers
	Speeds wound healing
		Citrus fruits
		Leafy greens, broccoli
		Most fresh fruits and
		  vegetables

D	Aids in calcium absorption
	May help prevent
	  certain cancers and
	  osteoporosis
		Fortified milk
		Fatty fish
		Sunlight

E	Protects against cell
	  damage from free radicals
	May help protect against
	  certain cancers and
	  cardiovascular disease
		Vegetable oils
		Nuts
		Leafy greens
		Wheat germ
		Mangoes

Calcium	Strengthens and
	  maintains bone
	Helps prevent osteoporosis
	  and arthritis
	Helps prevent muscle
	  cramps
		Milk
		Cheese
		Leafy greens
		Tofu
		Salmon
		Eggs

Iron	Increases energy Boosts the immune system Prevents iron deficiency anemia	Shellfish Wheat bran Brewer's yeast
Selenium	Keeps skin and hair healthy Boosts immune system Keeps eyes healthy Improves liver May protect against certain cancers	Tuna fish Wheat germ Bran Onions Tomatoes Broccoli

Zinc	Boosts the immune system
	May protect against
	  certain cancers
	Helps prevent and treat
	  the common cold
		Mushrooms
		Oysters
		Meat
		Whole grains
		Eggs

Herbal Remedies

Herbalism is an ancient and time-tested art that remains alive and well today. Many people take herbal remedies, from the popular Echinacea for colds to more complex preparations for every imaginable ailment. A good herbalist can help you treat your health problems naturally and can be an excellent complement to conventional medicine.

Herbal remedies can be infused into water for teas, decoctions, and infusions; syrup, to make herbs more palatable; alcohol for tinctures; oil, to rub into skin; they can be mixed with cream, for external application; they can be formed into tablets or put inside capsules for easy swallowing; or they can even be put into the bath.

Although you can buy many herbs at your local pharmacy or even at the grocery store, herbs aren't FDA regulated, so your best bet is to go to an accredited herbalist with a good reputation. Herbalists know about the side effects of different herbs and also how they interact with other medications. To find an herbalist, look in the phone book, ask the employees at your local health food store, or talk to friends for a referral. Some areas have directories of natural health care providers.

While many prescription medications are made from or derived from herbs, herbalists use herbal prescriptions to treat the whole person, not just an isolated condition. Herbalists believe that medical treatment should involve the least possible intervention and should strengthen the body's healing powers.

ALERT

The FDA doesn't regulate herbal supplements. So, you can never be completely sure the herbs you are buying are consistent in their ingredients or quality. It is best to stick with well-studied remedies and rely on a trained herbalist for additional remedies. Always check with your doctor before taking herbal supplements if you are taking or begin taking other medications, or if you have a health condition. Many herbs have side effects you should know about, and some could interact with other medications and even certain foods.

Homeopathy

Like herbalism, homeopathy is holistic, but the remedies, which can be purchased in many health food stores, are so diluted that they are safe for anybody to use. Homeopathy is a holistic healing therapy that works on the principle that like cures like. Herbs and other natural substances that cause certain symptoms in a healthy person are diluted and shaken again and again, resulting in an extremely dilute remedy that supports and encourages the body's own healing efforts. Homeopathy is based on a few basic principles: that symptoms of disease are a sign that the body is healing itself, so symptoms shouldn't be suppressed; that a substance that causes symptoms such as those of a particular disease will, in minute amounts, negate the effects of the disease; and that symptoms will clear up in the opposite order from how they appeared.

Because the remedies are so safe, you don't have to understand the whole philosophy behind homeopathy to try it. In fact, homeopathy is an exceptionally safe way to deal with health imbalances, although it typically works more slowly than conventional medicine. Many people prefer it because it is less invasive, has fewer side effects, and is more holistic than conventional medicine. Homeopathic remedies are effective for physical ailments such as colds, chronic problems such as arthritis or allergies, and emotional problems such as anxiety or depression. Plus, homeopathic remedies, which can be made with everything from herbs and berries to roots to minerals such as gold and oyster shells to whole honeybees dissolved in alcohol and diluted, are typically far less expensive than prescription medications because they contain such minute amounts of the actual substance on which the remedy is based.

Balancing Your Stress with Relaxation

Fortifying your body with sleep, water, nutritional supplements, and holistic health care will help to put you in good condition for managing stress. But what about that active mind, those tense muscles, that parade of worries that keeps running through your head like a looped videotape?

When stress hits and your body begins to experience its effects, knowing how to react to combat those effects before they can do too much damage is a powerful skill.

SSENTIALS

Remember high school science class? For every action, there is an equal and opposite reaction. When stressed, the body responds by releasing stress hormones that have certain effects. When relaxed, the body experiences something very different:

- Decreased oxygen consumption
- Muscle relaxation
- Decreased metabolism
- Change in brain waves

In his influential book *The Relaxation Response* (Avon Books, 1975), Herbert Benson, M.D., determined in his research that consciously and purposefully invoking the relaxation response through meditation involves the following four basic steps, no matter what your meditation technique:

1. A quiet environment
2. Something to focus on (a sound, an object, a thought)
3. A comfortable position
4. A passive attitude

It seems that the most important of the four for inducing a relaxed state is the passive attitude, or not judging oneself and one's relaxation efforts or becoming too distracted. Having a passive attitude can carry over into many areas of life and can be effectively invoked when you sense stress mounting. People get very stressed out when they are feeling pointedly *un*-passive about something. It could be a client's condescending comment, disrespectful words from your child, finding the toothpaste cap behind the toilet *again*, doing something clumsy like spilling your coffee on your computer keyboard, breaking your grandmother's crystal platter, or backing out carelessly and denting someone's car.

At times like these, especially when they seem like the last straw after a stressful day, you can feel like exploding. You experience a surge of cortisol. Your muscles tense. Your breathing increases. A recent study suggested that these sudden cortisol surges can cause tiny nicks and tears in your blood vessels.

ESSENTIALS

So, you know you've got a stressful day ahead of you. What can you do? Have a bowl of oatmeal for breakfast. Oats help to maintain a healthy nervous system, and a bowl of oatmeal for breakfast can help to promote a feeling of calm throughout the day. It has been demonstrated that oatmeal, more so than other breakfast foods, including cold cereal made with oat flour, can raise an athlete's endurance level. And studies show it can lower your cholesterol to boot.

When you feel a rage, a surge of irritation, a flood of despair, a panic, or a fit of yelling coming on, one way to circumvent the surge is to consciously adopt a passive attitude. You may not always be able to stop and meditate, find a quiet place, focus on a mantra (a word or sound you repeat while meditating that helps clear and center your mind, bringing a feeling of peace), or even get comfortable, but you can adopt a passive attitude. How? Two words: *Oh well*.

These two little words are extremely powerful. Really! Someone criticizes you? You spilled your coffee on your keyboard? Oh well. Something is broken, wrecked, ruined? Oh well. Your child talks back? Oh well.

This response may seem all wrong to you. Oh well? Won't that keep you from learning from your mistakes? Won't that encourage people to walk all over you? Certainly not. If your child talks back to you, that doesn't mean he or she shouldn't have to suffer the consequences, but it also doesn't mean you have to get all worked up about it. Besides, a serene parent dolling out consequences is much more in control than a flustered parent.

If you make a mistake, learn from it. Something happened. You'll be more careful next time. But "oh well" means you recognize that attaching negative emotions to a mistake will cloud your thinking rather than clear it up. If you aren't filled with rage, you'll be better able to respond and react appropriately. You'll calmly and politely respond to the client. You'll calmly clean your keyboard rather than throwing the whole computer against the wall. You'll write a sincere and heartfelt letter of apology to your grandmother that isn't stained with tears. You'll buy your own tube of toothpaste rather than get irritated with your partner for leaving off the cap.

"Oh well" can become a mantra of its own, reminding you at the onset of your stress reaction to let go of the stress part of the experience. It doesn't mean you ignore the experience itself. It means you stop your body from damaging itself with a surge of unnecessary stress hormones. Unless you need to fight or flee, you're better off without that cortisol surge.

So, relax. Say, "Oh well." You're balancing your stress response with the relaxation response. Good for you!

Relaxation Techniques

When you do have more time to work on relaxation techniques, you can certainly take your pick of many. Throughout the ages, different cultures all over the world have developed their own relaxation techniques. Some involve meditation, some breathing, some specific kinds of movement. Some work quickly; others are meant to take time. Some involve more physical effort but relax the mind. Others involve mental effort but relax the body. If you learn about them all, you'll be able to pick the kind of relaxation technique that suits you in any given situation. I'll tell you about a few of these techniques in the following sections, and you'll find out about more in later chapters throughout this book. Many of these techniques aren't designed specifically for relaxation, but relaxation is a side effect (such as with yoga and certain types of meditation).

Body Scan

The body scan is a popular relaxation technique that involves a mental scanning of the entire body in search of tension and the conscious release of that tension. You can do a body scan on your own, or you can have someone direct you by speaking out loud and naming the parts of the body, in order, so that you are cued when to relax what. You can also recite your own body scan cues onto a tape and play it back for yourself.

The body scan is a great way to wind down after work or to calm down before a stressful event. Practiced every day, it can become a way to maintain a tension-free body and a body-aware mind.

Different people do the body scan in different ways. Some people like to tense each area of the body in turn, then fully relax it. Others prefer to visualize the release of tension without actually contracting the muscles first. You can imagine breathing into and out of each body part, exhaling the tension one area at a time. Whichever way you choose is fine. You might try several ways to find out which one you prefer.

If you would like to make your own body scan tape, you can use the following script. Read this passage out loud on a tape (or have someone with a relaxing voice do it for you). Don't forget to pause after mentioning each body part to give yourself time to focus on relaxing and releasing tension. When the script tells you to pause, don't repeat the word *pause*, but actually pause in your reading for five to ten seconds or more.

Lie down comfortably on your back on a firm surface. Feel your shoulders, middle back, lower back, and hips settling into the floor. Relax your upper arms, lower arms, hands, thighs, calves, and feet. Let your feet fall open, away from each other. Relax your neck and let your head feel heavy against the floor. Breathe deeply. [PAUSE]

Become aware of your feet. Are they relaxed? Search for tension in your feet and let it go. Release all tension and strain from your feet. Don't forget to breathe. [PAUSE]

Feel your lower legs and calf muscles, from your ankles to your knees. Are your lower legs relaxed? Search for tension in your ankle. Let it go. Search for tension in your calf muscle. Let it go. Search for tension in your shin. Let it go. Search for tension in your knee. Let it go. Release all tension and strain from your foot. Keep breathing. [PAUSE]

Now, bring your attention to your upper legs—the muscles on the fronts of your thighs, the muscles on the backs of your thighs, and your hip joints. Search for tension. Let go of the tension in the fronts of your thighs. Let go of the tension in the backs of your thighs. Breathe it away. Let your hips go, relaxing them even further into the floor. Let all the tension out of your hip joints. Breathe deeply. [PAUSE]

Feel the muscles of your lower abdomen and your buttocks. Feel how these muscles hold tension, then let that tension go. Let the muscles relax completely, releasing all strain and tightness. Breathe. [PAUSE]

Now, bring your attention to the muscles over your stomach. You probably hold these muscles in all day. Let them go. Fully relax and release your abdominal muscles. Breathe deeply, and exhale all the tension. [PAUSE]

Feel the muscles that radiate around the sides of your body and extend into your upper back. Feel your shoulder blades, ribs, chest, and upper spine relaxing. Let the tension go. Breathe out the tension. [PAUSE]

Bring your attention to your shoulders and neck. Feel all the stress and tension lingering there, making your neck and shoulder muscles tight and tense. Slowly let it all go, taking several long deep breaths. Completely relax your shoulders and your neck. [PAUSE]

Feel the muscles in your upper arms—your deltoid muscles at the top, and your biceps and triceps around your upper arms. Search out any hidden pockets of stress and tension in your upper arms and let it go. Relax your upper arms and breathe. [PAUSE]

Feel your elbow joints, the muscles of your lower arms, your wrists, your hands, and each one of your fingers. Imagine a radiating circle of warmth moving down each arm and dissolving all tension from your elbows, lower arms, wrists, hands, and each finger and thumb. [PAUSE]

Now, feel the muscles in your head, feel your scalp, your facial muscles, your chin, your jaw. Release the tension in your scalp, along your temples, around your ears, in your forehead, around your eyes, your cheeks, your jaw, your mouth, your chin. Let it all go. Relax. Breathe. [PAUSE]

Now, imagine a warm radiant circle of light moving slowly up your body, starting around your toes, moving to the crown of your head, then slowly moving back down again. As it moves over you, it scans for any remaining areas of stress or tension and immediately dissolves them. You feel warm, deeply relaxed, and infused with a sense of well-being. [LONG PAUSE]

Lie still for a few more minutes savoring the feeling of total relaxation. Then, when you are ready, very slowly roll over to one side and carefully sit up. [PAUSE]

ESSENTIALS

Focusing on your peripheral vision can be deeply relaxing. The Kauna shamans of ancient Hawaii called this technique "hakalau," which means "to focus in and spread awareness." To use this technique, sit comfortably and relax. Pick a spot in front of you and relax your eyes, blurring your vision just slightly. Then, without moving your eyes, focus for a few minutes on what you can see in your peripheral vision. Instant relaxation.

Breathe Away the Stress Response

One of the easiest relaxation tips is as simple as breathing in and out. In fact, it *is* breathing in and out. Many people are in the habit of shallow breathing, or chest breathing. While this allows quicker respiration and is handy for emergencies, shallow breathing doesn't plumb the depths of the lungs the way deep breathing does. A few slow, purposeful, truly deep breaths can stop a stress attack in its tracks. Deep breathing also helps to expel more air from your lungs, which is important for efficient lung functioning.

When told to breathe deeply, people tend to gulp in a huge amount of air with a dramatic uprising of the chest. Actually, deep breathing happens much deeper, and it is the stomach and abdomen that should rise and fall, not the chest—and especially not the shoulders.

Also, in deep breathing, the *exhalation is the focus*. With a truly deep exhalation, the inhalation will take care of itself.

Breathing from deep in your torso is hard to do if you aren't used to doing it. You used to do it as an infant, but as an adult in a high-stress world, you may have forgotten how. The easiest way to retrain yourself to breathe deeply is to begin by lying down. Lie comfortably on your back and put one hand on your abdomen and the other on your chest. Then, do the following:

1. Begin by breathing normally. Be conscious of your breathing, but don't try to manipulate it. Which hand is moving more, the hand on your chest or the hand on your abdomen?
2. Now, try to exhale every last bit of breath slowly, making a "sss" sound. When you think you've exhaled every bit of breathe, give your lungs one more push and let out a final "sss" of air. As you exhale, feel the hand on your abdomen sinking in, lower and lower, as the breath empties out of the body.
3. After this deep exhalation, you'll naturally take in a deep breath, but don't try to suck in air. Just let your body take it in on its own. Don't try to suck air into your chest. Just let your body refill. As it refills, try to keep your chest and shoulders still. Be conscious of how the hand on your abdomen rises up again as breath enters the body.
4. Exhale again, slowly, as fully as possible, feeling the hand on your abdomen sinking in.
5. Repeat for ten deep breaths.

Once you've mastered the feeling of deep breathing, you can try it sitting up. Again, focus on the exhalation. A good calming breathing exercise is to measure your breathing by silent counting, making the exhalation twice as long as the inhalation. Try this exercise when you are feeling tense (before you say or do something you'll later regret!):

1. Slowly breathe in through your nose to a slow count of five, filling your torso, from the bottom up, with air. Keep your shoulders and chest still. Instead, feel your body expanding from the abdomen and lower back.
2. Slowly breathe out through your mouth, lips pursed, making an airy, whispering "whhhhhh" sound, to a slow count of ten. Keep your shoulders and chest still. Feel your body deflating from the abdomen and lower back.
3. Repeat several times, or until you feel calm.

You'll read more about breathing as a meditation in Chapter 8. In the meantime, let your breath work for you, as the ultimate no-frills, any-time, any-place relaxation tool.

Imagery Power

For instant relaxation, imagery can work for you. Imagery is simple and fun. Feeling stressed? Feeling anxious? Feeling hopeless? Go on vacation. No, don't leave your desk and head to the airport. Stay at your desk, close your eyes, relax, breathe, and use your imagination to visualize the place you would most like to be.

You remember your imagination, don't you? It was that thing that, as a child, allowed you to fly like a bird, stomp like an elephant, bark like a dog, save the world from disaster, go on safari, jump from an airplane with your parachute, and visit a land made entirely out of candy, all in one day. Remember that? Wasn't that fun?

Your imagination is still in your head, even if it's grown a little rusty from disuse. Time to take it out, brush it off, and use it in the service of stress management! You might not decide to imagine that you are a superhero (then again, you might, and why not?). But why not imagine wandering down a secluded beach at sunset, the balmy tropical winds rippling the turquoise sea? Maybe you would prefer cuddling in front of the fire with a special someone (even if you haven't met him or her yet) in a cozy cabin in the woods? Maybe images of the Far East, the rain forest, or hiking a glacier in Alaska invoke a sense of peace in you. Maybe you're partial to the desert . . . or a really fancy dessert! (Nothing wrong with visualizing a land made entirely out of candy!)

Let yourself daydream a little. Consider it personal time. Time to recharge. It's fun, and it's perfectly legal. It's also an excellent way to manage the stress that comes your way. After all, that's what vacations are for!

CHAPTER 7

Get Strong, Get Healthy

If you've ever tried to lose weight, you've heard the mantra, "Eat less, exercise more." The same prescription can help to decrease the effects of stress in your life. You should eat moderate amounts of food high in vitamins, minerals, complex carbohydrates, low-fat proteins, and fiber, and decrease your intake of highly processed food and food high in sugar and fat. Exercise builds muscle, increases lung capacity, improves cardiovascular function, and triggers the release of chemicals that counteract the effects of stress.

SSENTIALS Don't set yourself up for an energy crash by breakfasting on sugary sweets like doughnuts, cinnamon rolls, or sugar-loaded breakfast cereal. Complex carbohydrates and a little protein will keep your blood sugar levels steady and your energy steady, too. A whole wheat bagel with low-fat cream cheese, a bowl of oatmeal with a sprinkling of almonds or walnuts, a tortilla wrapped around a scrambled egg, or a peanut butter sandwich are all good choices.

Move It or Lose It!

Exercise may be one of the most perfect stress management tools, yet it's often the first thing to go when our schedules get too busy. Because there is no "deadline" associated with daily exercise, it's easy to bump exercise to the bottom of the priority list.

Or, *is* there a deadline? According to the Centers for Disease Control and Prevention (CDC), Americans are no more fit than they were in 1990. Now, as then, only about 25 percent of American adults get enough exercise to achieve health benefits. Many researchers believe that poor health habits—most essentially, lack of exercise, improper diet, and smoking—are responsible for a significant proportion of deaths from heart disease and cancer. Are we fast approaching our "deadline" without having established good health habits? Maybe it would be wise to move it so that we *don't* lose it.

But this book is only peripherally about disease prevention. It is primarily about stress, and moderate exercise, according to an increasing number of experts, may be the single most effective way to get stress under control. Are we sabotaging our own stress management efforts because we think we're too busy to get up and take a walk? We certainly aren't helping our body deal with the effects of stress by leading a sedentary life. Why?

I've told you how stress evokes the "fight or flight" reaction by releasing stress hormones into the body designed to give us sudden, quick reactions, extra strength, and endurance. When we don't respond to the stress response by moving quickly, using our strength, or taking advantage of the added endurance, our bodies are all geared up with no outlet for that energy. Muscles stay tense. Blood pressure stays high. Breathing stays shallow. Cortisol and adrenaline course through the body causing all kinds of problems when the body doesn't react the way it is being programmed to react.

ESSENTIALS To boost your energy when you just can't seem to get up and exercise, take a shower. A shower is your in-home hydrotherapy center. Start with body-temperature water for three minutes, focusing the shower stream on your major muscle groups. Then, turn up the cold water and stand for thirty seconds under the cooler stream. Jump out and get going! The stimulation of the water on your skin and the cool temperature at the end will jump-start your mind and increase the circulation throughout your body, helping you to feel awake, alert, and ready to move.

Exercise changes the picture, accomplishing two important things in the wake of the stress response:

1. Exercise allows the body to expend energy so that while your brisk walk around the block may not actually be "fight or flight," to the body, the message is the same. That extra energy available to your body is being used, signaling the body that it can, after exercise, return to equilibrium.
2. Exercise also releases chemicals like beta endorphins that specifically counteract the effects of stress hormones, alerting the body that the danger has passed and the relaxation response can begin.

In other words, exercise makes the obsolete "fight or flight" stress response relevant again. It lets your body respond the way it is trying to respond. Rather than sitting and fuming (what caveperson ever did that in response to a charging predator?), you are getting up and moving. "Ahh . . ." the body responds. "Ahh, this is what I want to do!"

But making yourself get up and exercise is the trick. While I don't mean to beat a dead caveperson, our prehistoric ancestors didn't have much of a choice: It was exercise or die. We have plenty of choices. We can get along just fine, thank you, without moving very much at all. We might move from room to room in the house, or from house to car to office desk to car to house, but that's relatively insignificant compared to the kind of day-to-day, hardworking, on-the-move kind of existence humans once knew.

Exercising enough is certainly possible, however, in modern life. Resources are widely available to help, making exercise easy to accomplish for those who really want to accomplish it. For some people, exercise is already a good habit, or a priority to keep energy high and weight under control. For others, exercising is akin to having a root canal. They don't like it, they don't want to do it, and they see absolutely no good reason to break a sweat.

Most of us are probably somewhere in between. We know exercise is good for us and we do it . . . occasionally—when the mood strikes or time permits. The trouble is, exercising in fits and starts isn't enough to accomplish long-term stress management or a decreased risk of developing chronic illness. How do you get in the regular habit of exercising?

The trick is finding an exercise plan you can stick with. Since you aren't compelled, you need to be motivated. When life is busy and full, forcing yourself to spend thirty minutes daily doing something you hate when nobody is making you do it . . . well, you do the math. It's not going to happen.

However, even if you are a die-hard exercise hater, you can probably find something you like. Maybe your idea of exercise is an aerobics class, but you can't stand the pressure of standing in the midst of all those young, fit, barely-twenty year olds. Maybe you're one of those twenty year olds, but you can't seem to master the fancy footwork. Or, maybe you think exercise is jogging, or team sports, or calisthenics, and you'd rather eat worms.

Whatever your preconception, fear not. Exercise is a broad term. Just about anybody can find some kind of exercise they actually enjoy. Maybe joining a gym is the answer for you—all those classes, all that equipment, the sauna and spa to relax you afterwards, even child care! Maybe you need something more tranquil than high-impact aerobics, and you'll find new inspiration in a yoga class. Maybe you just need to get out into the fresh air and take a walk. What could be easier?

Even if you find something you can only, at best, tolerate, try it for a while. Expand your fitness horizons and keep an open mind. Try one thing, then try another, then another. You'll accumulate a lot more hours of exercise than if you just sit there rejecting the prospect. Once you begin to experience the stress-relieving benefits of regular exercise, that daily trip to the gym or that yoga class may seem a lot more attractive, even an essential part of your day. You might even learn to like it!

ESSENTIALS   It seems that in the world of fitness, there's always a buzz, and one of the buzzwords in recent years is "core." Core strengthening through targeted weight machines, yoga, and Pilates exercises (I'll discuss the benefits of yoga and Pilates a little later in the chapter) means building the abdomen, lower back, and the other supporting muscles in the body's "core." These exercises do more than help hold in your tummy. Core muscles, when strong and supple, lend grace, lightness, and control to the entire body. Ask any ballet dancer about the importance of a super-strong torso.

Quiz: Your Exercise Profile

Are you exercising enough? Are you exercising too much? Are you doing the right kind of exercise to relieve your stress? Take the following quiz to determine if your exercise routine is the right prescription for you:

1. Which of the following best describes your opinion about exercise?

   A. Love it, love it, love it! Couldn't go without it!
   B. Sometimes it's fun, and sometimes it's tolerable, depending on my mood.
   C. It's a necessary evil.
   D. It's something other people do.

2. After exercise, how do you typically feel?

   A. Exhausted but satisfied
   B. Cranky and irritable
   C. Euphoric
   D. Relieved that it's over

3. How often do you exercise each week?

   A. One or fewer times per week
   B. Two or three times a week for fifteen to thirty minutes
   C. Daily for an hour or more
   D. On most days for thirty to sixty minutes

4. If you are unable to do your regular exercise routine, how do you feel?

   A. I feel panicked.
   B. I feel like I've been let off the hook.
   C. Inconvenienced, but I'll make up for it later.
   D. What regular exercise routine?

5. Which of the following is most likely to keep you from exercising?

   A. Nothing
   B. Boredom with the exercise routine
   C. Stress
   D. Lack of energy and motivation

You may be addicted to exercise if you identify with the following:

- You absolutely *have* to exercise every day, even if you are sick or injured.
- You often exercise longer than two hours.
- You have given up other activities you enjoy for exercise.
- You work out twice as long the day after a missed workout.
- You feel intense guilt and anxiety if you miss a workout.
- You suffer from a lot of exercise-related injuries.

Give yourself points according to the following:

1. A: 1, B: 2, C: 3, D: 4
2. A: 2, B: 4, C: 1, D: 3
3. A: 4, B: 3, C: 1, D: 2
4. A: 1, B: 3, C: 2, D: 4
5. A: 1, B: 3, C: 2, D: 4

If you scored between **5** and **8** points, you are super-motivated to exercise, and that's great . . . unless you have become so dependent on exercise that you get stressed out when you miss an occasional workout, or unless you have become addicted to exercise. If you are exercising too much, or if your exercise routine is controlling you rather than the other way around, it's time to ease off a bit and seek balance by developing other areas of your life that promote health. For example, you could concentrate on eating a nutritious diet, drinking plenty of water, getting sufficient sleep, and enjoying spiritual renewal such as meditation and relaxation. Don't forget to spend time with the people you love, too, and every now and then, see if you can relax and do absolutely nothing at all.

If you scored between **9** and **12** points, you have probably established exercise as an integral part of your routine and you are already reaping the benefits. Just remember to stay flexible, vary your routine, and stay balanced in the other areas of your life, too. You should feel great that you've been able to master this most effective stress relieving technique. Good for you! When stress does interfere with your regular routine, don't be afraid to do something easier and more relaxing for exercise, such as take a slower walk or do an easy yoga routine.

If you scored between **13** and **16** points, you know exercise is good for you and manage most of the time, but you aren't always happy about it. You may need to try another form of exercise to keep yourself motivated. Consider your likes and dislikes and try to match them with something that will get you moving, like a cool new exercise machine at the gym or a hike in the wilderness.

If you scored between **17** and **20** points, you just don't like exercise, or you just can't find the time to fit it in. Whether you are worried that you won't know how to exercise the right way or burned out from too much stress and a too-hectic lifestyle, you are letting the most effective stress relieving technique out there pass you by. Don't be afraid to start slow and build up to a more moderate exercise routine at a comfortable pace. Exercise shouldn't be painful or unpleasant. The more regular your exercise becomes, the more you'll be able to see it working its magic in your life.

The Whole-Body Effects of Exercise

You've heard exercise is good for you. You even feel better after you do it, so you know it's doing something good. But what does it do, exactly, and how can it help relieve stress? Exercise benefits the body in very specific ways. Here are some of the benefits of moderate exercise:

- Stronger muscles
- Better flexibility
- Increased heart and lung efficiency
- Decreased risk of developing heart disease
- Decreased risk of developing lung disease
- Improved overall circulation
- Reduced cholesterol levels
- Reduced blood pressure
- Strengthened immune system
- Decrease in excess body fat
- Increased energy
- Decreased symptoms of depression
- Decreased symptoms of arthritis
- Decreased risk of diabetes and decreased risk of complications from diabetes
- Decreased risk of osteoporosis and decreased risk of complications from osteoporosis
- Improved quality of sleep and decrease in insomnia
- Increased mental acuity
- Improved posture
- Improved self-image
- Decreased frequency of injuries in daily life

- Decreased effects of stress
- Improved ability to manage stress

Not only does exercise help the body to deal with the physical effects of stress, but it helps the mind to feel more in control and able to manage stress. Add to that the positive effect exercise has on so many other disorders and its ability to help prevent so many physical problems, and you've got a stress management tool that is both preventive and proactive.

SSENTIALS

If you crave variety in your exercise routine, vary your workouts (sometimes called cross training) to keep yourself interested and motivated. Walk one day, go to the gym the next, play tennis with a buddy the day after that. On the weekend, drive somewhere interesting and go on a hike to explore uncharted territory. You might even forget to call it exercise!

Finding a Movement Plan You Can Live With

So many types of exercise, so little time! Of course, not all of the types of exercise in the following sections will appeal to you, but maybe you'll get some new ideas. Here are brief descriptions of some of the more common types of exercise. Don't be afraid to try something new, especially if you feel like you are in an exercise rut or need inspiration to get you started.

If you are very overweight, have a health problem, or haven't exercised in over six months, please consult your doctor before beginning any exercise program.

Walking

Walking is great. It's easy, fun, and can get you out in the fresh air or can provide an opportunity for socializing with friends while you all shape up together. Walk at a brisk pace for thirty to sixty minutes at least three times each week, and preferably five to six times per week.

FACTS

From 1975 to 1995, walking declined among American adults by 42 percent, according to the U.S. Department of Transportation. Some blame urban sprawl, or spread-out suburbs in which walking is unsafe and/or impractical. In fact, the Centers for Disease Control and Prevention is studying the connection between urban sprawl and the 60 percent increase in obesity in adult Americans in the past decade.

Swimming

Swimming is great for people who love the water, people with joint or orthopedic problems, and people who have a lot of weight to lose. The water buoys the body so that joints, bones, and muscles don't feel the impact of exercise, making injuries less likely for people who are vulnerable to the impact. Work up gradually to thirty to sixty minutes of steady swimming. Varying your strokes—freestyle, breaststroke, backstroke, sidestroke—will help work all your muscles.

Water aerobics is very popular and fun, too. Water aerobics can be tailored to any fitness level. Check your local pool or health club for water aerobics classes. Some areas even offer water yoga classes.

Join a Gym

For some people, joining a gym is the inspiration they needed all along. A gym provides fellowship, a wide range of fitness possibilities from aerobics classes (step aerobics, cardio funk, kickboxing, and many other types of aerobics are offered these days) to yoga to racquetball to swimming to weight lifting to the latest in exercise machines, from high-tech treadmills to no-impact elliptical trainers. In many clubs, you can also find personal trainers, nutritionists, sports leagues, child care, as well as other amenities such as massage therapists, saunas, spas, steam rooms, and snack bars filled with healthy fare.

Plus, if you've paid for a membership, you might be more inspired to get your money's worth. Going to the gym can be a mini-break, a special treat, something you look forward to every day.

FACTS

A recent Duke University Medical Center study showed that thirty minutes of brisk exercise three times per week was just as effective as drug therapy in relieving the symptoms of major depression. A follow-up study revealed that only 8 percent of the study's exercise group experienced a depression relapse, while 38 percent of the drug-only group and 31 percent of the exercise-plus-drugs group experienced a depression relapse.

Yoga

Yoga is an ancient Indian method of exercise designed to "yoke" body and mind. Yoga involves specific postures, breathing exercise, and meditation. Hatha Yoga, most popular in the West, consists primarily of the postures and breathing exercises.

Yoga is an excellent fitness activity on its own and also makes the perfect complement to other fitness activities because it increases strength, flexibility, circulation, posture, and overall body condition. Yoga is great both for people who have a hard time slowing down (you'll learn how great it feels and how important it is to move your body with slow control) and for people who have a hard time engaging in high-impact or fast-paced exercise (yoga is adaptable to all fitness levels and it's decidedly low impact).

Yoga is among the more perfect stress management exercises. Its original purpose was to gain control over the body and bring it into a state of balance in order to free the mind for spiritual contemplation. Yoga can help you to master your body so that it doesn't master you.

Pilates

Pilates is an increasingly popular core-strengthening routine that uses either special machinery or a simple mat. Pilates concentrates on strengthening and gaining control over the body's core, or the torso, especially the abdominal and back muscles. Many fitness centers and certified individuals offer Pilates classes. The exercises are part yoga, part gymnastics, and part ballet. Because Pilates have become so popular, classes and even do-it-yourself Pilates books are widely available. However, nothing beats the expertise of a certified Pilates instructor to help you get the exercises right. Many Pilates exercises are advanced and doing them incorrectly could cause injury, so be careful. Once learned from an expert, Pilates can easily be practiced at home on your own.

Tai Chi/Qigong

Tai chi and its precursor, Qigong, are ancient Chinese Taoist martial arts forms that have evolved to fit the twenty-first century. Rarely used today as methods of defense, tai chi consists of a series of slow, graceful movements in concert with the breath designed to free internal energy and keep it flowing through the body, uniting body and mind, promoting good health and relaxation. Tai chi is sometimes called a moving meditation. Qigong involves specific movements and postures as well as other health-maintenance procedures such as massage and meditation to maintain and improve overall health and balance the body's internal energy (called "chi" in China).

FACTS

While the average life expectancy is in the mid to upper seventies today, the longest a human has ever lived, according to documentation many believe is authentic, is 120 years. Shirechiyo Izumi of Japan died of pneumonia at 120 years old in 1986, leading some scientists who study longevity to speculate that under the right conditions, humans could feasibly live to 120 or beyond.

The Great Outdoors

If you feel particularly inspired by great views, fresh air, and the lovely and varied smells of the natural world, choosing an outdoor exercise can inspire you to keep up the habit. Whether you walk, jog, run, bicycle, roller blade, cross-country ski, hike, or climb mountains, exercising outdoors is good for your body and soul. And who says you can't take a walk in the rain or the snow? Exercising outside, even for just a little while each day, can also help to keep you in touch with the natural world, which helps to put things in perspective—and that all on its own can relieve a lot of stress!

Dance

Whether you take an organized class—ballet, jazz, tap, ballroom dancing, swing dancing, country dancing, square dancing, Irish dancing, to name a few—or go out dancing with your friends every weekend, dancing is great cardiovascular exercise and also a lot of fun. Something about music makes exercise seem less like exercise, and dancing, especially for fun, even alone in your house with the music blaring, is about as "unexercise-like" as you can get, but with all the benefits. Vigorous dancing can also be an excellent way to relieve tension and anxiety. So, get up and shake it!

Team Sports

For people who like to play on a team and are motivated and energized by the energy of others, team sports can be an excellent way to get exercise and a social life at the same time. Weekend football games, tennis leagues, racquetball tournaments, playground basketball games, beach volleyball, or whatever else is available in your area and interesting to you can be so much fun that you'll forget you're exercising!

Variety Is the Spice of Exercise

No matter what types of exercise you choose, you'll work a wider range of muscles and reap a wider range of benefits if you vary your exercise. Try a different kind of activity once a week.

Also, varying your pace can add up to increased health benefits. Author and exercise physiologist Greg Landry, M.S., suggests interval training, a simple way to vary any exercise you're already doing. Landry suggests warming up for five minutes, then exercising at your regular pace for four minutes, then stepping up the pace for one minute. Then, for the rest of your workout, work four minutes at a regular pace, then one minute at a fast pace, and so forth. Interval training can help you to break past a weight loss plateau, help get you in shape faster, increase your energy and your body's rate of calorie burning by raising your base metabolism rate, and keep your workout more interesting. Changing pace every five minutes may also help to keep you more focused on your workout, too, which is a nice break for your busy brain.

Lift Weights! Yes, You

Weight lifting isn't exactly aerobic activity, but it's an important part of any fitness routine. Lifting weights is great for any adult. It builds bone mass and can reverse osteoporosis. It increases muscle tone and helps your body to burn more calories because the more muscle you have, the more calories you burn during the aerobic portion of your workout. Stronger muscles means everyday efforts, from lifting grocery bags and small children to carrying that box of office supplies into the supply room, are easier. You'll feel better, your posture will improve, and your body will look firmer and shapelier.

ALERT

When your day has been more stressful than usual, don't exercise beyond your limit. Focus on long walks in the fresh air, practice yoga or tai chi, or take a leisurely bike ride. Let your workout be gentle and meditative. Even if you know you need to get in shape, don't worry about it. When you get your severe stress under control, you can step up the pace.

Lift weights no more than every other day (or every day, but alternating which muscles you work). To find a good plan, talk to your health club trainer, find a good book on weight lifting that addresses your personal goals (toning or building), or subscribe to a magazine, such as *Shape,* that keeps track of the latest news and research on weight lifting and provides different routines with detailed explanations on technique and benefits.

At about age thirty-five, people start to lose bone mass; with that loss of bone mass comes a greater susceptibility to fractures. Weight lifting can counteract bone loss. It's never too late to start. As soon as you begin a regular program of weight lifting, your bones start getting stronger. What an easy way to ward off a broken bone!

Massage Therapy

After all that exercise, your muscles might be sore, especially if you are just getting into the exercise habit. While you shouldn't push yourself to the point of pain, movement and effort often result in sore muscles, achy joints, and injuries such as strained ligaments and pulled tendons.

Massage therapists are trained to knead and manipulate the muscles and connective tissue in the body to help the body find its equilibrium after exercise. Regular massage is great even for nonexercisers. It activates muscles and skin, improving circulation and even organ function.

Massage is an excellent stress management tool. It helps your body and mind to relax as it encourages the body to help heal itself. Massage can also give you a feeling of control and mastery over your body as it responds to the targeted effects of massage. Pain may disappear. Posture may improve. Muscles and joints may begin to work better and more easily.

Massage also feels great and shouldn't be relegated to the status of occasional indulgence. Consider regular massage as a serious stress management tool. Massage can equal mental and physical maintenance.

Your doctor may be able to refer you to a professional massage therapist, and, in some cases, massage therapy and even acupuncture is covered by insurance. If you are interested in less mainstream types of massage therapy such as reflexology, acupressure, or Reiki, talk to friends, a natural health provider, a yoga teacher, or the employees at your local natural health food store for recommendations. Some areas have directories of natural health care providers. Here are some of the common types of massage.

Swedish Massage

This common form of massage involves a massage therapist applying oil to the body and certain types of massage strokes—namely, *effleurage* (gliding), *petrissage* (kneading), *friction* (rubbing), and *tapotement* (tapping)—to increase circulation in muscles and connective tissue, help the body to flush out waste products, and heal injuries. Swedish massage induces a feeling of deep relaxation and increases range of motion. Some Swedish massage therapists also use hydrotherapy, or massage through soaking, steaming, or applying jets of water to the body.

Shiatsu and Acupressure

Shiatsu is the Japanese word for "finger pressure" and is sometimes known as acupressure. Shiatsu is an ancient form of massage, still widely practiced, that involves the application of pressure through fingers, palms, elbows, or knees to pressure points in the body. Pressure points are certain points along energy meridians that the Japanese and other Asian cultures have defined within the body. Pressure on these points is thought to release energy blockages that cause pain and disease, resulting in balance, equilibrium, and greater physical health. Acupuncture is based on the same principle but uses very thin needles painlessly inserted into pressure points. Although the idea may sound strange to a Westerner, much research has supported the effectiveness of both acupuncture and acupressure in the relief of pain and the treatment of certain disorders.

Reflexology

Reflexology is a little like acupressure, but in reflexology, all the pressure points are in the hands and feet. The theory goes that the entire body, including all the parts, organs, and glands, is represented in a "map" on the hands and feet, and that pressure applied to the right area of the "map" will help to balance the problem in the associated area of the body. Knowing the map allows people to work on themselves by rubbing their own hands or feet in the appropriate area.

You can perform reflexology on yourself! Here's one to try. To stimulate your brain when you really need to think clearly, hold up one thumb, then squeeze the tip with the thumb and index finger of your opposite hand. Squeeze in the middle of your thumb's tip, then make little squeezes in seven slow circles around the tip of your thumb, never fully releasing pressure. Repeat on your other thumb.

Reiki

Reiki (pronounced RAY-KEY) is an energy healing technique based in ancient Tibetan practices. Practitioners of Reiki put their hands on or just above the body in order to balance energy by acting as a sort of conduit for life force energy. Reiki is used to treat physical problems as well as emotional and psychological problems, and it is, more positively, also used as a tool to support and facilitate positive changes. Becoming a Reiki practitioner is a complex process and also is somewhat mysterious. Advanced Reiki practitioners are even thought to be able to perform long-distance healing.

Rolfing

Rolfing is a deep massage designed to restructure the body's muscles and connective tissue to promote better alignment. If you like your massages hard, this one's for you. Some people claim that the deep tissue massage actually releases deeply buried emotions and that emotional outbursts are common during the course of the ten-session program.

Alexander Technique

The Alexander technique is less massage than movement instruction. Clients are taught to move and hold their bodies with full consciousness and in a way that releases tension and uses the body to its best advantage. People say that practicing the Alexander technique makes them feel lighter, easier, and more in control of their bodies. The Alexander technique is popular with actors and other performing artists.

Applied Kinesiology

This is a muscle testing technique that helps people determine where in the body they are experiencing an imbalance or problem. Then, massage as well as movement of certain joints, acupressure, and advice on diet, vitamins, and herbs are offered as treatment. Applied kinesiology should be practiced by health care professionals such as doctors, osteopaths, chiropractors, or dentists who are trained and licensed to diagnose illness.

Many holistic health practitioners are highly qualified, experienced, competent, and trustworthy. Because the industry is still largely unregulated, however, be careful when choosing someone who specializes in alternative or complementary therapies. Get referrals from friends and ask about credentials and experience.

Polarity Therapy

Polarity therapy is a little like Reiki in that it is designed to free and balance the body's internal energy, but polarity therapy is more of a melding of Eastern and Western approaches. It includes massage, dietary counseling, certain yoga exercises, and psychological counseling for a full mind-body approach to energy balancing.

Self-Massage

If you learn about acupressure, Swedish massage, reflexology, and many other techniques, you can perform massage on yourself. You can massage your own neck, scalp, face, hands, feet, legs, arms, and torso. Many yoga postures also result in internal and external massage by bending the body in certain ways against itself or by using the pressure of the floor against certain parts of the body.

Fueling Up: The Stress Connection

If you're going to exercise (or even if you aren't), you have to eat. But what will you choose to eat? Americans are notorious for making less than ideal dietary choices, and statistics reveal that over half the population is overweight. But whether or not you are cursed with a sweet tooth or a penchant for pepperoni pizza with extra cheese, stress can make you less likely to keep compulsive eating under control.

What's worse, stress-related eating may be particularly dangerous to your health. In a recent ABC news special on stress, one segment was devoted to recent research that reveals the difference between "regular fat" and "stress fat." Stress fat, the segment explained, is not the lumpy, bumpy stuff you can see jiggling on your thighs and upper arms. Stress fat is the fat that accumulates deep inside the body, specifically around the internal organs of your torso.

This "stress fat" is the only fat that is known to contribute to heart disease, cancer, and diabetes. *The only kind!* And you can't even see it. This dangerous fat may be directly related to stress (among other things, including estrogen levels). Research shows that compulsive eating related to stress is more likely to result in fat accumulation around the internal organs.

Other studies suggest that while cortisol is a powerful appetite stimulant and can trigger excessive eating in the stressed-out among us, cortisol may actually encourage the body to accumulate fat in the abdominal region, especially in "apple-shaped" women—women who tend to gain weight around the middle rather than in the buttocks and legs (the so-called pear shape).

Stress-related eating is the beginning of a vicious circle. You feel stressed, so you eat foods that are likely to increase your susceptibility to stress. Consequently, you feel more stressed and eat more of those same stress-promoting foods. How do you stop the madness?

Knowledge is power, and although knowledge may not equal *will*power, it is the first step. Certain foods are known to have a disruptive effect on the body's equilibrium, while other foods are known to have a more balancing effect. Many cultures have discovered this food/body connection. Ayurveda, an ancient Indian system of health maintenance and improvement still popular today, focuses on balancing the body through food as well as other practices. (I'll tell you more about ayurveda in Chapter 9.) Many contemporary researchers and health promoters also emphasize the link between good health, balance, energy, and the food we eat.

QUESTIONS?

If you can't see stress fat, how do you know you have it?
Lie on your back on the floor and look at your abdomen. If it protrudes above your hip bones while you are lying down—that is, stays inflated, in the shape of a pregnant belly or a beer belly, when you're on your back—that protrusion is caused by stress fat. The fat deep in your belly is pushing up the outer, visible fat. This fat can seriously damage your health. Isn't it time to start doing something about it?

Diet-of-the-Week

It's easy to find fad diets that promise miraculous results, and it's equally easy to find people to proclaim how this or that diet was the only thing that worked for them. Many of these diets are controversial. Some people swear by the diet that suggests different blood types should focus on different foods. Others are devoted to the low-carb diets such as the Zone Diet, the Atkins Diet, the Protein Power diet, and the Carbohydrate Addict's diet. Some people choose a vegetarian or vegan (no animal products at all including dairy and eggs) diet. There are countless others.

Maybe one of these diets will work for you. They all make interesting points and include healthy eating plans (not everybody agrees they are all healthy, but then again, not everybody agrees on anything).

The blood-type diets are all low in calories and high in natural, minimally processed foods. The low-carb diets make a good point: Refined carbohydrates tend to spike insulin levels, and in some people, insulin fluctuations seem to cause food binges and unusual weight gain. For the last few decades, the common wisdom has been "carbs, carbs, and more carbs." Now, the low-carb diets suggest that we need to get more protein back into our lives, and for some people, it's the answer to carbohydrate binges and can put a stop to massive weight gain.

Vegetarian and vegan diets have merit, too. Animal products have been associated with an increased risk of certain diseases, and many available animal products, from rich cheeses to marbled meats to the preservative-infused lunch meats we feed to our children, are high in saturated fat, calories, and, in the case of the cured meats, salt and preservatives, some of which are known carcinogens. Vegetarians tend to eat more vegetables, fruit, whole grains, beans, nuts, and seeds, and other healthy, unprocessed foods. That's certainly an improvement over lunch at the fast-food drive through (although more fast-food restaurants are serving healthier fare, by popular demand).

But if all the diets out there baffle you, you can feel comforted. They all boil down to a few simple rules that, when applied, will help just about anybody to reach and maintain a healthy weight, feel energized, and manage stress from a dietary perspective:

- Whenever possible, eat food as close to its natural state as you can. Eat an orange instead of drinking orange juice, but drink orange juice instead of orange soda. Eat a broiled, free-range, organic chicken breast instead of a minced, shaped, breaded, fried chicken patty. Choose brown rice over white, old-fashioned oats over instant flavored oatmeal, instant oatmeal over a toaster pastry. Eat whole wheat bread or, better yet, sprouted wheat bread instead of plain white bread, and spread it with natural, organic peanut or almond butter.
- Choose nutrient-dense foods instead of foods that are mostly empty calories. For example, dried fruit is more nutrient-dense than candy, broccoli and carrots with yogurt dip are more nutrient-dense than chips or popcorn, and freshly squeezed fruit or vegetable juice is more nutrient dense than soda. Less nutrient-dense food can be useful to help fill you up if it is low in calories and you are trying to lose weight (popcorn, for example, can help stave off hunger pangs, as long as you don't pour butter all over it).
- Start and end the day with protein and complex carbohydrates rather than simple carbohydrates such as sugar.

- Eat a hearty breakfast, a moderate lunch, and a light dinner, or if you aren't a breakfast person, a light breakfast, a hearty lunch, and a light dinner.

FACTS

Foods that exacerbate the negative effects of stress in the body are those that are high in the following:

Sugar	Fat, especially saturated fat
Caffeine	Calories
Salt	

Foods that help to ease the negative effects of stress in the body include the following:

- Vegetables, especially organic
- Fruit, especially organic
- Low-fat, organic or free-range protein sources such as fish, chicken, turkey, lean beef, soy products such as tofu and soy milk, low-fat dairy products, and legumes
- Monounsaturated sources of fat such as olive oil and canola oil
- Complex carbohydrates such as whole grain breads, pastas, and cereals

- Stop before you are stuffed and don't eat more calories than you need.
- Don't let more than about 30 percent of your calories come from fat, and try to eat fat mostly from sources that contain a higher proportion of monounsaturated fat (olive oil, canola oil, avocados, walnuts, and walnut oil) and omega-3 fatty acids (in fatty fish like salmon and tuna), rather than saturated fat (meat and dairy products), trans-fatty acids (in margarine, vegetable shortening, and partially hydrogenated oils), and polyunsaturated fats (prevalent in many vegetable oils).

Rethinking the "Treat"

Some people eat pretty well some of the time but can't get over the notion that on special occasions or when they've had a hard day (and lately, most of them have seemed pretty hard), they deserve a treat. If you are one of those people, you can rethink the "treat" concept.

It is so easy to eat in response to stress. Many people do it. After all, don't you deserve it? Don't you deserve a treat?

Sure you do. But a treat doesn't have to be about food. A treat could be a movie, a day trip, a full hour of doing nothing, a visit to the salon, a game of golf in the middle of the afternoon on a Wednesday, letting yourself go to bed at 9:00 P.M. There is so much that is wonderful, fun, and rewarding in life that has nothing to do with food. So, get in the habit of thinking creatively about how to reward yourself.

Binging on any food, no matter how healthful the food itself, contributes to physical stress because the body isn't designed to process huge amounts of food at one time.

And if you just have to reward yourself with food, make it absolutely worth the indulgence. A little bit of something superb is a far more rewarding and sensual experience than a whole huge bunch of low-quality anything. A single piece of the highest quality imported chocolate, a thin slice of cake and a tiny cup of espresso from the best dessert café in town, a small but perfect filet mignon wrapped in the best bacon, or whatever your indulgence—savor every bite and don't do anything else while enjoying it. If the television is off, no one is talking to you, you aren't reading the newspaper, you are simply experiencing your treat, then that tiny bit will be plenty. You'll feel supremely satisfied. And so elegant, too!

Your Personal Eating Plan

How will you go about changing your ways (if they need changing)? Like anything else, you'll do it one step at a time. It may sound tedious, but if you get in the habit of keeping a food diary in which you write down every single thing you eat each day and how you were feeling when you ate it, you'll be surprised at how obvious your bad habits become. You might notice that when you are feeling stressed or insecure, you eat sugar, and that when you are feeling confident or calm, you eat really well. Keep at it until you feel in control of your eating habits; if you start to slip again, go right back to it.

Here is a sample food diary. Notice that food choices seem directly connected with mood. Yours may not be this obvious, but you'll probably see patterns after keeping the diary for a while.

DATE: October 23rd

TIME	WHAT I ATE	HOW I FELT	COMMENTS
7:00 a.m.	Two slices of wheat toast with butter 1 cup orange juice 1 apple	Tired but in a good mood	This was a good breakfast.
10:15 a.m.	Four handfuls of M&Ms	Insecure and vulnerable	Jenny just told me I messed up that report.
12:00 noon	Large plate of pasta with meat sauce and cheese Large salad with ranch dressing Three breadsticks	Anxious and stressed out	I can't get over my mistake. How could I have done that? I hope everyone doesn't think I'm incompetent!
3:35 p.m.	Four more handfuls of M&Ms	Depressed	I'm thinking of quitting.
6:45 p.m.	2 cups of stir-fry with shrimp and lots of vegetables ½ cup brown rice	Happy and energized	Jenny told me not to worry about the mistake and said I'm doing a great job.

Following is a sample food template for you to copy and use. Eat well and keep moving! You'll be feeling strong and stress-proof soon.

DATE:

TIME	WHAT I ATE	HOW I FELT	COMMENTS

CHAPTER 8

Stress Relief for Your Mind and Spirit

Stress management techniques that strengthen and reinforce the body will also help to strengthen the mind's ability to resist the negative effects of stress. But some stress management techniques directly deal with the mind—the thought processes, emotions, intellect, and, extending beyond the mind, the quest for spiritual meaning. In this chapter, we'll look at meditation techniques, which are the most effective techniques targeted to your mind and spirit.

The Negative Mental Effects of Stress

- An inability to concentrate
- Excessive, uncontrollable worrying
- Feelings of anxiety and panic
- Forgetfulness
- Sadness, depression
- Nervousness
- Fatigue, low energy
- Irritability
- Restlessness
- Negativism
- Fearfulness
- Unrealistic expectations
- Despair

Yes, some of these symptoms of stress can be directly connected to the body, but these symptoms are often a product of the mind and its interpretation of and obsession with or attachment to stressful events. How do you stress-proof your mind? With mental stress management, of course.

Stress management for the mind and the spirit is specifically targeted to help still, calm, and quiet the overactive mind, which is so common in people who are experiencing stress beyond their stress tolerance levels. These techniques help you to recognize the thought processes that are increasing your stress, the attitudes that can trigger a stress response, and the way you tend to cling to ideas as if they were life preservers. They can also fulfill the desire for higher meaning that, when thwarted by a life that isn't what we wanted it to be, can slowly erode our happiness and self-esteem.

Some of these techniques are related to physical stress management techniques (specifically, relaxation techniques) because, again, mind and body are inextricably connected. But if you are experiencing even a few of the mental negative effects of stress or feel that your spirit is sorely in need of reinforcements and want to go straight to the source, try these stress management techniques for mind and spirit.

Meditation for Peace of Mind

Meditation is one of the most widely practiced stress management techniques worldwide. Meditation is an excellent way to cultivate control over your own mental processes, but in many cultures (including ours), meditation is often practiced for spiritual reasons, not for stress management at all. Stress management is merely a fringe benefit.

Westerners are more likely to practice meditation either solely for stress management or as a combination of the desire for stress management and the desire for a more spiritual life. Whatever your reason for meditation, the effects are consistent. Meditation has a profound effect on both the body and the mind. It helps to still the constant chatter in our heads so that we can think more clearly. It cuts through all our expectations and attitudes. It cultivates mental discipline and, in addition, is exceptionally relaxing.

Meditation teaches us, most significantly, to live in the now. Rather than letting our restless minds, worried thoughts, and anxious feelings carry us away into what might happen next or what we could have done before, meditation teaches us to still that mental ruckus. What's left? The perfection of the present moment, in which you are only and exactly what you are, with no need for improvement. And that doesn't leave much room for stress.

ALERT

Some people hesitate to meditate because they think it might be against their religion. Meditation, however, is a technique that crosses the boundaries of all religions and is equally effective apart from any religious practice. It is mental discipline, not religious ritual.

Why Meditation Really Works

Meditation works to relieve stress. Studies show that people who are meditating have lower blood pressure, slower breath and heart rate, and brain waves that signal a state of alert but, at the same time, deep relaxation. Meditation also works to train the mind to avoid negative patterns and thought processes, vicious circles of failure and low self-esteem, even the perception of chronic pain as an intensely negative experience.

The brain is a complex and amazing organ, and meditation can teach you to harness your mind's power, integrate your mind and body, and feed your hungry spirit. Meditation comes in many forms, including sitting meditation, walking meditation, mindfulness meditation, yoga meditation, mantra meditation, mandala meditation, visualization, and even prayer. Whether or not you are affiliated with any specific religious tradition, you can pray, either to God, to Goddess, or toward whatever makes sense for you—the universe, the spirit of love, positive energy.

As broad a category as meditation may be, it all boils down to one thing: the honing of focus. Modern life promotes an unfocused mind. We are constantly bombarded with stimuli, from the media, from our environments, from people, from our computers. Television switches shots every few seconds and breaks up each show with commercial after commercial. Movies move fast and don't often demand too much concentration anymore. Work is full of so much to do that it isn't easy or even possible to spend very much time on any one task, even if more time would result in higher quality. It's a get-it-done-fast-and-move-on-to-the-next-thing-quick kind of life for many of us, and so the mind gets used to multiple points of focus and constantly moving focus. The ability to concentrate becomes irrelevant and, consequently, begins to disappear.

ESSENTIALS

If your concentration seems really off, you can boost it with herbs in addition to meditation. Much research points to ginkgo biloba as an effective brain booster that improves circulation to the brain and, consequently, improves concentration, memory, and mental clarity. Because of possible drug interactions or side effects, you should always check with your physician before taking any herbal remedy, especially if you are on any other medication or have a health condition.

Think of your life as an all-you-can-eat buffet. You've got thirty minutes for lunch, and there you stand with your little plate, faced with a fantastic array of options: three kinds of lettuce, two kinds of tomatoes, carrots, cucumbers, cheese, hard-boiled eggs, hot peppers, olives, broccoli, cauliflower, eight kinds of dressing, cottage cheese, potato salad, macaroni salad, three different marinated salads, a taco bar, a pasta bar, four soups, three breads, ribs, wings, meatloaf, fish sticks, drumsticks, ham, turkey, pork, corn, mashed potatoes, strawberries, cantaloupe, honeydew melon, watermelon, peaches, pears, pineapples, three Jell-O salads, and four different colors of some kind of creamy whipped dessert (are you hungry yet?).

It doesn't take most people long to dive in and start loading their plates with the things they like. You may start out with good intentions—"I'll just get a small salad and a little of one entrée—" but with so many tempting options, most people end up taking just a little of this, and that, and this, and that, and this . . .

What often results is a plate filled with so many different things that it's hard to focus on or fully enjoy any one thing on your plate. It's such an overwhelming variety mounded on that little plate that the pleasure comes in the feeling of indulgent excess, the "Look at all this food!" response.

Never mind the food's quality. That's why all-you-can-eat buffets can get away with food of lesser quality than a restaurant that serves just a little of a few choice dishes. If you're impressed with the array of choices, you won't notice so much that everything isn't exquisite in taste. You might be charmed by the price. "Well, as long as it's all I can eat . . ." Or, maybe you are seduced by the possibilities of sampling lots of things you don't normally get to eat. "Wow. Five kinds of potato salad? I'll have to try them all!" The experience of the all-you-can-eat buffet can even become addictive. You lose sight of the pleasure of the food itself because you have become so enamored with the massive quantities and the impressive arrangement.

Now, let's carry over the metaphor. Life is full of stuff to think about. What you have to do today, what you didn't finish from yesterday, what to wear, where to go, who to go with, how to do things, not to mention what to eat. We've got schedules, lists, assignments, deadlines, and responsibilities. We've got dependents, friends, and pets. We've got houses or apartments and cars or trucks to maintain. Some of us have more than one house, more than one car or truck, even a boat. We've got to worry about looking right, acting right, making a good impression. What do others think of you? How well did you complete that task? How much money do you have and what should you spend it on? Or, should you save it?

The list of things the average human thinks about in one day far exceeds the list of items on any all-you-can-eat buffet, so just imagine how much more deluded and seduced into accepting the unacceptable our minds (like our buffet-abused palates) become. Our minds are pulled in different directions, at a pace that can be described, pretty accurately, as frantic. When the amount of information coming in and the thoughts being generated from within become overwhelming, we start to forget things, lose things, fail to pay attention, make more mistakes, have more accidents, feel more frustrated and less in control of our lives than ever.

But it's hard to stop. Thinking and taking in information can be even more addictive than the indulgent prospect of five kinds of potato salad. Have you ever turned the television on to watch while working on your laptop, even though you have a lot to get accomplished and know the din will slow you down and distract you? Have you blasted the stereo while reading or called one person after another on your cell phone while driving the car? We can't stop generating input! We feel comforted, dulled perhaps, or at least lulled by the incessant din of media, noise, distraction.

But the price is high. Going through life without ever really paying attention means going through life as a watered-down, lukewarm version of yourself. Maybe spending your days distracted and only partially aware feels safe because you don't have to confront the big questions, the strong emotions. Or, maybe you would like to cut down on all that distraction but don't have the first idea how to start or, for that matter, time to figure it out. But to go through life with your mind going in so many directions all at once isn't really living, and it certainly isn't living up to your potential.

Meditation puts a slow, painless end to this life-numbing process. It hangs a "closed" sign on the buffet restaurant's door for just a few minutes each day. And those few minutes give your mind the opportunity to slow down, wake up, come out of its stupor, and pay attention. To what? To you. To who you are, how you feel, what you are right now, regardless of all the incoming information, regardless of all the internal worries, anxieties, thoughts, and emotions. Meditation also helps you to pay attention to the world around you while helping you to remain unengaged and caught up in that world. You can step back and look, an uninvolved observer, and that can be pretty enlightening.

ESSENTIALS

If you are ill or in pain, meditation can help to support the healing efforts of your health care practitioners. Meditate on your illness or pain with an open mind and without judgment, as an observer, apart from the negative feelings attached to your condition. As you become comfortable with this process, pose the question, What can I do to help you heal? Don't grasp for an answer. Just stay open. This technique taps into your intuition. Eventually, very specific thoughts may arise about what you can do to support your body's healing efforts.

How to Meditate

If you are interested in starting a meditation practice of your own, first read the following sections in which many different meditation techniques are described to find one that appeals to you. Then, set aside a time each day—first thing in the morning, just before dinner, or just before bed are all popular choices—and practice. Practice, practice, practice. At first, meditation can be tough. You'll probably find it hard to keep your mind focused. Soon, you'll learn to recognize your mind's wanderings as natural, and, as you gently redirect your mind to its point of focus, you'll stop judging yourself and learn simply to be. And learning simply to be is a crucial and significant step toward a lifetime of successful stress management.

Meditation Techniques

Meditation comes in many shapes and sizes. Here are a few of the most popular meditation techniques. One is sure to be right for you.

Zazen

Zazen is the sitting meditation of Zen Buddhism, but many so-called "Zennists" who don't practice Buddhism practice zazen. Zazen can be accurately defined as "just sitting" and is exactly that—just sitting. It doesn't require any religious or philosophical affiliation. All it requires is the ability to apply the seat of the pants to the floor and stay there for a while. Sounds easy, you say? Hardly. For those of us accustomed to accomplishing something at every moment of the day, just sitting is quite a challenge.

But just sitting accomplishes something amazing if it is practiced every single day for an extended period of time. The mind becomes calmer. The muscles stay more relaxed. Stress fails to get the rise out of your body and your mind that it once did. Suddenly, you hold the reins, not your stress. Suddenly, priorities seem clearer, truths about life, people, and yourself seem more obvious, and things that used to stress you out seem hardly worth consideration anymore.

FACTS

The Rinzai sect of Zen Buddhism is most known for its meditation technique of koan contemplation. Students are given a koan, or an enigmatic question or statement, by the Zen master, such as, *What is the sound of one hand clapping?* During meditation, they must contemplate the koan until they exhaust all rational understanding and their minds shift into a more enlightened state.

Just sitting doesn't remove you from the world, however. Choosing not to worry, dwell, and obsess about things means you can concentrate on the real business of living. Just sitting teaches you how to be, right now, in the moment. As your mind opens up, the world opens up, too. All those anxieties suddenly seem like ropes that were tying you down. Just sitting can dissolve the ropes and set you free to really be who you are and live the life you want.

That may sound like pretty powerful stuff, especially as a result of just sitting there. Can just sitting really do all that? Believe it or not, it really can, and you'll only begin to perceive its power if you try it and stick with it. The power of zazen isn't really so mysterious. Just as exercise trains the body and just as regular, targeted exercise can train the body to do truly amazing things (think about gymnasts, acrobats, Michael Jordan . . .), zazen trains and exercises the mind.

All those worries and anxieties, the panic, the nervousness, the restlessness, the inner noise are holding you back from your true potential the same way being out of shape and undisciplined holds you back from athletic potential. Just sitting is the way to train your mind to let that stuff go.

From the Buddhist perspective, zazen is thought to be the path to enlightenment because thousands of years ago the Buddha attained enlightenment while "just sitting" under a bodhi tree in India. He sat and sat and sat and continued to sit, and legend has it that he proclaimed (I'm paraphrasing), "I'm going to sit here until I perceive ultimate truth, and that's final." Supposedly, it took about one night. Then, he understood the meaning of all existence. This was, of course, after six years of intensive searching for truth.

Enlightenment may or may not be your goal. But whatever the case, learning to sit, cultivate stillness and inner silence, and become fully and totally aware of the present moment makes for powerful stress management.

ALERT

If enlightenment sounds foreign, strange, or even a little scary, don't worry. Enlightenment isn't weird. It just means you become fully aware of who and what you are. You are still you. You just know more! Also, there is nothing wrong with you if you never "attain" it. Some people don't even believe such a thing exists.

How to Practice Zazen

You can learn zazen at a zendo, a place where Zennists or Zen Buddhists gather to meditate together. The rules for meditation will depend on the individual zendo and whether or not the zendo is based in Soto or Rinzai Zen (differences include things like whether you will sit facing the center of the room or the wall).

Or, you can learn zazen on your own. While, ideally, you should be able to practice zazen under any circumstances, you can help yourself along, especially in the initial stages, by practicing zazen in a quiet place where you're not likely to be distracted. Set aside about five minutes your first time out, then gradually work up to fifteen to thirty minutes once or twice each day. Increase your meditation session by about two minutes each week.

To begin zazen, sit cross-legged or on folded legs (sitting on your feet), with a firm pillow under your hips so that you aren't sitting directly on your legs. Make sure you are wearing enough clothes to stay warm, or wrap yourself in a blanket. Sit up straight, feeling a lift from the crown of the head toward the ceiling and an open feeling in your spine. (In other words, don't scrunch over.) Keep your shoulders back, your chest open, and place your tongue on the roof of your mouth. Look down, but don't hang your head. Your focus points should be slightly downward and your eyes relaxed. Now, unfocus your eyes just a little so that you don't really see what's in front of you. This will help you to focus inwardly.

Rest your hands in your lap in either of these two positions: Rest your left hand, palm up, in the open palm of your right hand. Bring your thumbs together so the tips touch just slightly; or make your left hand into a loose fist and rest it inside the open palm of your right hand. Rest your hands against your body about two inches below your navel.

Keep your mouth closed and breathe through your nose. At first, practice concentrating by counting each breath. In your mind, count from one to ten, with each full breath (inhalation and exhalation) constituting one number. Or, simply follow your breath, keeping your awareness focused on the sound and feel of your breath moving in and out of your body. Don't try to control your breath. Just notice it.

Soon, you'll probably notice that you aren't paying attention to your breath, or even counting. Your mind has wandered! Notice it, then bring your attention back to your breath. Keep going for five minutes. Once you get really accomplished at focusing, you won't even have to count. You'll just sit, breathe, and be.

And that's it. Sound too simple to be true? Zazen is simple, but it isn't easy, for several reasons. Let's be frank:

- It's boring, especially at first.
- It's really hard to sit still.
- It's difficult to "just sit" when you know how much you have to do.
- It's hard to justify the time when you don't see immediate results. (We are so impatient!)
- Your mind will try to talk you out of it. Discipline is hard and your mind will resist the effort.
- At first, you'll think you are hopeless and could never do it.
- It's frustrating when you can't concentrate on anything.
- It's frightening to confront some of the emotions that arise unexpectedly.
- Dropout rate is high. Most people don't keep it up long enough to see the benefits.

But what happens if you don't drop out? What happens if you sit through the boredom, sit despite the other things you think you should be doing, sit out the frustration and the fear, sit until you've learned how to really sit still, physically and mentally? The answer is simple: Clarity, peace, acceptance, satisfaction, and, yes, a whole lot less stress.

ESSENTIALS

You can practice zazen without any props, but if you become devoted to your practice and want to spend the money, you can buy several props to make your meditation more comfortable. A zafu is a firm, small, round cushion to sit on during Zen meditation. A zabuton is a larger mat on which to place the zafu. You can also buy a small wooden bench designed so that you don't actually put weight on your legs. Look for these and other meditation tools in specialty stores and catalogs. You might try your local health food store, New Age bookstore, or meditation center.

Walking Meditation

In Zen, walking meditation (kinhin) is the counterpart to sitting meditation (zazen), but walking meditation doesn't necessarily have anything to do with Zen. It is what it sounds like: meditation on the move. Walking meditation is different from sitting meditation because you have to be thinking about what you're doing so that you don't wander into traffic or bump into a tree. On the other hand, it isn't really so different, because in sitting meditation, you become acutely aware of your surroundings. They just aren't changing the way they change when you walk.

Walking meditation is excellent as an alternative to sitting meditation. Some people like to sit for most of their meditation session but then spend the last few minutes in walking meditation, and for some, who practice sitting meditation for longer periods of time, walking meditation gets the body moving periodically without breaking the meditative flow.

Walking meditation is more challenging than sitting meditation for the same reason that it is more interesting to many people: You've got more to look at. With more to look at comes more temptation to let the mind get frantic again. For this reason, walking meditation is often best practiced as a counterpart to sitting meditation.

But for most people reading this book, walking meditation is a great way to enjoy walking and reap the benefits of meditation at the same time. It's also great for people who simply refuse to sit still. Walking meditation can be a good way to ease into the meditation concept without the commitment of sitting (and sitting for even five minutes is a fairly serious commitment for some people). It's an enjoyable form of meditation that can serve as the basis for a meditation practice, or as an occasional alternative to any other form of meditation.

How to Practice Walking Meditation

To practice walking meditation, first decide where you will walk. You can do walking meditation outside or around the room. You should have a prepared path in mind so that you don't spend time thinking about where to go during the meditation. Know exactly where you are going: around the block, to the end of the path, around the periphery of the living room.

Begin by spending a moment focusing and breathing, to center yourself and prepare for the meditation. Then, taking slow, deliberate steps, walk. As you walk, notice how your breath feels as it comes in and out of your body. Notice how your limbs move, how your feet feel, how your hands and arms hang, the position of your torso, your neck, your head. Don't judge yourself as you walk. Just notice.

Once you feel you've observed yourself well, begin to observe the environment around you as you walk. Don't let it engage you. If something you see sets you off on some long, involved path of thought that has nothing to do with how you feel walking through the place you are walking, then as soon as you catch your mind so wandering (and it will so wander), gently bring your thoughts back to your breathing.

While new to walking meditation, stay with your breath for a good long while. Before you can start noticing and focusing on the rest of your body and your environment, you need to be able to focus on the breath. Otherwise, your mind will be all over the place.

Start with five minutes and add two minutes every week until you're up to fifteen to thirty minutes of daily walking meditation. Or, alternate walking meditation with another form of meditation every other day. Or, once you are up to fifteen to thirty minutes of daily meditation, spend the first or last five to ten minutes of each session in walking meditation.

Yoga Meditation

Yoga, practiced in India for thousands of years, even before Hinduism arose, may be the oldest of all meditation traditions. While hatha yoga, the yoga most known to people in the West, focuses on postures and exercises, these are designed to get that troublesomely twitchy and unfocused body under control, so that meditation can be more easily practiced.

While yoga has many different sects that believe slightly different things and orient their meditation and other techniques toward slightly different directions, many forms of yoga have certain things in common:

- They believe that throughout the body, channels of energy run up and down. Along these energy channels are chakras (wheels of light), or spinning energy centers (see "Chakra Meditation," a little later in this chapter). Chakras are focal points for energy in the body and represent different organs in the body, different colors, and different aspects of the personality and life force.
- They believe that deep at the base of the spine is the seat of kundalini energy, sometimes called "serpent energy" or "serpent power" and likened to a coiled serpent waiting at the base of the spine to be awakened. Kundalini energy is thought to be a powerful force that, through the proper practice of postures, breathing, and meditation, can be activated or awakened. As kundalini energy awakes, it rises through the body, activating each of the chakras in turn until it reaches the seventh chakra at the crown of the head, resulting in an intense physical experience that actually, it is said, physically restructures the body.

Most of the yoga practiced today is profoundly influenced by a text called the *Yoga Sutras*, which describes and explains yoga via a long list of aphorisms that were written thousands of years ago by a man named Patanjali. Many of these aphorisms can be seen as ancient and interesting approaches to stress management, which, in a sense, they were, for isn't stress what keeps us from enlightenment, and isn't seeking enlightenment about ridding ourselves of obstacles like stress so that we can perceive the truth and finally be wholly happy?

In the *Yoga Sutras*, Patanjali described the Eightfold Path to enlightenment. The steps aren't necessarily to be followed in order; in a sense, though, they are progressive. (Note the placement of meditation.)

1. **Yamas,** or lifestyle guidance. If you want to make your path to enlightenment (and your path away from stress) easier, these are the things you should not do. You should not lie, steal, be greedy, commit violence, or let yourself get carried away by lust or disrespect of other humans. Pretty good advice!
2. **Niyamas,** or more lifestyle guidance. These take the form of healthy places to focus your attention and energy, including purity (keeping both mind and body clean), contentment, discipline, studying oneself, and being devoted to something. Also good advice.
3. **Asanas,** or yoga postures. These are designed to help you gain mastery over the body.
4. **Pranayama,** or breathing exercises. These are specifically designed to infuse the body with life-force energy (called *prana* in yoga).
5. **Pratyahara,** or learning to become detached. Now, we're getting into familiar meditation territory. This step is about learning to step back from the world and your own thoughts, feelings, emotions, and sense impressions, to view them with an unengaged, unbiased eye.
6. **Dharana,** or learning concentration. This is also familiar meditation territory. It involves concentrating on something—a sound, an object, a thought—until the boundaries between you and the object dissolve and you are one.
7. **Dhyana,** or meditation. In this step, all the previous steps come in to help out. The lifestyle guidance sets the stage, the asanas and pranayama prime the body, and the detachment and concentration discipline the mind. The goal of yoga meditation is to recognize your ultimate oneness with the universe, which can result in a state of pure, joyful bliss called samadhi.
8. **Nirvana,** or ultimate bliss. This is the final step and the final goal of the Eightfold Path. It is what happens when we finally recognize truth and our oneness with the universe. It is enlightenment. (And it's a pretty stress-free way to live!)

Maybe the yoga path interests you, and if so, you should certainly go out and learn everything you can about it. If not, don't be put off by all these steps. This is just for your information. You can still practice yoga meditation without committing yourself to an all-out yoga lifestyle.

How to Practice Yoga Meditation

To practice yoga meditation, first choose a quiet, comfortable, warm place where you are unlikely to experience distractions. If possible, turn off any sources of noise and anything that emits electricity (TV, stereo, computer—but leave the refrigerator plugged in so as not to spoil the food!). Take off any jewelry, especially anything metal. Electrical currents, metal, and anything encircling a body part can disrupt the flow of energy.

Wear something comfortable. Take off your shoes but keep your socks on if you think your feet will get cold. Wrap yourself in a blanket to keep warm if necessary.

Sit cross-legged, or in the half lotus position, with one foot placed, sole facing up, on the opposite thigh. Or, if you are very flexible in the hips or experienced with yoga asanas, sit in the full lotus position, with legs crossed and each foot placed, sole facing up, on the opposite thigh. To create additional stability, sit on a small, firm pillow so that your knees point toward the ground, forming a tripod.

ESSENTIALS

The full lotus position isn't for beginners because it requires quite a lot of hip flexibility. However, once mastered—through the practice of other yoga exercises that work up to it and then the practice of the position itself—the lotus position is the most stable sitting position. It can be held for long periods of time. And some people claim to have fallen asleep in this position without tipping over.

Next, put your right hand, palm up, on your right knee and your left hand, palm up, on your left knee. You can leave your fingers open or make a circle with each index finger and thumb or middle finger and thumb. Making these circles with your fingers is meant to keep energy concentrated in the body rather than allowing it to escape from the fingertips during meditation.

Rock back and forth and side to side on your sitting bones to find a nice, stable, center position. Imagine the crown of your head being lifted up as the tip of your tailbone sinks down, lengthening the spine and straightening the posture.

Next, simply begin to notice your breath as it flows in and out. Inhale and exhale through your nose, or inhale through your nose and exhale through your mouth. Once you feel relaxed, think or say a syllable, word, or phrase, called a mantra. The traditional mantra of yoga meditation is the sound/word "Om." Say it slowly on the exhale of the breath. Let the "M" resonate through your body.

"Om" is meant to imitate the sound of the universe, from which everything originated and of which everything is a part. Some people think of it as the sound of God. By saying/making this sound, you can feel a connection with the universe, and that is the philosophical basis of yoga (and Hinduism)—we are all one with the universe; all matter, all energy, everything is connected; everything ultimately merges together; beneath the surface of reality, which we experience with our senses, all is really just one. Some people who practice meditation like to use the mantra "One" instead of the mantra "Om" because it more directly evokes, to them, this idea.

Repeat your chosen sound with each exhalation for five minutes on your first time out, then increase the time in meditation as instructed. Yoga meditation feels good. It feels spiritual. It can be a counterpart to any religion or practiced by itself. It can be an energizing spiritual reinforcement, which is important for getting stress under control. If you are feeding your spiritual side, you tend to be less stressed out by the less important things in life.

FACTS

Many who practice yoga meditation and other forms of mantra meditation (described later in the chapter) believe that the sound vibrations produced within and from the body with the chanting of a mantra actually have a physical effect on the body, helping it to align and reinforce its life-force energy.

Shavasana

Shavasana, or the corpse pose, is actually a yoga asana, or exercise—one of those postures designed to help keep the body under control so that it doesn't interfere with the pursuit of meditation. And shavasana does just that—it helps to rein in the body and get it working the way it is meant to work. For that very reason, shavasana is an excellent stress management technique.

Many yoga teachers consider shavasana to be the most important of all yoga asanas. It is both easy and challenging because all you do is lie on your back and relax, but . . . you actually have to lie on your back and relax!

How to Practice Shavasana

To practice shavasana, find a comfortable spot on the floor. A bed usually isn't supportive enough, but you can lie on a mat. Lie on your back with your legs about two feet apart and flat on the floor, your arms flat and away from your body, your palms facing up. Let your feet fall to the side.

Now, begin to relax as you breathe in and out through your nose. As you breathe, concentrate on fully relaxing your body: bones, joints, muscles, everything. Let it all sink comfortably down toward the floor. Don't worry about how you look or what you should be doing. Just let it all go. Relax deeply. Stay in this position for five minutes to start, and work up to fifteen or twenty minutes.

ALERT

One problem with shavasana is that if you are tired, lying on your back with your eyes closed and relaxing is likely to result in a catnap. Don't chide yourself! If you fall asleep in shavasana, you probably need the rest. Just try again when you are better rested. (And get to bed early tonight! Your body is sending you a message!)

This pose is great after a yoga routine or any other kind of workout. It's also an energizing way to start the day and a relaxing way to end the day. Doing shavasana is like pushing the RESET button on your personal computer. It lets your body reset itself, realign itself, re-energize itself, and reverse that insidious stress response.

Breathing Meditation

Breathing meditation is part zazen and part pranayama, which are the breathing techniques associated with yoga. Breathing meditation takes qualities from both. In zazen, you watch your breath without judging, following it in and out. In pranayama, you control the length and character of the inhalation and exhalation.

Breathing is, obviously, a vital function. We do it throughout our lives. It constantly infuses our body with oxygen and, according to some traditions, life-force energy. Our breathing rate is also directly connected with our stress level. When stress chemicals pump through the body, breath rate increases. What happens when we consciously slow our breath rate? We send a message to our bodies to relax. We defuse the stress reaction. And it's so easy to do!

How to Practice Breathing Meditation

First, practice breathing deeply (see Chapter 6). Then, when you feel you can breathe from the lower part of your body rather than from your upper chest, sit comfortably (don't lie down for this one), either on the floor, in one of the positions described in previous meditations, or in a chair. Sit up straight so that you aren't scrunching up your body's breathing space. Imagine you are being suspended from above so that the effort of sitting up straight feels effortless.

Now, take a long, slow, deep breath through your nose, and in your mind, count slowly to five. When you've inhaled fully at five, hold the breath for five more counts. Then, slowly release the breath through your nose to the count of ten.

As you breathe and count, your mind will need to concentrate on the counting. This will help you to stay focused. Eventually, when you get used to the rhythm, your mind won't have to stay so occupied. Now, it's time to focus on the sound and feel of the breath, as in zazen meditation. Focus completely on the breath as it enters, waits, and exits the body. When your mind wanders, guide it gently back to the breath.

Keep breathing in this way for several minutes. Increase your breathing meditation time by two minutes per week until you've reached fifteen to thirty minutes once or twice each day. After a session of breathing meditation, you will feel directly and immediately energized. Try it in the middle of a stressful day, at the end of the day, at the beginning of the day when you need a boost . . . any time you need a shot of energy. In addition to infusing your body with energy, you also are filling it with the oxygen it needs to nourish itself.

Breathing meditation can be practiced anywhere, anytime, even for only a few breaths. Even in small amounts, it is instant stress relief.

A L E R T

While most meditation techniques suggest breathing through the nose, mouth breathing is fine if you have nasal congestion or if you feel more comfortable doing it that way. Better to do your breathing exercises through your mouth than not at all.

Mantra Meditation

Yoga meditation is a mantra meditation, but there are many other kinds of mantra meditation. Any concentrated focusing while repeating a sound can be called a mantra meditation, whether it's Sufi chanting or the recitation of the rosary prayer. Some people believe that the sounds of a mantra actually contain certain powers; others believe that the key to mantra meditation is not the sound but the repetition itself. In either case, if you choose a word that means something to you, you may feel your meditation has a more personalized meaning and feeling to it. Your mantra can even be an affirmation like "I am happy."

Any word or phrase will do. Maybe you already have something in mind. If not, here are a few you "might try (the possibilities, of course, are endless):

- "Om"
- "One"
- "Peace"
- "Love"
- "Joy"
- "God"

- "Sky"
- "Mind, body, spirit"
- "I am happy" (or good, perfect, special, loving)
- "Hallelujah"
- "Shalom"

- "Goddess"
- "Earth"

- "Amen"

Mantra meditation is an ancient tradition practiced by many different cultures in many ways. If time is the ultimate test, then mantra meditation may be the ultimate form of meditation. It disciplines the mind, hones the focus, and even improves the depth of the breath and the capacity of the lungs. It's also supremely relaxing.

ESSENTIALS

Another stress management benefit to practicing mantra meditation is that, like Pavlov's dog, you learn to associate a sound with something positive. After practicing your mantra many times during meditation and experiencing the benefits of relaxation, calm, and inner peace, the mere mention of the word can immediately invoke some of these feelings. For example, if your mantra is "One," then in a stressful situation, just say "One" the way you say it during your regular meditation. Notice the immediate feeling of calm.

How to Practice Mantra Meditation

To practice mantra meditation, find a quiet place to sit, in the position described for yoga meditation or Zen meditation or even in a chair. Get situated, centered, and in a comfortable position. Take a few relaxed breaths, than slowly begin to repeat your mantra with every exhalation of your breath. Repeat for five minutes at first, then build up by two minutes each week, until you've reached a comfortable period of time between fifteen and thirty minutes once or, if possible, twice each day.

Mandala Meditation

In mandala meditation, which is a significant kind of meditation in Tibetan culture, the focus of meditation isn't placed on a sound but on a beautiful object: a mandala. Mandalas are circular pictures, sometimes very plain, sometimes highly ornate, that are used for meditation. The round form and, often, the inner lines of the picture (whether painting, drawing, mosaic, sculpture, or something else), draw the eye to the center of the mandala, helping the mind to focus on that center point.

In Tibet, fantastically complex and beautiful, brilliantly colored and intricately designed mandalas, large and small, are made with colored sand, then brushed away. The making of mandalas is an art form in Tibet. Mandalas are thought to be a symbolic representation of the universe, making them the perfect point of focus. Again, the concept of oneness with the universe recurs. But you don't have to believe that concept to practice mandala (or any other kind of) meditation. You can learn all about the philosophy behind it if you choose, or you can just practice it to help train, discipline, and teach your mind to be still and clear.

How to Practice Mandala Meditation

First, you need a mandala. You can find mandalas in books, in stores that carry imported items from Tibet, and in stores that carry meditation supplies. Or, you can make one yourself, one as simple as a circle with a center point, or as complex and ornate as you want to make it.

Hang or place the mandala at just below eye level from a sitting position, and sit four to eight feet away from it, depending on how comfortable you feel (and how well you see!). Sit comfortably cross-legged, in a kneeling position, or on a small bench or a chair. If sitting on the floor, use a cushion to make yourself more comfortable. Take a few relaxed breaths.

Then, look at the mandala. Instead of following your breath or a sound, use the mandala as your point of concentration. Examine it in detail. Notice everything about it. Notice how your eyes move toward and away from the circle. Let the mandala become the entire focus of your concentration.

FACTS

The labyrinth in the Chartres Cathedral in Paris is a modified version of a mandala. Walking along the path of the maze-like pattern is a concentrated form of walking meditation designed to mimic the journey into the soul and back out again.

When your mind starts to wander (which it will) and you realize it has wandered—"Hey, what am I doing thinking about what we're having for dinner tonight?"—gently guide it back to the mandala.

The more you practice mandala meditation, the easier it becomes. It also becomes more challenging, because after many sessions, you are still looking at the same mandala and your mind must learn to continue to find it a point of complete focus. It's great mental exercise.

Start with five minutes, then add two minutes every week until you are up to fifteen to thirty minutes of mandala meditation once or twice each day.

Chakra Meditation

According to yoga and other traditions, chakras are those centers or "wheels" of energy at key points along the energy channels in the body. Each chakra is thought to represent different parts of the body, both physically and emotionally. Each chakra also has a color. Meditating on the chakra that represents an area in your life that needs reinforcement can be an effective, even life-changing form of meditation. Meditating to open and energize all the chakras is also an effective technique for freeing the body to do the work of extinguishing the negative effects of stress.

While the body is filled with minor chakras, the seven major chakras exist on a line from the base of the spine to the crown of the head. Different people put them in slightly different places and attribute slightly different meanings to each one, but you'll find the following basically in line with standard interpretations of the chakras:

- *The First Chakra* is located deep at the base of the spine. Its color is red. This is the seat of instinct, including appetite, the instinctual sexual urge, aggression, violence, fear, and that instinctual, nonintellectual joyful response to the satisfaction of the basic urges and needs. Meditate on this chakra if you are having trouble controlling your primal urges.
- *The Second Chakra* is located behind the navel or just slightly below. Its color is orange. This is the seat of creativity, including both procreation and the deep-seated urge to create art. This is

also the seat of passion. Meditate on this chakra if you are having trouble with blocked creativity, including reproductive problems.

- *The Third Chakra* is located just behind the solar plexus in that indentation beneath your rib cage where both sides of your ribs meet. Its color is yellow. This is the seat of action and consumption. Your digestive fire lies here, turning food into energy. Meditate on this chakra if you are having trouble with your appetite, for food or for life. If you have difficulty taking things in, work on this chakra.
- *The Fourth Chakra* is located just behind the heart. Its color is green. This is the middle chakra of the seven, and the center of compassion, emotion, and love. This is the chakra of giving away, in contrast to the third chakra, which takes and consumes. Meditate on this chakra if you are having trouble giving of yourself, being compassionate or loving, or feeling emotions.

FACTS

Some people believe that chakras can be energized or unblocked by placing crystals corresponding to that chakra's color over the area of the body in which that chakra lies. Crystal healers place crystals on the body to balance the energy of the chakras and promote the flow of life-force energy through all the chakras.

- *The Fifth Chakra* is located in the throat. Its color is sky blue. This is the seat of communication energy. Meditate on this chakra if you are having trouble communicating your feelings or expressing yourself, or if you have writer's block.
- *The Sixth Chakra* is located between and just above the eyebrows. It is sometimes called the Third Eye chakra. Its color is deep, dark blue or indigo—like the night sky, as opposed to the fifth chakra's color of bright blue sky. This is the center of intuition, unclouded perception, and psychic abilities. Meditate on this area if you want to develop your intuition or if you feel your intuition is blocked.
- *The Seventh Chakra* is located at the crown of the head. This is the highest chakra, sometimes called the Thousand Petalled Lotus chakra. Its color is violet. This is the source of enlightenment and knowing your

true self. If enlightenment is your goal, meditate on all the chakras and the energy that flows between them, culminating in the seventh chakra.

How to Practice Chakra Meditation

To practice chakra meditation, choose a quiet spot where you are unlikely to be disturbed, and sit comfortably. The yoga meditation positions are most common for chakra meditation, but you can also sit in a chair or even lie on the floor (but don't fall asleep!).

Rock yourself into a straight position. The primary energy channels in your body run along your spine and into your head. If you keep your spine straight, energy can flow more easily through the chakras. Close your eyes and breathe easily.

Then, focus either on the first chakra, if you plan to move through all of them, or the chakra on which you want to focus. Imagine the chakra's color and feel the color pulsing in the area of that chakra. Think about what that chakra represents. Reflect on those qualities in your own life. Don't judge yourself. Just observe and let thoughts come and go.

For example, if you are meditating on the fifth chakra, because you are feeling creatively blocked, imagine a bright blue color, like the color of the sky on a breezy, sunny spring day. Feel the blue color cooling and opening your throat, letting your thoughts and ideas come pouring forth. Think about your creativity. Do you wish to be a writer but have trouble getting yourself to try it? Do you love to write but have trouble getting started? If you find yourself lecturing yourself or berating yourself ("Why can't I just sit down and write?"), notice what you are doing and let that go. Concentrate on your throat, the bright blue color, and the creativity in your life in an observer sort of way.

This kind of meditation often brings up surprising solutions. If you let go of the worry and the blame in the area of your concentration, simply letting yourself see and reflect, ideas arise like bubbles, breaking loose from the side of a glass and floating to the top. Pop! The answers become clear.

If you don't get answers or don't feel renewed after one try, keep at it. Sometimes it takes awhile to get used to this kind of concentration and reflection, but with persistence, you can open and energize your chakras. Your body will help you to let go of unnecessary stressors and heal the negative effects of stress. You'll find your consciousness breaking into new territory.

To meditate on all the chakras, as a kind of whole-self-maintenance, start with the first chakra, its color, its function, and concentrate on it for two to five minutes. Then, imagine the energy rising into the second chakra, and concentrate on it for two to five minutes (don't worry about watching a clock—try to feel when it's right to move up). Keep going until you reach the seventh chakra. If you feel more blocked in any one area, spend a little more time there.

Chakra meditation is a superb stress management meditation. You feel that you are really doing something to take care of yourself. And it's a lot cheaper than therapy! (It's also an excellent complement to therapy.)

FACTS

In addition to colors and aspects of the self, the seven primary chakras also have associated planets, vibrational syllables, and glands!

- First chakra: Saturn, sound is LAM, glands are sex glands
- Second chakra: Jupiter, sound is VAM, glands are adrenals
- Third chakra: Mars, sound is RAM, glands are digestive
- Fourth chakra: Venus, sound is YAM, gland is thymus
- Fifth chakra: Mercury, sound is HAM, gland is thyroid
- Sixth chakra: Sun, sound is OM, gland is pineal
- Seventh chakra: the universe, sound is also OM, glands are pituitary and hypothalamus

Mindfulness Meditation

Mindfulness meditation is different than other meditations because it can be practiced anywhere, anytime, no matter what you are doing. It is simply focusing on total awareness of the present moment. Mindfulness meditation is inherent in many other forms of meditation but can also be practiced while walking, running, playing basketball, driving, studying, writing, reading, or eating. Anything you are doing, you can do with mindfulness. Your entire day can be one long mindfulness meditation—although it's pretty hard to sustain.

Mindfulness meditation has been popularized by both Easterners who have come West, such as Thich Nhat Hanh, the Vietnamese Buddhist monk, and Westerners such as Jon Kabat-Zinn, Ph.D., the founder and director of the Stress Reduction Clinic at the University of Massachusetts Medical Center. It is easy to do for short periods. It is tough to do for an extended time, because our minds resist staying in the present moment. But it is a rewarding mental discipline that teaches us to cherish and relish the miracle of the present moment, no matter how ordinary. It is also supremely relaxing and satisfying.

How to Practice Mindfulness Meditation

Wherever you are, whatever you are doing, you can practice mindfulness meditation by consciously making the decision to be fully and completely aware of everything around you. Notice the impressions from all your senses—see, hear, feel, smell, taste. When your mind begins to think about something else, gently bring it back to the present moment. Don't judge the impressions of your senses. Just observe. You may be amazed at what you notice about yourself and the world around you.

FACTS

A famous Buddhist aphorism (paraphrased here) asks, "If you hear a dog barking, do you think of your own dog, or do you think only 'bark'?" Thinking "bark" means you are practicing mindfulness. Thinking of your own dog means that you are making an association and that your mind is somewhere else.

If practicing mindfulness anywhere sounds overwhelming, you can start out practicing it while doing something very specific, like eating. Pick a single thing to eat—not a fancy dish with lots of ingredients, but a vegetable, a piece of fruit, some simple broth, or a piece of bread. Eat it slowly, slowly, and notice everything about the process. How do you bring the food to your mouth? How do you put it in? How does it feel in your mouth? How does it taste and smell? How does the food look? What spurs you to take another bite? How does your body react to the food?

Practicing mindfulness meditation while eating is a good way to hone your mindfulness skills. It is also a way to help overcome mindless eating, a common problem especially among stressed-out Americans.

Prayer

Several studies that continue to baffle the mainstream medical establishment suggest that when hospitalized patients were prayed for, *even when they didn't know they were being prayed for,* they recovered more quickly than those who weren't prayed for. These studies suggest that people can experience stress relief if others pray for them.

ESSENTIALS

If you're stuck for words when trying to pray and aren't really associated with any religious tradition, borrow a prayer from any of the world's religions. The Lord's Prayer, the Rosary Prayer, the Hail Mary prayer, a Gregorian chant, one of the Kabbalah's twenty-five names for God, the Jesus prayer of the desert fathers, a Sufi chant, a Buddhist chant, a Hindu chant. Go to the library and do some research. It's a place to start. Once you get comfortable, you can generate your own words.

Any practice of centered, reverential concentration is a form of at least a cousin of meditation, and they all work to relieve stress. The meditation traditions of all cultures have common themes and techniques. The Eastern mantra meditation in which "Om" is chanted is similar to the Western practice of saying prayers.

What is prayer? Prayer is a focused, concentrated communication, statement of intention, or opening of the channel between you and divinity, whatever divinity is for you. A prayer can be a request, thanks, worship, or praise to God. It can be an intention of being thankful directed to the universe. It can be used to invoke divine power or an attempt to experience divine or universal energy directly. Many different traditions have many different modes and types of prayer. Prayer can mean whatever you want it to mean for you.

How to Practice Prayer

To practice prayer, first decide what you want your prayer to be. To whom, to what, or toward whom or what is your prayer addressed? What is the substance of your prayer? Are you praying for healing for yourself or someone else? Are you praying for something you want or need? Are you praying to say thank you for everything you already have? Are you praying to praise, to express your inner joy, to release your inner sadness?

Once you have a specific intention in mind, sit or lie quietly in a place where you are unlikely to be disturbed. Focus your thought on your prayer and say it, out loud or in your mind. Stay focused on your prayer and the energy of your prayer. Imagine where it is going. Let your prayer continue to radiate from your heart toward its intended source. As you open this channel from your heart to the outside, also allow a space for a return message. You may be filled with a warm, joyful feeling. Or, you might receive a message. Or, you might not.

Whatever happens, continue to focus on your prayer as it flows from you and don't judge the results. Just let it happen and let this outpouring of positive energy from your heart fortify and strengthen you. Because, as we all know, the more you give, the more you receive!

Imagery Meditation and Visualization

Imagery meditation and visualization are meditations that use your imagination to make positive changes in your thinking and even in what happens to you. The purpose of imagery meditation is to imagine yourself in a different place (the beach, the mountains, Paris) or circumstance to effect instant relaxation. Visualization is a technique for imagining something you want (a different job, the love of your life) or a change you would like to see in yourself (to be less reactive to stress, more self-confident, perfectly organized). Imagining and visualizing have two separate effects:

1. Instant stress relief because of the positive feeling you associate with what you are visualizing
2. Life changes because continually visualizing something can help to bring those changes about in your life

Even if your imagination is a little rusty, you can practice imagery meditation and visualization. It's fun! Maybe you will use imagery meditation to take a five-minute seaside vacation in the middle of your workday. Maybe you will use visualization to help you change your eating and exercise habits to finally achieve a healthy body and a healthy weight. Whatever you use them for, these imagination generators are powerful stress management techniques, both in the short and the long term.

How to Practice Imagery Meditation

Get comfortable, either sitting or lying down. Close your eyes. Take a few deep, relaxed breaths, then form a picture in your mind. Maybe it is the place you wish you could be right now, a place you visited in the past and loved, or a place you invent. What does the place look like? What do you see around you? What colors, what textures? Notice everything about the place you are visualizing.

Then, imagine touching things around you—sand, water, grass, trees, great art or architecture, your favorite person. Listen. What do you hear in this place? Wind, waves, rustling leaves, traffic, talking? Next, think about what you smell. Freshly cut grass? Salt? A storm? Cooking food? Perfume? Focus on each of your senses and explore the place you've created or remembered in your mind. Stay here as long as you like, but for at least five minutes. Then, slowly, let the images fade away and open your eyes. Instant relaxation!

How to Practice Visualization

Get comfortable, either sitting or lying down. Close your eyes. Take a few deep, relaxed breaths, then form a picture in your mind of some kind of positive life change. Maybe it's a career goal, a change in health or appearance, situation, confidence, or anything else. Keep it simple and stick to one thing. You can always tackle other areas in a separate session.

Imagine yourself in your new situation. How do you look, act, feel? How do you like being this new way, looking like this, having this job?

Explore yourself in your new situation. If you like it, if it feels right, then stick with your visualization every day and imagine it with fervent and confident intention.

As your life changes, your visualizations may change and grow. That's fine! You may realize, for example, that as your life becomes less stressful and more rewarding, you don't really need to be financially wealthy, because you have gained emotional and spiritual wealth instead. The trick is to keep it up. The more you use your imagination, the stronger it becomes, just like a muscle.

With a strong imagination, you become a more creative problem solver, and your brain works better. You'll be better able to manage the stress in your life as you work on eliminating it.

To add power to your visualization, use an affirmation as a mantra for your meditation, worded as if the change has already taken place, and worded positively (rather than, "I won't be sick," say, "I will be well"). Use the affirmation as a mantra while you visualize your goal.

SSENTIALS

Examples of positive affirmations:

- "I am healthy, strong, and well."
- "My body is healing quickly and growing stronger."
- "I am confident and self-assured."
- "I am relaxed, calm, and tranquil."
- "I have found the perfect life partner for me."
- "I am rich in many areas of my life."

Meditation Tips for Sticking with It

Once you've started to meditate, you may find that the charm wears off after a few sessions. How do you stick with it so that you can reap all the benefits of a regular, long-term meditation practice?

Here are some tips:

- Stick with one kind of meditation most of the time so that you feel focused and practiced at your chosen technique.
- If you absolutely can't stand the thought of meditating on a given day, choose a different type of meditation, just for a change of pace.
- Put meditation into your schedule just like any other appointment. It's an appointment with yourself, and you should be the most important person in your life!
- Meditate at the same time or times each day, to get into a rhythm and cement your meditation into your schedule.
- If possible, meditate on an empty stomach, either before a meal or two hours after (one hour after a light meal). Your body will be able to focus more easily if it isn't busy digesting.
- Meditate at a high-energy time of day rather than a low-energy time of day. If you are a morning person, meditate in the morning. If you get going at night, meditate at night. You'll lessen your chances of nodding off, and you'll have better focus and concentration.
- Throughout your day, make a point to remember the feeling of meditation. Recalling the relaxing feeling of meditation can re-invoke that feeling, helping to extend meditation's stress-relieving effects all day long.
- Start meditating with a friend. Whether you meditate together, at the same time and/or in the same place, or maintain your separate meditation practices, you can call each other on those days when you don't feel like meditating and give each other encouragement and motivation.

ESSENTIALS   Your stress management journal can be part meditation journal. After meditating each day, make an entry that includes the date, time, how long you meditated, and how it felt. Your entries can be as long or short as you wish, but a journal will help you to keep a record of your practice and your progress. You might also detect patterns in your mood and energy level that affect your practice.

Above all, just keep practicing. Practice, practice, practice. Practice may not make perfect (because nobody's perfect), but practice is what will eventually make dramatic changes in your life, your health, and your stress management mastery.

CHAPTER 9

More Stress Management Tools

We've already covered a number of highly effective stress management techniques, but the world is a wide and interesting place, and many more tools for mastering stress management exist. In this chapter, I'll list some techniques that don't fall into the categories already covered. Browse through this list with a spirit of exciting possibility, in search of stress management tools you can use. Maybe one or more of these will be just what you are looking for.

Attitude Adjustment

Remember that country song about giving people an attitude adjustment on the top of the head? The attitude adjustment technique in this book has nothing to do with violence. It's about subtly changing one's attitude.

Negativity is a huge drain on your energy and exacerbates any stress in your life, magnifying it until it seems huge and uncontrollable. Many people are in the negativity habit. Are you?

What's your attitude? Are you a glass half-full or a glass half-empty type? Do you see the upside or the downside first?

Being negative is a habit. It may be a habit brought on by lots of past suffering, and that's perfectly understandable. But it can stop right now. Even in suffering, you don't have to be negative. Some people remain positive through tragedy; others despair. What's the difference? Attitude.

How do you change your negative attitude? First, become aware of when you tend to be negative. Keep a negativity journal. Whenever you feel like being negative, don't express it out loud. Write it down in your journal. Once you get it out of your system on the page, you can look it over more objectively later. Eventually (as with any kind of journaling), you'll start to see patterns.

Has stress sapped your sense of humor? Try to keep your sense of humor when life gets stressful. A lighthearted approach is much less stressful, and sometimes a funny face or a well-timed joke can put an immediate and happy end to an escalating situation.

Once you know what kinds of things trigger your negativity (it may be triggered by many things), you can begin to catch yourself in the act. When something unexpected happens, do the first words out of your mouth tend to be a frantic "Oh NO!"? If so, stop yourself after that first "Oh . . ." Notice what you are doing. Tell yourself, "I don't have to respond this way. I should wait and see if a full-blown, all-out 'Oh NO' is really warranted." This stopping of your thought process and your negative reaction can help you be more objective and, eventually, more positive about any situation. Even if, after stopping, you realize that an "Oh NO" really *is* warranted, you won't be calling wolf at every little mishap. You'll save your "Oh NOs" for when you really need them.

Just like any habit, the more you get used to halting your negative reactions and replacing them with neutral or positive reactions, the less you'll find yourself reacting negatively. Instead of "Oh NO," react with silence, taking a wait-and-see attitude. Or, react with an affirmation: "Oh . . . I can learn something positive from this!"

You might encounter obstacles along the way, and that's to be expected. Maybe in your negativity journal you'll discover that you are comforted by or even *enjoy* being negative. Maybe it makes you feel safe: If you always expect the worst, you'll never be disappointed. But obstacles are meant to be overcome. Even if a negative attitude is comforting in some ways, is it worth the drain on your energy and happiness? Keep working through it and being honest with yourself. You may discover that your negative reactions are all about protection and that you can find much better ways to protect yourself than that. How about quality friends, a really fulfilling hobby, a regular meditation practice?

If you are serious about kicking your negativity habit, you can adjust your attitude. It just takes some attention. (For a related technique, see "Optimism Therapy," later in this chapter.)

You can oppose your own tendencies to think irrationally by evaluating your feelings. Ask yourself these questions:

1. Is the situation or just my perception causing me stress?
2. Am I expecting things to be other than they are?
3. Am I stressed because of someone else's mistake?
4. Conflict requires two people. Am I contributing?
5. Am I wasting time looking for a cause of this situation instead of changing my behavior now?

Autogenic Training

Autogenic training, or autogenics, was designed to reap the benefits of hypnosis without the need for a hypnotist or the time typically involved in a hypnosis session. Autogenics uses a relaxed position and the verbal suggestion of warmth and heaviness in the limbs to induce a state of deep relaxation and stress relief. Autogenics have been used to treat muscle tension, asthma, gastrointestinal problems, irregular heartbeat, high blood pressure, headaches, thyroid problems, anxiety, irritability, and fatigue. It can also increase your stress resistance.

The verbal suggestions of autogenics are designed specifically to reverse the body's stress response. The suggestions have six themes:

1. Heaviness, which promotes relaxation of the voluntary muscles of the limbs, reversing the tension in the limbs typical of the stress response
2. Warmth, which opens the blood vessels in your arms and legs, reversing the flow of blood to the center of the body typical of the stress response
3. Regular heartbeat, which helps to normalize the heart rate, reversing the quickened heart rate characteristic of the stress response
4. Regular breathing, which helps to normalize breath rate, reversing the quickened breath rate characteristic of the stress response
5. Relaxation and warming of the abdomen, which reverses the flow away from the digestive system typical of the stress response
6. Cooling of the head, which reverses the flow of blood to the brain typical of the stress response

In other words, all the major symptoms of stress in the body caused by the release of stress hormones are systematically targeted and reversed through the suggestions in autogenic training.

If you feel stress or discomfort during autogenic training, skip to the next area. If you suffer from ulcers or other gastrointestinal problems, skip the step that warms the abdomen and stomach.

You can do autogenic training on your own, but visiting a professional autogenic training instructor to learn how to do it correctly may be a good idea. If you can't find one in your area, look for books on the subject and follow their directions. Or, simply find a quiet place to relax where you are unlikely to be bothered, get comfortable and warm, turn down the lights, and sit or lie comfortably, then focus on each of the six areas in the following manner, repeating the verbal suggestions listed and concentrating on what you are saying to yourself and on the named area. Don't force yourself to concentrate, however. Keep your attitude passive and accepting. However it happens is fine. You can't do it wrong. If you want to consult a professional, check with psychotherapists in your area who practice hypnotherapy, or check with licensed holistic health practitioners such as chiropractors, herbalists, or massage therapists who might be able to refer you to someone nearby.

You can put these suggestions onto an audiotape, or you can memorize them. Repeat each phrase slowly four times before moving on to the next phrase:

1. My right arm is heavy.
2. My left arm is heavy.
3. My right leg is heavy.
4. My left leg is heavy.
5. My right arm is warm.
6. My left arm is warm.
7. My right leg is warm.
8. My left leg is warm.
9. My arms are heavy and warm.
10. My legs are heavy and warm.
11. My heartbeat is slow and easy.
12. My heart feels calm.
13. My breathing is slow and easy.
14. My breathing feels calm.
15. My stomach is warm.
16. My stomach is relaxed.
17. My forehead is cool.
18. My scalp is relaxed.
19. My whole body is calm.
20. My whole body is relaxed.
21. I am calm and relaxed.

Voilà! Good-bye stress response.

Ayurveda

Ayurveda (pronounced I-YOUR-VAY-DA) is an ancient science of living a long and healthy life, defying disease and aging, and promoting well-being and good health through a variety of practices. Ayurveda may be the oldest known health care system, probably over 5,000 years old! Amazingly, it is still widely practiced today. In fact, thanks to the efforts of Dr. Deepak Chopra, physician and author, the science of Ayurveda has enjoyed a new surge in popularity in the last decade.

In Ayurveda, stress equals imbalance. When the body isn't balanced, pain, illness, injury, disease, and psychological and emotional problems result. The theory of Ayurveda is complex, but to simplify, it uses certain foods, herbs, oils, colors, sounds, yoga exercises, cleansing rituals, chants, lifestyle changes, and counseling to put the body and mind into the ultimate state of health. It also has at its heart a very specific philosophy that suggests disease and even the aging process can be halted, even reversed, through certain practices.

ESSENTIALS

While Ayurveda treats dosha imbalances in many ways, here are some generalizations:

- **Vatas** benefit from warm, moist, comforting foods (oatmeal, soup) and holding to a regular daily routine. They feel aggravated by the cold.
- **Pittas** benefit from cold food, anger management, and long walks. Heat and spicy foods aggravate them.
- **Kaphas** benefit from warm, dry foods, stimulating events, and exercise. Too much sugar and fat aggravate them.

The ayurvedic system divides people (and everything else—weather, tastes, seasons, temperatures, and so on) into three main dosha types. Many people are a combination of two or even a balance of the three doshas, but most people lean toward one dominant dosha. One's dosha determines what kinds of foods, herbs, oils, colors, sounds, yoga exercises, cleansing rituals, chants, lifestyle changes, and counseling will be most beneficial.

VATA	PITTA	KAPHA
Thin build; if overweight, irregularly so, with spongy rather than solid tissue	Muscular or average build; easily builds muscle	Heavyset, or large boned; when overweight (common for Kapha), body is solid
Curly, thin, brown hair; can be frizzy	Reddish hair, either dark or strawberry blonde; redhead complexion, freckles, rosy skin	Dark, thick, glossy or oily hair, smooth skin, full lips, creamy or olive complexion
Small, darting eyes	Sharp, piercing, somewhat bloodshot eyes	Large, wide, white eyes
Dry, cracking joints	Loose, soft joints	Large, thick, sturdy joints
Can't keep to a schedule; erratic eater, sleeper	Good appetite, eats fast	Low constant appetite, eats slowly
Low or variable endurance	Moderate endurance but heat intolerant	Strong, steady endurance
Prone to pain, arthritis, and disorders of the nervous and immune system	Prone to infections, fever, and inflammatory diseases	Prone to respiratory diseases, swelling, and obesity
Fast, unsteady, erratic lifestyle	Purposeful, goal-oriented, assertive lifestyle	Slow, steady, elegant lifestyle
Sensitive to noise	Sensitive to bright lights	Sensitive to strong odors
Adaptable but sometimes indecisive	Intelligent but sometimes critical	Steady but sometimes dull

An ayurvedic physician can determine your dosha, sometimes through nothing more than feeling your pulse. Typically, a rigorous and detailed analysis is made of a patient who seeks ayurvedic therapy, including detailed questions covering everything from physical makeup to habits, likes and dislikes, and profession. Many do-it-yourself quizzes are available in books and Web sites to help you determine your own dosha. Some people choose to visit ayurvedic centers or in-patient ayurvedic treatment programs. Others take dietary and lifestyle advice only.

Ayurveda is a fascinating and complex system, and this book can only scratch the surface. But just to get you started, here are some qualities commonly associated with each of the dosha types. This list is by no means exhaustive and is meant to give you a very general idea about the three doshas.

Even though most people have one dominant dosha, every person has all three doshas and can experience imbalances in any dosha. Vata goes out of balance first, then pitta, then kapha. Ayurveda treats dosha imbalances in many ways.

If Ayurveda interests you, do some research. Books and other sources of information on this ancient science of life and longevity are plentiful. Here are a few I like.

BOOKS

✎ *Ageless Body, Timeless Mind,* by Deepak Chopra, M.D. (New York: Harmony Books, 1993)

✎ *Creating Health,* Revised Edition, by Deepak Chopra, M.D. (Boston: Houghton Mifflin Company, 1991)

✎ *Perfect Health,* by Deepak Chopra, M.D. (New York: Harmony Books, 1991)

✎ *The Ayurveda Encyclopedia,* by Tirtha, Swami Sada Shiva (Bayville, NY: Ayurveda Holistic Center Press, 1998)

WEB SITES

- Ayurveda Holistic Center: *ayurvedahc.com/index.htm*
- The National Institute of Ayurvedic Medicine: *niam.com/corp-web/index.htm*
- Everyday Ayurveda: *www.everydayayurveda.org*

Biofeedback: Know Thyself

This high-tech relaxation technique, designed to teach the body how to directly and immediately reverse the stress response, puts you in control of the bodily functions once considered to be involuntary. Biofeedback was developed in the 1960s and was popular in the 1970s and 1980s. A biofeedback session involves getting hooked up to equipment that measures certain bodily functions such as your skin temperature, heart rate, breathing rate, and muscle tension. A trained biofeedback counselor then guides the patient through relaxation techniques while the patient watches the machine monitors. When heart rate or breathing rate decreases, for example, you can see it on the monitor. You learn how your body feels when your heart and breathing rate decrease. Eventually, after a number of sessions, you learn to lower your heart rate, breath rate, muscle tension, temperature, and so on, on your own.

The first time some people try biofeedback, they actually experience a heightened stress response. This is normal and natural. Once the subject gets comfortable with the process of monitoring physical reactions, body functions normalize.

Because biofeedback requires special equipment and a trained counselor, it isn't something you can figure out on your own at home, but once you've learned the technique, your vital functions are in your own hands—or head!

To find a certified biofeedback counselor near you, search your city on the Biofeedback Certification Institute's Web site at *www.bcia.org/generalinfo_findpractitioner.cfm.*

Creativity Therapy

Creativity therapy is the use of drawing, painting, writing, sculpting, or playing music as a form of stress relief and also as a way of dealing with emotional or psychological problems. Art therapy has a long history of helping patients work through problems and unblock creativity through certain techniques, and requires a trained art therapist. Creativity therapy is a more general term for using creativity on your own to help relieve your own stress. Art therapy is a kind of creativity therapy, but it is not the only kind. In creativity therapy, you can write poetry, play the piano, even mold homemade playdough to help relieve your own stress and express your creativity.

Creativity therapy is an excellent way to relieve stress. When you become immersed in creation, you can achieve a kind of intense, all-consuming focus similar to the intense focus and concentration you can achieve through a meditation practice. Allowing yourself to become one with your creation—your painting, your drawing, your poem, your short story, your journal entry, your sculpture, your music—helps you to let go, even for a little while, of the stresses in your life. Your body responds by relaxing, counteracting the effects of too much stress.

As with meditation, creativity therapy teaches your mind to concentrate for a long period of time on a single thing—it's great practice and a great way to hone your mental power. Creativity therapy can also help you to feel good about who you are. Rather than spending your entire day doing what you're supposed to do or what other people want you to do, creativity therapy gives you a space solely for yourself, during which you can express your innermost thoughts, feelings, problems, anxieties, joys, and the imagery that sits deep within your subconscious waiting to be released.

How do you do it? Set aside thirty to sixty minutes each day. Choose your creative outlet. Maybe you will write in your journal, or practice the cello, or paint with watercolors, or draw the flowers in your garden, or dance to classical music in your living room. Whatever you choose, commit to this time as you would to a meditation time. Make it an unbreakable appointment. Then, sit down in a quiet place where you are unlikely to be disturbed, and start creating (or dancing or playing or whatever you are doing).

Try not to look at your creations or analyze your own performance, at least not carefully, until you've practiced creative therapy for one month. When the month is over, look carefully at what you've accomplished. Do you see patterns? Motifs? Themes? Words and images that recur in writing or painting or drawing are your personal themes. Movements or sounds can also have meaning for you, personally, if you are dancing or playing music. Spend some time meditating on what they could mean for you. What is your subconscious trying to tell you?

SSENTIALS

Let your creativity therapy be a private event. Whether you are painting, drawing, writing, sculpting, or playing, the important thing is not to try to create a "masterpiece." This is private creation. This is just for you. Promise yourself you won't show it to anyone—at least not for a month, and then you can decide. For now, just let whatever is inside you flow out through the medium.

It doesn't even matter if you don't know how to draw, paint, write poetry, or whatever you choose to do. This is not work to be judged, analyzed, or displayed. This is work that comes directly from your subconscious. It is a process of releasing what you are holding onto, mentally, deep inside. And that feels good.

Here are some tips to remember when engaged in your creativity therapy:

- As you work, don't stop. Write or draw continuously. If you stop, you'll be more likely to judge your work.
- Don't judge your work!

- Try creating when you are very tired. Sometimes fatigue dulls your conscious, organized, critical mind, allowing more images from the subconscious to flow through.
- Promise yourself you won't read what you wrote or survey what you drew until the session is over. Otherwise, you're likely to start judging.
- Don't be critical or disappointed in what you come up with. There is no wrong way to do this, unless you are judging yourself.
- Stuck? Faced with a blank page? Just start writing or drawing without any thought or plan, even if you end up writing "I don't know what to write" for three pages or drawing a page full of stick figures. Eventually, you'll get tired of that and something else will come out.
- Commit to the process. Even if it seems like it isn't working at first, thirty minutes (or just ten to fifteen minutes when you first try it) each and every day will yield dramatic results if you stick with it.
- Don't think you can't do creative therapy because you "aren't creative." Nonsense. *Everyone* is creative. Some people just haven't developed their creativity as much as others, and creativity therapy is just as helpful (if not more helpful) for nonartists, who aren't already indoctrinated into how they are "supposed to" create something.
- Most importantly, enjoy the process! Creativity therapy is illuminating, interesting, and fun!

Dream Journaling

Dream journaling is similar to creativity therapy because your unmonitored creativity can tap your subconscious in the same way your dreams do. While "the stuff that dreams are made of" is still a matter of some controversy, many people believe that dreams tap the subconscious mind's hopes, fears, goals, worries, and desires.

We all dream, but it isn't easy to remember your dreams, and some people claim they never remember their dreams. Dream journaling is a way to begin keeping track of the images, themes, motifs, and emotions in your dreams. Because it helps you to work on your own mind and train your mind to dream in a way that benefits you, dream journaling is a good stress management tool. Its mental training helps the mind to become more stress resilient. Also, the information you may uncover in your dream journaling may help to root out and dispose of unnecessary stress in your life.

First, find a journal you like that is pleasing to write in. This could be your stress management journal or a separate journal you keep by your bed. Also, find a pen that is easy and pleasing to write with. Keep these items on your bedside table, in a place that is easy to reach while you are lying in bed.

When you are in bed and ready to go to sleep, close your eyes and tell yourself: "I will remember my dreams tonight." This sets your intention in your mind. It may not work the first night, the second night, or even for a few weeks. But eventually, it should work.

In the morning, the second you wake up, before you get up to do anything, as you are opening your eyes, reach for your dream journal and immediately start writing. If you remember a dream, write about it in as much detail as you can. Even if you don't remember a dream, just start writing whatever impression is in your head. As you write, dream impressions, even full dreams with elaborate plots, may come into your head. If they don't, you'll still be writing from the subconscious, which is more accessible in the first few minutes after awakening.

Write until you've recorded all the dreams you remember, or until your awakening thoughts are exhausted. Then, the next night, state your intention to remember your dreams again, and record them again in the morning.

FACTS

Dreams of flying may symbolize a feeling of freedom, power, success, or a new perspective. Dreams of falling may symbolize a feeling of insecurity, anxiety, failure, or the inability to control one's situation. Both flying and falling dreams are quite common. To learn more about what your dreams mean, check out *The Everything® Dream Book,* by Trish and Rob MacGregor (Adams Media Corporation, 1998).

As with creativity theory, try not to look back on your dreams for about a month. Then, after a month has passed, go back and read your journal. Do you see themes, motifs, recurring images? These are probably signals from your subconscious. Reflect on what they might be telling you about the direction your life is going, your health, your relationships, and your happiness. Your dream journal may give you clues about ways to reshape and de-stress your life.

Even if you don't find any obvious messages, persist in your dream journaling. Like meditation, this process helps you to focus and concentrate your thoughts and will also help you to tap into your inner creativity and to feel more connected to yourself. People who devote time each day to themselves and engage in inner reflection tend to feel better about themselves and are less likely to suffer from the negative effects of stress. Let your dreams lead you to a feeling of groundedness and connectedness with your inner self.

Flower Remedies

Flower remedies or flower essences are substances made from water and whole flowers, then preserved with alcohol. They contain no actual flower parts, but people who use and prescribe them believe they contain the flower's essence or energy and can promote emotional healing. The remedies are thought to work in a vibrational, rather than a biochemical, way on the body. The typical dosage is four drops of the flower remedy under the tongue four times per day.

ALERT

Flower remedies are preserved with alcohol, and while the alcohol in the remedies is minute, it could be enough to trigger problems in anyone who is sensitive to alcohol or recovering from alcohol addiction; those who are should not take flower remedies. Also, only choose flowers that you can identify, specifically those used in traditional flower remedies. You wouldn't want to drink a remedy made with poison ivy, even if the leaf didn't remain in the remedy.

Flower remedies are a noninvasive, safe, gentle way to balance the emotions. Yes, you drink them, but they are considered noninvasive because no actual flower parts remain in the remedy. You are drinking spring water with a little alcohol for preservation and the vibrational energy of a flower.

Different remedies directly address the emotional effects of stress without any side effects. They are a lovely, natural way to treat the emotional effects of stress. And while some holistic therapists prescribe them, you can make them and take them yourself. In fact, the actual process of making flower remedies is a fun and relaxing way to combat stress and could even become an interesting hobby!

Of course, many of the remedies that are effective for certain emotional imbalances will come from flowers that aren't available in your area. Bach flower remedies, the most widely known, and other brands of flower essences are available in health food stores and from holistic health care professionals.

Different flower remedies address different emotional imbalances, helping to clarify the mind, "unstick" the emotions when they get stuck in one place or mode, and help to restore rational and productive emotions. Often, several remedies are prescribed in combination. According to the *Illustrated Encyclopedia of Natural Remedies,* by C. Norman Shealy, M.D., Ph.D. (Element, 1998), flower remedies were created to be so easy to make and use that people could treat themselves. If you would like to try making your own flower remedies, look for books that tell you how to do it, or talk to your holistic health care practitioner. If you don't wish to do this, or if you need a remedy from a flower not available in your area, you can buy flower remedies from health food stores or holistic health practitioners.

ESSENTIALS

Flower remedies are often used to help pets overcome emotional imbalances, too. Holistic pet supply stores and catalogs often offer different remedy mixes to help pets overcome separation anxiety, nervousness, hyperactivity, even depression. Always see your vet first, to rule out a medical condition.

Find your emotional symptom of stress in the table on page 206 to see what kind of flower remedy might benefit you.

SYMPTOMS	FLOWER REMEDY
Hiding problems behind a cheerful demeanor	Agrimony
Constant worry, anxiety, racing thoughts	White Chestnut Flower
Strong feelings of hopelessness and despair	Gorse
Inability to find a life purpose or direction	Wild Oat
Always on the move, can't stand to wait, rushing, can't slow down	Black-Eyed Susan
Resignation, passivity, apathy	Wild Rose
Selfish, sulky, self-pitying, ungrateful	Willow
Self-condemnation, disgust with self	Crab Apple
Self-obsessed, unable to listen to and share with others	Heather
Sensitivity to other people, obsessive worrying that something horrible will happen to loved ones	Red Chestnut Flower
Procrastination, exhaustion from work, inability to get motivated to work	Hornbeam
Compulsion to constantly give to others, disregarding one's own need, resulting in depletion	Centaury
Weak will, tendency to follow or imitate others	Cerato
Possessive, selfish, nagging, manipulative	Chicory
Excessive daydreaming, not living in the present, living in a fantasy world	Clematis
Nervous, stammering, intelligent but slow to learn	Bush Fuchsia
Being judgmental, overcritical, intolerant	Beech
Discouragement, despondency, and mild depression due to circumstances	Gentian
Intense fear, terror, nervousness, panic	Rescue Remedy, made from Rock Rose, Cherry Plum, Impatiens, Clematis, Star of Bethlehem
Obsessed with past, nostalgia, feeling that past was wonderful and future is bleak	Honeysuckle
Intense negativity, hatred, jealousy, suspicion, or revenge	Holly

Friend Therapy

Friend therapy is simple: Let your friends help you manage your stress! Research shows that people without social networks and friends often feel lonely, but often won't admit it. Loneliness is stressful. Holding in your feelings is even more stressful.

Some people tend to turn to friends automatically when things get tough. Others tend to isolate themselves during stressful times, just when they could most use a listening ear and a few words of encouragement.

Some people already have a group of friends they can turn to, but when things get stressful, it's often easy to stop calling them. Do you stop returning e-mails, calling your buddies, or going out with your group when you are feeling stressed? Engage in some friend therapy and give those buddies a call. Warn them you are feeling stressed. Ask them to listen without offering advice, if you don't want advice. Or, maybe you do!

If you don't have a ready-to-go group of friends or have lost touch with yours, you may have to start from scratch. One of the easiest ways to make friends is to join something. Take a class, join a club, attend a church, find a support group. You might need to try a few different things before you meet people you can really relate to, but if you keep trying, you'll do it.

Don't use the excuse that you can't fit anything else into your schedule. Set something up with a coworker you like, make an overture to another parent at your child's school during a school event, or call a friend you haven't been in touch with for a while to meet for lunch. You're going to eat lunch anyway, right?

Treating your stress with friend therapy doesn't mean you sit at home alone and wait for your friends to come to you. It means you take the initiative and get out there to make contact. Sometimes, it just takes a few words to find someone who is in the same position as you and needs friend therapy, too.

Friend therapy isn't complicated. All it entails is human contact—not cyber-contact (although that's better than no contact). Phone contact can be helpful, but nothing beats the real thing. Just being with another person—talking (even if it's not about your problems), having fun, taking a break from the daily routine—is a great way to relax, raise your self-esteem, and have the chance to be there for somebody else, too. You don't have to do anything in particular with your friends to make it friend therapy. You just have to get a social life.

Of course, there are limits to what friends can and should do for you. Part of friend therapy is giving as well as taking. A productive friend therapy relationship should certainly be reciprocal. If you use your friends for constant unloading but never allow them to unload on you, they won't be your friends for long!

ESSENTIALS   One way to start up a friendship is to ask a favor. Acquaintances and neighbors are often hesitant to ask favors, but asking a favor starts a reciprocal relationship. If you ask your neighbor to borrow her snow shovel or the proverbial cup of sugar, your neighbor will feel easier about asking you for something later on. Asking a favor is more effective than offering a favor "any time" because people are usually more willing to do you a favor than to ask you for one. Go ahead and ask for what you need. You may forge a friendship.

Hypnosis: Hype or Help?

People tend to have preconceptions about hypnosis: the swinging pendulum, the controlling therapist with the German accent, the hypnotized person running around on a stage clucking like a chicken. While hypnosis has certainly been used (or misused) by those seeking applause, hypnosis and hypnotherapy are legitimate tools that are also used to help people put themselves into more positive mental states. Hypnosis is, in essence, deep relaxation coupled with visualization.

Hypnosis is *not* some mysterious state in which you are completely at the mercy of the hypnotist. While hypnotized, you retain your awareness, but your body becomes extremely relaxed and disinclined to move, your awareness becomes narrow, your thinking tends to become literal, and you become much more open to suggestion than you would be in a nonhypnotic state. This suggestibility is what makes hypnosis work.

During the course of life, we may often want to change things about ourselves—our habits, our reactions to stressful circumstances, our tendency to worry, our inability to sleep—but just telling ourselves, "stop that!" or "just go to sleep!" doesn't often work. We've got so much to do. We are caught up in patterns. Our minds are uncontrolled and racing. We are tense. All these things keep us from doing what we know we should do, such as quitting smoking or worrying too much.

Hypnosis is a state similar to sleep. The body becomes so profoundly relaxed that it ceases to be a distraction. The mind becomes highly focused and, thus, more able to do what we want it to do. This focus makes the imagery we use to direct our behavior and feelings more real, so real that our bodies respond to it. This is nothing new. When watching a movie or even hearing a story, our bodies often respond as if we were part of the action—we may experience a faster heart rate at an exciting part, a surge of emotion at a poignant part, feelings of anger at an injustice.

Hypnosis uses the body's ability to react to the mind by directing the mind in specific ways while the body is relaxed. That's all there is to it.

Hypnotherapy is the use of hypnosis by a trained therapist to help the patient heal from the trauma of a past event, reframe negative health habits, or regain control over certain behaviors. Hypnotherapy is frequently used to help people stop smoking or overeating. It is a common therapy for people experiencing chronic fatigue. It is also effective for improving self-esteem, confidence, and social anxiety.

When you are hypnotized, you can't be made to do something that would harm yourself or others (unless you would do so anyway). You also can't be made to do things against your will. The hypnotic state is merely a highly relaxed state in which the mind is more open to suggestions from visualizations and verbal cues.

You can even hypnotize yourself, although not everyone is as open to being hypnotized. You do have to be willing to try it and to follow the hypnotic suggestions. The following exercises, adapted from *The Relaxation & Stress Reduction Workbook,* by Martha Davis, Ph.D., Elizabeth Robbins-Eshelman, M.S.W., and Matthew McKay, Ph.D. (New Harbinger, 2000), can be used to begin training your mind to respond to suggestion. You can also use these tests to see whether you would be a good candidate for hypnosis. If you don't respond to them after several tries, hypnosis may not be helpful to you.

EXERCISE 1

1. Stand with your feet about shoulder-width apart, your arms hanging loosely at your sides. Close your eyes and relax.
2. Imagine you are holding a small suitcase in your right hand. Feel the moderate heaviness of the suitcase and the way the suitcase pulls your body to one side.
3. Imagine someone takes the suitcase and hands you a medium-sized suitcase. This suitcase is heavier and bulkier than the small suitcase. Feel the handle in your hand. Feel the heaviness of the suitcase weighing down your right side.
4. Imagine someone takes the suitcase and hands you a large suitcase. This suitcase is incredibly heavy, so heavy you can hardly hold on to it, so heavy it pulls your entire body to the right as the weight of the suitcase sinks toward the floor.
5. Keep feeling the weight of this heavy suitcase for two to three minutes.
6. Open your eyes. Are you standing perfectly straight, or has your posture swayed, even a little bit, to the right?

EXERCISE 2

1. Stand with your feet about shoulder-width apart, your arms hanging loosely at your sides. Close your eyes and relax.
2. Imagine you are standing outside on a small hill in the middle of an expansive prairie. The breeze is blowing and the sun is shining. It is a beautiful, clear day.
3. Suddenly, the breeze begins to pick up, and the wind starts to blow. You are facing into the wind, and as it blows harder and harder, gusting around you, you feel it pushing you back, blowing your hair back, even blowing your arms back a little.
4. The wind is now so strong you can barely stand up. If you don't lean into the wind, you'll be knocked backward! You've never felt wind this strong, and each forceful gust nearly pushes you off your feet!
5. Feel the strength of the wind for two to three minutes.
6. Open your eyes. Are you standing perfectly straight, or leaning into the wind, even just a little?

EXERCISE 3

1. Stand with feet about shoulder-width apart, both arms straight out in front of you, parallel to the ground. Close your eyes.
2. Imagine someone has tied a heavy weight to your right arm. Your arm has to strain to hold up the weight that hangs from it. Feel the weight. Imagine how it looks hanging from your arm.
3. Imagine someone ties another heavy weight on your right arm. The two weights pull your arm down and down. They are so heavy that your muscles have to tense and strain to hold them up.
4. Imagine someone ties a third heavy weight on your arm. The three weights are so heavy that you can barely keep your arm raised. Feel how the weights pull down your arm.
5. Now, imagine that someone ties a huge helium balloon to your left arm. Feel the balloon pulling your left arm higher and higher, tugging it skyward.
6. Feel the weights on your right arm and the balloon on your left arm for two to three minutes.
7. Open your eyes. Are your arms still even, or is your right arm lowered and your left arm raised, even just a little?

If your body didn't respond at all to any of these exercises after several tries, hypnosis may not help you. If you still want to try it, however, of course, try it! The mind is powerful, and wanting it to work is half the battle. Many researchers believe almost anyone can learn self-hypnosis.

FACTS

Studies show that self-hypnosis is among the most effective methods for reducing migraine headaches in children and teenagers.

Hypnotizing yourself is done pretty much the same way you would hypnotize somebody else. While trained hypnotherapists and hypnotists may be able to hypnotize you right away, with some practice, you can learn to hypnotize yourself. You'll need to decide very specifically what you want to work on, say, quitting smoking or not falling apart every time your mother-in-law comes to visit.

Then, self-hypnosis involves a detailed process of breathing, muscle relaxation, and visualization, beginning with the descent down a staircase to the backward-count of ten to one. After some detailed visualization to engage and focus the mind, the hypnosis session ends with a posthypnotic suggestion to trigger you to act the way you want to act. Phrase the suggestion positively: "I feel strong, confident, and in control of the situation when my mother-in-law is in my house," not, "I don't want to burst into tears every time my mother-in-law makes a comment about my housekeeping ability."

After the posthypnotic suggestion, you can bring yourself slowly out of the hypnotic state by counting to ten, telling yourself that at the number ten, you will be alert, refreshed, and wide awake.

Several good books on self-hypnosis will explain in great detail how to do it. Or, if you aren't comfortable doing it on your own, visit a qualified hypnotherapist. Either way, hypnosis can be an effective, deep relaxation technique that can help you to get a handle on the stress you thought was out of your control.

Your physician may be able to refer you to a psychotherapist or colleague who practices hypnotherapy or knows someone who does. You might also check the phone book, or get recommendations from a practitioner you are familiar with.

Never practice self-hypnosis in a situation where you need to be alert, such as while driving. The deeply relaxed state could keep your body from responding quickly enough to stay safe.

Optimism Therapy

So, you think you are a confirmed pessimist? Optimism therapy is like an attitude adjustment but focused on reframing responses as an optimist. Optimism may have a reputation as a deluded view of the world through rose-colored glasses, but, actually, optimists are happier and healthier because they tend to assume they have control over their lives, while pessimists tend to feel that life controls them.

Psychologists determine optimistic and pessimistic character based on a person's explanatory style when describing an unfortunate event. The explanatory style has three parts:

1. **The internal/external explanation.** Optimists tend to believe that external factors cause misfortune, while pessimists tend to blame themselves (the internal factor).
2. **The stable/unstable explanation.** Optimists tend to see misfortune as unstable or temporary, while pessimists tend to see misfortune as stable or permanent.
3. **The global/specific explanation.** Optimists tend to see problems as specific to a situation, while pessimists tend to see problems as global—that is, unavoidable and pervasive.

How does an optimist body differ from a pessimist body? Profoundly. Studies show that optimists enjoy better general health, a stronger immune system, faster surgical recovery, and longer life than pessimists.

ESSENTIALS

You can use a fun behavioral technique called "thought stopping" to nip your pessimistic tendencies, and any other mental stress reaction. To practice thought stopping, think of a negative thought you tend to have. Associate the thought with a clear image. Set a timer for three minutes, close your eyes, and concentrate on the image. When the timer rings, shout, "Stop!" Repeat several times. Then, whenever the image recurs, whisper, "Stop!" The interruption will stop the thought and give you the opportunity to consciously substitute the thought with a more positive one.

Because of their tendencies, pessimists may feel like they are under more stress than optimists, even though both are under the same amount of stress. How the stress *feels* may directly determine how the body reacts, making the stress response more severe in pessimists. Optimists are also more likely to engage in positive behaviors such as exercising and eating well. Pessimists may adopt a fatalistic attitude that what they eat or how much they exercise doesn't matter anyway, so they might as well do what is easiest. Pessimists also tend to be more socially isolated, lonely, or have friends with negative influences—other pessimists or people with habits that are destructive to health and well-being.

But what if you are a pessimist? Can you change? Sure you can. You just need to engage in a little optimism therapy! Studies show that smiling, even when you aren't happy, can make you feel happy, but optimism extends far beyond a forced smile. Pretending to be an optimist can actually make you feel like one and can help your body learn to respond like an optimist, too.

If your pessimism is temporary or recent, you can probably help yourself through your own personal optimism therapy sessions. At the beginning of each day, before you get out of bed, before you have time to get too pessimistic, say one of these affirmations out loud several times:

- "No matter what happens today, I won't judge myself."
- "My life will improve from the inside out."
- "Today I will enjoy myself in healthy ways."
- "No matter what happens around me, this will be a good day."
- "This can be a good day, or this can be a bad day. I choose to make it a good day."

Then, choose one single area or part of your day and vow to be an optimist in that area only. Maybe you'll choose lunchtime, or the staff meeting, or the time with your kids before dinner. During that period, every time you begin to think or say something pessimistically, immediately replace the words or thought with something optimistic. Instead of responding to a spilled coffee cup with, "I'm so clumsy!", respond with, "Whoops! That cup slipped right out of my hand." Instead of responding to a critique of your work with the thought, "My supervisor always hates my work," change your thought and tell yourself, "She didn't like this part of this particular assignment, but the rest of it was great!"

You may feel forced and unnatural doing this at first, but like anything else, the more you do it, the more it becomes a habit. You can adopt the optimist habit. It's good for your health!

If you are a serious and fully committed pessimist, and/or if you suffer from depression, you could probably benefit from visiting a trained psychotherapist for cognitive therapy. Cognitive therapy is a kind of therapy in which the therapist helps patients discover the effect of pessimistic or depressed thoughts on mood, and also helps patients to discover the ingrained nature of these thoughts in order to catch themselves in the pessimistic act. Cognitive therapy can be very successful for depression, and some studies show it is as effective as antidepressant medication (for many people with depression, a combination of cognitive therapy and medication work best).

Reward-based Self-Training

If you've ever trained a dog, you probably know about positive reinforcement training because it is what most animal trainers use today. People (and dogs) do things for two reasons:

1. To benefit or be rewarded
2. To avoid something negative

The first reason is much more compelling and positive. You see a piece of chocolate cake. You know you shouldn't eat it because you could gain weight (negative reinforcement), but you want to eat it because it tastes good (positive reinforcement). Which is more fun, eating it or not eating it?

If you can frame your stress management in terms of positive reinforcement (not to mention your other habits and the life changes you are trying to make), you are much more likely to be successful. Even if you are successful with negative reinforcement—you didn't eat the cake—it won't be as enjoyable, and you may be less likely to stick with it. What if not eating the cake was rewarded with a stroll through the park on a nice day or with an afternoon matinee? That's more inspiring, isn't it, than the mere promise of not gaining weight?

But who has time to go see a movie for every good behavior? Your rewards needn't be so time-consuming. They need only be rewards. No, you probably don't do flips for dog biscuits, but that doesn't mean you don't like treats. Make a list of your personal "people treats," and every time you think you've got a tough battle ahead in which you know you'll encounter stress, promise yourself a treat from your list. You'll get through it on your best behavior, and the promise of a reward will help to keep you thinking positive, feeling relaxed, and enjoying the "training session"! That's a *good* girl! That's a *good* boy!

FACTS

Dog trainer Jean Donaldson lists the five things dogs consider most rewarding. How easily could you adapt this list to fit yourself?

1. Food
2. Access to other dogs
3. Access to outdoors and interesting smells
4. Attention from people and access to people, especially after isolation periods
5. Initiation of play or other enjoyed activity

Your personal treat list might look something like this, but, of course, these are just suggestions to get you started. Your list will be as individual as you are.

- Order in or go out instead of cooking tonight.
- Get a massage (paid for, or ask a loved one).
- Go to yoga class.
- Go to bed early.
- Watch your favorite movie . . . again!
- Make time to call a friend and chat.

Continual rewards make life a lot more fun and a lot less stressful. They also help to boost and maintain your self-esteem because you are taking time for yourself and celebrating yourself by paying yourself (through rewards) what you're worth. So, let yourself enjoy life with positive reinforcement!

CHAPTER 10

De-stressing the Nuts and Bolts

Stress management techniques are great to add to your routine so that you can manage the stress of daily life. But what about that daily life? What about all those things you *have* to do? What about managing your money, your time, your work, your home—managing your *life*? There are many ways you can de-stress these daily have-tos by making them simpler, easier, less time-consuming, and even a little more fun. In this chapter, you'll find ways to de-stress the nuts and bolts of your life so that you have more time for the fun.

Your Money

On the list of things that stress you out the most, how high is money? For many people, money is one of the primary causes of daily stress, usually because we don't think we have enough of it, and sometimes because we have enough but are worried about how we are managing it.

There is a lot more to managing your money than getting the bills paid with a little left over or maintaining a productive portfolio. As humans, we have lived with money in one form or another for thousands of years, and it has become deeply ingrained in our psyches. We have all kinds of hidden and not-so-hidden feelings about money, emotional blocks, obsessions, and pretty strange ideas. The phrase "It's only money" might be something you say sometimes, perhaps to justify an extravagant expense or to make yourself feel better when you don't have any of it, but very few of us really believe that the green stuff is "only" anything.

FACTS

Studies show that income level has no apparent link with reported happiness or life satisfaction.

Money is important to us. It is important to our culture. Some might even say it rules the world. But it shouldn't rule you.

In *The 9 Steps to Financial Freedom,* certified financial planner and investment advisor Suze Orman lists "Seeing How Your Past Holds the Key to Your Financial Future" as step number one. Money memories from childhood can hold the key to how we feel about money right now, even if we don't realize it.

Maybe you grew up knowing a family with a lot of money whose members weren't very kind to you. Did you learn to look askance at people with a lot of money, thinking they surely didn't understand about the important things in life such as love and family? Or, maybe you grew up in a family that didn't have to struggle with money and had contact with a less fortunate family whose members weren't trustworthy. Did you learn to be suspicious of people with low incomes?

Maybe money was highly valued in your family, or not valued much at all. Maybe you were taught to manage it, but many of us weren't given those skills and, as adults, don't have the slightest clue what to do with the money we earn beyond paying the bills and buying the groceries.

Added to our personal experiences are cultural stereotypes galore. Television shows, movies, and books often represent rich people as heartless snobs, poor people as slovenly thieves. Old misers who hoard their riches must be a little crazy. Generous souls who give all their money away must be angelic. Sometimes, it seems like a sin to have or try to get money. Yet, it also seems to be a crime if you don't have enough.

ESSENTIALS
One place to look for wasted money is right in your own kitchen. How much food do you buy every week that goes uneaten? How much rotten produce do you toss out? How many plastic containers filled with unidentifiable leftovers are there? How many food items sit in your cupboard month after month, things you bought on a whim but can never quite get yourself to eat? Planning your meals, avoiding impulse buys, and learning to cook an appropriate amount of food can save you hundreds of dollars each year.

In America, the "middle class" has been consistently held up as the ideal and has grown to be such a broad category that most people now consider themselves to be part of it. Most of us aren't in poverty, but wouldn't call ourselves rich, either. And isn't that what makes us comfortable? Yet, we remain obsessed with money . . . with wealth, with the fear of poverty, with the material objects it can buy. Isn't that what capitalism is all about?

If it's "only money," why does it obsess us so? Money is no simple matter. But that doesn't mean it has to be complicated for you. To de-stress your financial life, you need to do several things:

- Understand *exactly* how you really feel about money, including your prejudices and preconceptions.
- Continue to recognize with vigilance your financial preconceptions so that they don't control you.
- Have very specific financial goals, for both present and future.
- Have a very specific plan to meet your financial goals.

- Know *exactly* how much is coming in and how much is going out.
- Start by building a financial cushion.

Many excellent books are devoted solely to this subject and are worth reading. However, this book covers the subject only with stress relief in mind. I hope you'll start here, then be inspired to learn more from other sources. Let's start by looking at these steps one by one.

How Do You Really Feel about Money?

To get you thinking about how you *really* feel about money (which may be different from how you *think* you feel about money), answer the following questions here, or in your stress journal.

1. How do you feel, emotionally, when you think about your financial situation right now?

_____

_____

_____

_____

_____

2. Examine any negative feelings about your financial situation. Why do you think you have these negative feelings?

_____

_____

_____

_____

_____

3. How do your parents feel about money?

_____

_____

_____

_____

4. When you were a child, what was your family's attitude toward people who had more money than you did?

_____

_____

_____

_____

5. When you were a child, what was your family's attitude toward people who had less money than you did?

_____

_____

_____

_____

6. Describe an incident from your childhood that revealed your family's attitude about money.

_____

_____

_____

_____

7. Describe a specific book, movie, television show, or other source that you think could possibly have affected your feelings about money in some way.

    _____

    _____

    _____

    _____

8. If you had all the money you could possibly ever spend and you knew you would continue to be wealthy for the rest of your life, how would it make you feel?

    _____

    _____

    _____

    _____

9. List the things in life that you honestly believe are more important than money.

    _____

    _____

    _____

    _____

10. What, specifically, has to change in your life so that money no longer causes you stress?

    _____

    _____

    _____

Continue to Recognize Your Financial Preconceptions

Look back at your answers now, for clues to some of your financial preconceptions. Keep those in mind as you work on simplifying your financial life. If you have the preconception that there is something wrong with having money, you may have been sabotaging yourself your entire life, subconsciously keeping yourself from financial security. Maybe you strongly believe that money shouldn't be important, but the lack of it in your life is controlling you, and now, in its absence, money has become the most important thing in your life. Maybe you believe that self-worth is related to financial worth and you feel like, apart from money, you aren't worth much. Maybe you believe that money can, indeed, buy happiness, or that it is, indeed, the root of all evil.

Whatever you believe, know that you believe it, and continue to question your preconceptions so that they don't sabotage your financial life. Your relationship with money should be completely clear and unimpeded by prejudice. Otherwise, your financial life will probably always be at least a minor source of stress.

Many people don't realize they are afraid to earn more money than their parents earned. This is natural but something to be overcome. The fact that wealth is uncharted territory in your family doesn't mean you can't be a trailblazer.

Have Very Specific Financial Goals

If you don't know exactly what you want your money to do for you, it won't do much for you. No matter how much money you make, whether you dabble in stocks or can't make your monthly rent, you must have specific financial goals. If you know where you are headed, financially, your life will be less stressful. You'll know where you are going, even if it will take a long time to get there.

How much money do you need to be able to spend each month? (Most people underestimate this number.) How much do you want to have saved by retirement? Do you need college funds for the kids? A down payment for a house? Would you like to be able to have extra money for investing? How much do you need in savings to cover your expenses for six months if you should become unable to work?

Make a list of your financial goals, no matter how impossible they seem, either on your own or with the help of a good financial planner.

1. _____

2. _____

3. _____

4. _____

5. _____

6. _____

7. _____

8. _____

9. _____

10. _____

SSENTIALS

Every car, the second it is owned, becomes a used car, and it is said that a new car drops about 30 percent in value as soon as it is driven off the lot. Used cars can save you money and, in many cases, eliminate the need for a monthly payment and extra interest charges. Many dealerships even include warranties with used cars. Make sure to have your car checked out by a reliable mechanic to ensure it doesn't have a major problem, and enjoy your savings!

Have a Specific Plan

It isn't enough just to have goals. You also have to have a workable plan to meet them. If this seems overwhelming to you, visit a good financial planner to help you. Anybody can work toward financial goals, and financial planners are trained to show you how. Or, if you aren't ready for that or feel you can figure it out on your own, start reading books on the subject.

FACTS

According to feng shui, the ancient Chinese art of placement, the upper right-hand corner of any room, as you enter from the door, is the prosperity corner. Keeping this corner clear, clean, uncluttered, and decked in the prosperity colors of purple, red, green, or gold will help to direct financial energy your way. (There's more about feng shui a little later in this chapter.)

Part of meeting your financial goals might be focused on how to live on less rather than how to make more. Simplicity, frugal living, and other downscaling trends have been popular in the last decade as people realize they've been making lots of money and not getting much in return in the way of spiritual rewards. Books, Web sites, newsletters, and other sources are rich with information on this trend. Here are some tips for de-stressing your financial life by simplifying your financial needs:

- Become aware of the way advertising works and how it tries to make you think you need things you don't really need.
- Every time you are about to spend money, stop for a moment, take a deep breath, and ask yourself, "Do I really want this, or do I just think I want this in this moment?"
- Before you spend money, stop for a moment, take a deep breath, and ask yourself, "Is this item worth the time out of my life I took to earn the money I'll pay for it?"
- If you decide you really do want something, that it really is worth the money for you, even if it would be frivolous to someone else (dinner at a restaurant when you can't face cooking, that one special piece of Early American pottery you've been seeking for years, that pair of shoes that feels perfect), buying it will probably be less stressful than letting it go.

- Make a list of things you can do with your family and/or friends that don't cost any money. Be creative. Then, use that list!
- Slow down. You don't have to keep moving, going, spending. Why not relax at home with your family or friends and just do nothing for a change?
- Drive less. Walk, bike, or take public transportation more.
- Do you really need all those extra movie channels? Would basic cable satisfy you?
- Cooking can be fun, and home-cooked meals are less expensive than frozen dinners.
- How often do you go to your gym? Are you throwing away money when you'd rather just take a walk or a jog or a bike ride for free? For some people, the gym is really worth it. For others, it's a needless money drain.
- Growing a garden has an initial investment (small or large, depending on how frugally you go about it), but it yields free food and the opportunity for exercise and fresh air all spring and summer.
- Focus your energy on getting rid of the stuff you don't need rather than adding to it.
- Learn the joy and freedom of simple living!

Know *Exactly* How Much Is Coming In and Going Out

It isn't easy to keep track of every single penny that comes in and goes out, the way many books on financial planning would have you do. However, if you don't do this, at least for, say, a representative week or two out of each month, you will never know where your money is going. And boy, can it go when you aren't looking! Like anything else, keeping track of your money is a matter of *habit,* and this is a good habit to get into. If you know where your money is going, you can make a realistic budget that works, not one of those fanciful dream budgets you think should work but never does.

Plus, writing down every single penny you spend every single day has another surprising effect: major stress relief. Simply knowing where it is going is incredibly calming because even when you know you don't have any money left, at least you have a feeling of understanding about where it went. Have you ever spent an hour driving yourself crazy trying to figure out how that $20 bill you just took out of the ATM machine disappeared? Knowing is half the battle. When it comes to your money, knowledge really is power.

When you know how much you spend, you can also ferret out wasteful spending. Can you *believe* you spent $75 on caffeinated beverages this month? Is that ridiculous? If you think it is (maybe you think it's worth it, but if you don't . . .), then you know exactly what you need to change.

Financial stress is largely a product of not knowing, wondering, hoping, fearing—all because you have no idea what your money is doing. You'd think money had a life of its own! But if you know, you are in control. You say where it goes and where it doesn't go. And even if there isn't much coming in, that control feels really good.

These days, many financial experts advise more conservative investing, such as in CDs and mutual funds rather than aggressive stocks. The days of letting your investments save for you may be temporarily over, so save, save, save. Don't depend on investment gains to make up your savings.

Build a Financial Cushion

Financial stress is also largely a product of knowing that you don't have enough money in the bank if an emergency arises. What if you car breaks down, or you incur some major medical expenses, or the roof springs a leak, or Uncle Jerry needs bail and you don't have any backup cash? When events such as these occur, your stress level is likely to go soaring.

But if you have a cushion—many experts recommend six month's worth of monthly income stashed away in an easily accessible savings or money market account—then you will rest easier, even when you don't need the money, just because you know it's there. Whenever you have to tap your account, make paying yourself back your first priority.

How do you get a cushion? It can be tough if you think your paycheck barely covers your expenses, but successful savers say they put 10 percent or more of every single penny they make into savings before they ever have the chance to spend it. Setting up a system in which that 10 percent is automatically deducted from your paycheck, just like it is for taxes, is even easier. You don't ever have your hands on the money.

If you get used to doing this, you won't ever miss the money. You'll readjust to get by on just exactly what you are making, minus the 10 percent. Then, when things get really tight, you'll be okay for a while.

Make this your top priority—it's an easy way to give yourself financial peace of mind. Figure out what you need each month, then multiply that number by six. That's your cushion goal. Put 10 percent of your very next paycheck in that cushion fund.

If you put away just 10 percent each month, you'll reach a six-month cushion in five years, if you never use the money. To get there faster, put extra money in your cushion fund whenever it comes along—say, gifts for holidays, windfall money, and so on. Or, put away 10 percent this year, 20 percent next year . . . some people make it their goal to be able to live on 50 percent of their monthly income and save the rest. Now, that's smart savings! This may not be a realistic goal for you if your income doesn't permit it, but the more you adjust and learn to live more frugally, the more you'll be able to save, and the better and less stressed out you'll feel.

QUESTIONS?

What about the stress that comes from never being able to splurge or be financially frivolous and always feeling as though you have to save and budget?
It isn't fair! That's understandable. Many people on a tight budget describe how, when under financial stress, all they want to do is go out and spend money—but if they do, they get further in the hole. Just remember: You can get in the habit of enjoyable rewards that don't cost money, and an occasional *controlled* splurge is both reasonable and safer than binge spending.

The Five Golden Rules of No-Stress Money Management

Before we leave the subject of money, let's look at the five golden rules of no-stress money management. No matter what your tendencies, income, financial preconceptions, or savings account balance, these five golden rules will help to de-stress your financial life each and every day. Copy them. Post them. Live by them.

They aren't all easy to achieve right away. Add them to your list of financial goals if necessary. Working toward these rules will put the money that is (or isn't) in your life in its proper and rightful place: as a tool you use with total control and good sense to maintain and improve your life.

1. **Live within your means.** In other words, don't spend more than you make each month. Don't use credit unless it is absolutely necessary. If you don't have the ready cash to go on a shopping spree, don't go on a shopping spree. Of course, to accomplish this rule, you need to know exactly how much ready cash you have available to spend each month (see the earlier section "Know *Exactly* How Much Is Coming In and Going Out").

2. **Conquer your debt.** Make chipping away at those high-interest debts your top priority. Debt may not be something you can hold in your hand, but neither are a lot of the things that cause you chronic stress. Just knowing you've got huge debts is enough to activate the stress response in some people. First, purge the debt. Then, start saving. Even as you start to pay off your debts, you'll feel as though a black cloud is lifting from over your head. Don't listen to people who tell you debt is necessary, the American Way. Nonsense. A mortgage and a car payment, maybe. Other than those, pay them off, pay them off, pay them off, and breathe more freely.

3. **Simplify your finances.** Set up a simple system for financial management. Go through a single bank for all your transactions. When possible, have your paycheck automatically deposited into your bank account, and have payments made automatically or make them

online so that you don't have to run to the bank all the time. If you invest, go through a single firm. If the thought of investing stresses you out, don't do it.

4. **Know your money.** Know how much you earn. Know how much you spend. Know where all your money is. Know how much your investments are earning you. Know (and trust) your broker. Or, if you invest on your own, keep track of everything you do. Keep your checkbook balanced and your bank statements reconciled. You'll never have to get stressed out because you don't know whether a check will bounce, whether your investments are earning or losing, or how much you have saved.

5. **Plan for the future.** Save. Save. Save. The short-term sacrifice of buying something you don't really need and probably won't use very much, the decision not to do the expensive remodeling or get the really high-profile SUV, the decision to move to a smaller and more manageable house, to stop eating out so much, to spend more time at home, all in favor of saving, saving, saving, is well worth it in many ways. Your life will be simpler. It will be easier. You'll have a nest egg. All that adds up to a lot less stress.

Time Keeps On Slippin' . . .

Maybe money doesn't stress you out nearly as much as your basic lack of time. If you never seem to have enough time to get anything finished, you might feel constant, chronic stress. But although technically we all have the same amount of time each day (twenty-four hours), time is mysteriously malleable. Have you ever noticed how an hour can fly by like five minutes or crawl by like three hours? Sometimes, your workday is over in a flash, and sometimes it feels like 5:00 P.M. when it's only 11:00 A.M. Can you make this malleability of time work for you?

You bet you can! Although they say "time flies when you're having fun," time also flies when you are scattered and disorganized. If you have three hours to get something done and you don't manage your time efficiently, those three hours will fly by in a rush of half-finished jobs and flitting from task to task with dispersed energy.

If, instead, your time is organized and you are able to devote your full concentration to one task at a time, time seems to expand in quantity and quality. You get something—even one thing—finished. You feel a sense of satisfaction. The time won't crawl by, like it does when you are enduring something unpleasant. The time may seem to go fast, but because you will have accomplished something, you'll enjoy a feeling of accomplishment, a boost of self-esteem, and the relief of stress.

ESSENTIALS

Time that rushes by seldom seems well spent, or sufficiently spent. Time that expands, time in which something real is accomplished, seems more significant, more worthy of the ticks on the clock. The trick to making the most of your time is focus. Focus entirely on what you are doing, and although the time may be luscious and enjoyable, flowing smoothly along, each moment will be full and rich.

Learning how to manage your time efficiently takes some practice, but if you have a plan, time management is easy. Many great books and even Web sites will help you to get organized and manage your time. Begin managing your time to free yourself of the unnecessary stress that comes from scattered energy and the inefficient use of your day by observing the Ten Commandments of Time Management:

1. **Start small.** If you start with too many goals, too long of a to-do list, or too high expectations for yourself, you are setting yourself up for failure. Begin with one single time management step, such as laying out your clothes for the next day the night before, to save time in the morning, or by vowing that the counters will be free of dirty dishes every single night, to ease the breakfast rush. As you master each step, you can add more.
2. **Identify your time management issues.** Are you perfectly efficient at work but your time management skills fall apart in the unstructured, unscheduled environment of your home? Are you able to keep the house straight but whenever the family is home, life seems rushed and hectic, with no relaxed "together time"? Do you spend all day dealing

with other people's crises and taking care of busywork, never getting enough time to sit down and really concentrate on your job? Know your trouble spots—the places where time is getting frittered away.

3. **Identify your time management priorities.** Make a list ranking the things on which you most want to spend your time. Would you like to add family time first, then household organization time, then some personal time? Would you like more time for work and less time for dealing with other people's crises? Would you like to make time for your favorite hobby, time for yourself, or time for romance? Would you just like more time to sleep?

4. **Focus on your top five.** Look at the top five items on your Time Management Priorities list. Focus on those. Be very wary of letting yourself take on anything that takes your time if it isn't focused on one of your top five priorities.

5. **Have a strategy.** When the day starts, know where you are going. Know what you will do. Time unplanned is often time wasted. That doesn't mean you can't allow for spontaneity or a lovely, unplanned, unscheduled hour or two. Even a whole day of purposefully unplanned time is well worth it. But time unplanned in which you frantically try to accomplish ten different things is time wasted, and that's stressful. Resources abound for helping you make a strategy that works for you (see Appendix B for some ideas).

6. **Just say no.** Your time is valuable, even more valuable than money. Why should you just give it away to anyone and anything that asks for it? Learn to say no to requests for your time unless that time spent would be something very important to you. You don't have to be on the committee. You don't have to join that club. You don't have to go to that meeting. Just say no and watch that stress that was waiting to descend upon your life float away in another direction.

7. **Let it go.** If you've already taken on too much, learn to start purging. Don't let anything waste your time. Time spent relaxing by yourself isn't wasted if it refreshes and rejuvenates you. Time spent pacing and worrying is wasted time. Time spent enduring a committee meeting you don't really enjoy is wasted time. Time spent actively engaged in a committee whose cause inspires you is time well spent. Cut out the dross and let everything go that isn't really important.

8. **Charge more.** If you are self-employed, don't waste time on jobs that don't pay you for what your time is worth. (This is difficult until you are well-established.) But this rule doesn't just apply to work and actual money. Everything you do takes time. Is the reward payment enough for the time spent? If it isn't, ditch it.

9. **Do it later.** Do you really need to do every single cleaning chore every day? Do you really need to check your e-mail every ten minutes? Do you really need to change the sheets, vacuum the car, mow the lawn today? If doing it later is just procrastination, you'll spend the saved time worrying. But sometimes, when your time is at a premium, you can relieve your stress and make your life easier by postponing the less crucial chores. Even though many chores do need to be accomplished, they don't always need to be accomplished right now.

10. **Remember that not having enough time is always an excuse, never a reason.** You can make time for anything if it's important enough. You just have to stop spending time on something less important. You have control over your time. Time doesn't control you.

Stress-Proofing Your Work Life

For a few lucky people, jobs are sources of rejuvenation, personal satisfaction, and stress relief. For many others, even though work is sometimes or often rewarding, it is also a major source of stress. The more people work and the longer the workday becomes, the more we dream of being able to retire early. Who doesn't waste just a little time thinking about what we would do if we won millions in the lottery? Would we finally tell off our bosses? Quit with a flourish? *Never work again?*

Actually, research that has followed up on the life satisfaction of lottery winners reveals that very few were happier and that many were less happy after quitting their jobs (winning the lottery brings about its own kind of stress). Although any job can be stressful and sometimes monotonous, our work lives often bring us more than a paycheck. We gain self-esteem, purpose, and a sense of worth from our jobs. We benefit from the social contact, the structure, and the responsibility.

But maybe your job isn't giving you these benefits. Perhaps you should consider a change. Nowadays, people are more likely to change careers more often than ever before, voluntarily or not. Is a job change in order for you? Examine the following list. How many items apply to you?

- I dread going to work on most days.
- I come home from work too exhausted to do anything but watch television or go to bed.
- I am not treated with respect at my job.
- I'm not paid what I'm worth.
- I'm embarrassed to tell people what I do for a living.
- I don't feel good about my job.
- My job doesn't allow me to fulfill my potential.
- My job is far from being my dream job.
- I would quit in a second if I could afford it.
- My job is keeping me from enjoying my life.

If two or more items on this list apply to you, you might want to consider a job change. If you aren't qualified to do what you want to do, you need a plan. Find out what would be involved in getting trained in a field that holds more interest for you. Work on saving up some money so that you can start your own business. If you aren't sure what you would like, visit a career counselor who can help you discover what kind of work might be more fulfilling for you.

FACTS

According to the National Institute for Occupational Safety and Health, job stress is "the harmful physical and emotional responses that occur when the requirements of the job do not match the capabilities, resources, or needs of the worker."

If you like your job but certain aspects of your work are more stressful than you can comfortably handle, you can take steps to get your job stress under control. Remember, some stress can be good. It can get you motivated and boost your performance. You just don't want to exceed your stress tolerance level—at least not too often.

First, identify what areas of your work life are causing you the most stress. Maybe the work itself is fine but the coworkers are difficult. Or, maybe it's the other way around. Think about each of the following areas of your work life and write a few lines about how you feel when you think about these aspects of your job. Writing about each area may help you to understand more clearly where your stress lies.

Write your answers here or in your stress journal.

1. This is how I feel about the people I work with:

_____

_____

_____

_____

2. This is how I feel about my supervisor:

_____

_____

_____

_____

3. This is how I feel about the environment in which I work:

_____

_____

_____

_____

_____

4. This is how I feel about the values and purpose behind my place of employment:

Is your work environment ergonomic? If you are uncomfortable in your workstation, don't risk a lifetime of pain from a repetitive motion injury. Talk to your employer about making ergonomic changes—getting new furniture or equipment, or shifting tasks more often.

5. This is how I feel about the actual, day-to-day work I do:

6. This is how I feel about the importance of the work I do:

7. My favorite thing about work is:

_____

_____

_____

8. My least favorite thing about work is:

_____

_____

_____

9. My work utilizes my skills in the following areas:

_____

_____

_____

_____

10. My work fails to utilize my skills in the following areas:

_____

_____

_____

_____

11. My needs unmet by work are or aren't being met elsewhere (explain):

_____

_____

_____

12. I wish my job could change in these ways:

_____

_____

_____

_____

After answering these questions, it may have become more clear where your dissatisfactions with your job lie, and where things are fine. Now, make a list of the things about your job that cause you stress. After each item, circle O if you think you can live with this stressor, and X if you think you *can't* live with this stressor:

1. _____ O X

2. _____ O X

3. _____ O X

4. _____ O X

5. _____ O X

6. _____ O X

7. _____ O X

8. _____ O X

9. _____ O X

10. _____ O X

Look at the items for which you circled X. There aren't any? You're in pretty good shape. If there are one or more, these are the areas you need to manage.

A noisy work environment could be stressing you out, even if you aren't aware of it! A recent study out of Cornell University showed that people whose work area was open and allowed them to hear the noises of other workers showed higher levels of epinephrine (adrenaline) in the blood than workers whose work area was quiet, even though members of the "noise" group didn't necessarily report feeling more stressed.

Of course, how you manage the stressors at your job depends on what those stressors are. You can take a few different approaches:

- Avoid the stressor (such as a stressful coworker).
- Eliminate the stressor (delegate or share a hated chore).
- Confront the stressor (talk to your supervisor if he or she is doing something that makes your job more difficult).
- Manage the stressor (add something enjoyable to the task, give yourself a reward after completion).
- Balance the stressor (put up with the stress but practice stress-relieving techniques to balance out the effects).

Work is a big part of your life. If you can do something to avoid, eliminate, confront, manage, or balance the stress that comes from your work life, your entire life will be more balanced and less stressful. The key is to deal with the stressor in some way rather than ignoring it and letting the negative effects from work stress build until you are so stressed that you begin to miss work or find yourself putting your job in jeopardy, even though you know it really is a good job.

Building a Personal Sanctuary

After a long, stressful, busy day at work, you come home to your castle, your home sweet home, your haven of peace and comfort and . . . there you are, faced with a pile of dirty laundry, a mound of dirty dishes, a stack of newspapers and another of magazines to be sorted through and recycled, footprints in the kitchen, a pile of boxes to inch around to get to the dining room (you'll go through those later), and, oh no, there are those videos you were supposed to return yesterday, and what the heck are you going to have for dinner . . . ? Suddenly, it doesn't seem so relaxing to be home—as you grab a pizza coupon and start turning over piles looking for the cordless phone.

FACTS

According to a CBS Evening News report, September 1999, the fifth annual Labor Day survey found that more than half of American workers are somewhat or extremely stressed at work. One in six workers reported being "angry enough to hit a coworker." One of the most common sources of stress was, ironically, that modern convenience that supposedly makes life easier: technology.

But coming home doesn't have to be like this. Coming home at the end of the day or staying home all day long can be a relaxing, peaceful, or even positively exhilarating experience if that's what you want it to be. It's your home. It can be what you make it, and it shouldn't be just one more great big stressful burden. If your home isn't the place you want it to be, it may just require a little stress management.

Your Home and Office as Metaphor

According to feng shui, the ancient Chinese art of placement, our environment is a metaphor for our lives and the energy that comes and goes in our lives. Problems in your environment mean problems in your life.

Consider for a moment that this idea is true. If your home is a metaphor for your life, how does your life look? Take a good look around you. Is your life cluttered with stuff you don't need? How's the circulation? How long has it been since you've done preventive maintenance on your life?

Your office, either at home or at your work away from home, can also be a metaphor for your life. Is your life scattered with unpaid bills, things to file, scraps of information that take up energy but don't give anything back, malfunctioning equipment, unstable piles of books, files, binders, and folders?

If what you find in your home or office space is not exactly what you'd like to have in mind for your life, then take matters in hand. Let your home and office continue to be a metaphor for your life, but shape that metaphor in a way that suits your life. Remove the clutter. Keep it clean. Build a relaxing, positive atmosphere in which to decompress at the end of each day.

Once you've gotten into the habit of keeping your house in order, you'll find how calming and rejuvenating it is to be in your home. And whenever things start to get out of order again, you'll have an immediate and visible clue that stress is creeping into your life.

ESSENTIALS

Changing your external environment mysteriously and automatically seems to change your inner environment. You may never recognize how stressed you are because of the clutter in your environment until you get rid of it and experience how tranquil you feel living in your home the way you knew it must look beneath all the extra stuff. When you can see the things you love, find the things you need, and move unimpeded through your living environment, everything else seems easier.

1-2-3 Simplify

To make your home a less stressful, more tranquil place, one of the easiest things you can do is to simplify. Spend some time in each room of your home and list all the things you do in each room. What are the functions of the room? What is impeding that function? And what would make each room simpler, its functions simpler?

Simplify your cleaning chores by creating a system for getting everything done a little bit each day. Simplify your shopping by buying in bulk and by planning your menu a week in advance. You can simplify the way your home works and consequently reduce your stress while in your home in many ways. Many excellent books, magazines, and Web sites are devoted to simple living. See the resource list at the end of this book for further reading. Here are some more simplicity tips for your home:

- Wear your clothes a little longer (unless they get stained) to cut down on laundry.
- Choose a wardrobe in which everything matches.
- Change your bedding less often. Who's going to notice?
- Get rid of or pack away household items that complicate your life without giving you very much back—ornate items that require constant dusting, house plants that require constant watering, dishes you can't put in the dishwasher, clothes you have to have dry-cleaned.
- Hire a student or a neighboring teenager to mow the lawn, rake the leaves, run errands, or baby-sit. Consider hiring a housecleaning service.
- There are always more ways to simplify. Keep looking for them.

Making More Space

Some people feel comforted by a room full of stuff, but there is something relaxing and calming about a clean, clutter-free surface, a wall with a single hanging, an expanse of carpet without any toys, books, or discarded clothes, even a room with just a few basic pieces of furniture, just what is necessary. While not everyone would like to live in a home that is completely utilitarian, chances are that over the years, yours has accumulated a couple of layers of decor.

Why not put away or give away some of that stuff and free up some space? As you make space on your surfaces, floors, walls, and rooms, you'll feel like you are making space in your mind. You'll feel more relaxed and calmer in that clean, organized, uncluttered space. If you donate stuff, you'll also get the feeling of satisfaction that you've helped others. Or, if you give clothing or other items to sell on consignment, you can make a little pocket money.

De-clutter, De-stress

Clutter does more than keep your home, your desk, or your garage looking messy. It keeps your mind messy, too. The more stuff you have, especially the disorganized, unmatched, lost, or high-maintenance stuff, the more you have to worry about it, find it, maintain it, keep it, deal with it, have it. Getting rid of the clutter in your home is the most important thing you can do to make your home a stress-free haven of tranquility.

But getting rid of clutter is hard to do, especially for those who can't bear to throw anything away. Are you a pack rat? How many of the following statements would you agree with?

- I keep a lot of clothes that I think I might be able to fit into someday.
- I have at least one junk drawer filled with spare parts and other small items I might need someday, even if I'm not sure what most of them are.
- I have at least a year's worth of magazines that I know I'll look at sometime.
- All the storage spaces in my house are overflowing with stuff—I'm not sure what it all is.
- I record more movies, television shows, or music than I can keep up with watching or listening to, but I save all the tapes because I think I'll get to them all . . . eventually.
- I buy more books than I can read, but I just might read them someday.
- I have at least five different collections.
- I think I need to move into a bigger house because the house I'm in is overflowing with stuff.

If you check more than one item on the list, you're probably a pack rat. That means de-cluttering is trickier for you than for someone who doesn't have a problem letting go of stuff. If getting rid of clutter is actually *more* stressful than living with it, than go with what is the least stressful for you.

If you love your things and love to be surrounded by them, the trick to keeping your home stress-free is to have your things well-organized.

If everything is kept neat and you know where everything is (so you aren't constantly in a panic trying to find things when you need them), then your abundant collections and favorite things can bring you as much joy, comfort, and calm as a de-cluttered, spare space might bring somebody else.

ESSENTIALS

Sometimes people are actually more comfortable with clutter. They actually seem to need extra stuff all around them. You may be one of them if you are a collector, revel in the joys of bulk purchasing, or save everything. If you love your things, that's fine. You probably wouldn't feel relaxed in a sparse environment. The trick is to organize what you have so that it is neat and accessible.

Stress-Free Feng Shui

The ancient Chinese art of placement, called feng shui, has become a popular and important trend in decorating in the West. Feng shui masters are widely available for hire by those decorating a home or office, or designing and building a home or office building. Feng shui classes are hot, and it's easy to find books on how to decorate or redesign your home using feng shui techniques.

Feng shui is a highly complex system that uses Chinese astrology, mathematical calculations, and Chinese philosophy. There are several different schools of feng shui that advocate different methods. But like many things that come from the East to the West, feng shui has begun to transform for use by Westerners. The methods are simpler and more intuitive.

The basic premise of feng shui, particularly Westernized feng shui, is the same as the concept mentioned earlier in this chapter: environment as metaphor. People who practice intuitive feng shui decorate according to what "feels right," what arrangements, items, configurations, and colors make the energy feel good and flowing in a room. If you've ever arranged your furniture a certain way or placed an item somewhere and thought, "Oh yes, that's just right!", then you understand at least a little about intuitive feng shui.

Many feng shui experts use the bagua, an eight-sided shape that you imagine overlying your house. The corners are filled in to make a square. In the bagua, each of the eight sides represents a different area of life, such as money, relationships, creativity, health, and family. Whatever part of the home is in this area represents that part of your life.

But working with the bagua is just one way to apply feng shui to your home. Besides the colors, shapes, and elements associated with the different sides of the bagua, feng shui also uses light, movement (wind chimes, mobiles), water, plants, crystals, and symbolic representations of positive things to activate and enhance different areas of the home.

ESSENTIALS

Energy can get "stuck" in corners and particularly in alcoves or other irregular shapes in rooms. Cobwebs in corners of the room are a sign of stagnant energy. Keep your corners dusted and keep those feng shui areas of concern particularly cobweb-free. Wind chimes or crystals hanging in corners can get the energy moving out of the corner and back into the main flow of energy through the room. Hanging bamboo flutes is also auspicious.

Feng shui should be personalized. Your date of birth, for example, can determine specific feng shui prescriptions, such as which way to position your bed, even which direction to face if you want to appear more powerful during a meeting. (See Appendix B for sources that are devoted more fully and completely to feng shui techniques.)

The tips that follow are general feng shui tips designed to enhance the positive energy and decrease the negative energy in any household. Just remember, feng shui is most effective when used intuitively; try any of these suggestions that appeal to you or feel "right," but don't worry about following those that seem difficult, uninteresting, or even silly. To be truly stress free, feng shui should be fun and feel good. Take your pick from the following tips:

- Remember, symbolism is everything. Pictures of love birds or people in love encourage a romantic relationship, correctly placed coins or dollar bills attract wealth, a picture of a far-away destination encourages the likelihood of travel. Use symbolism everywhere to attract the appropriate energy and set your intention in your own mind. Arrange it, see it, think it . . . make it happen!

- A crystal, mobile, source of moving water (fish tank, desk fountain), or wind chime will energize any area of your home you think needs activation.
- Keep your cupboards and refrigerator well-stocked with fresh, healthy food, which represents abundance.
- Never leave your broom sitting in plain view. A visible broom symbolizes death or other catastrophe.
- To increase energy for prosperity, keep your stove immaculately clean.
- If your bathroom is in your prosperity corner—the corner to your upper left as you enter the room—your wealth could be getting symbolically flushed down the toilet. Keep the toilet lid down, keep the bathroom door shut, and hang a mirror on the outside of the bathroom door.
- Make sure you can't see yourself in a mirror when you are lying or sitting up in bed. If you can, cover that mirror at night. Seeing your shadowy image in the dark can be frightening.
- If you have a television in your bedroom, cover it at night. The energy it emits can negatively affect many areas of your life, including your health.
- Healthy living things add positive energy to any environment: a well-kept fish tank or turtle, dogs, cats, birds, and healthy plants all improve your home's feng shui.
- Use fresh flowers in the living room, but not in the bedroom. Toss out flowers and plants as soon as they begin to wilt.
- Don't sleep with a beam on the ceiling crossing over you, or with a beam dividing your bed if you sleep with someone.
- Don't sit, stand, or sleep with a corner or any sharp object facing you. Sharp objects send off "poison arrows" or negative energy that can have a detrimental effect.

- Don't position your bed directly facing the door. Corpses are carried out feet first!
- Good hygiene, clean clothes, clean sheets, and a healthy diet are all good feng shui.

To reiterate, feng shui is far more complicated than I can begin to explain here. The most important way to use feng shui in a stress-free manner is to have fun with it and not worry too much about it. Because feng shui works so well when used intuitively, if things feel right and good to you in your home, don't worry if they don't match one particular book's advice about furniture positioning or color or anything else.

FACTS

In Chinese, the word for the number eight sounds like the words for growth and prosperity. Eight is considered lucky, and in China, many wealthy people will pay huge sums of money to have an eight anywhere on their car license plates.

Because the actual, original version of feng shui is so complex, you have to take any contemporary all-or-nothing feng shui prescriptions with a grain of salt. Any easy-to-understand feng shui text is by necessity simplified and could easily be, in your particular case, inaccurate or misconstrued.

In other words, use advice from feng shui sources if you find it enjoyable and it results in a living environment that pleases you. If feng shui is starting to stress you out, well, that's certainly not the point—pick another hobby. If your home feels good, if you feel good while in your home, that's good stress management, and that's all that matters.

CHAPTER 11

De-stressing for Women Only

S tress comes in many shapes and sizes, and it also comes in different ways, depending on who you are. Women have unique and particular symptoms of and reactions to stress because of their biology and because of culture. The aging process is stressful for biological, psychological, and cultural reasons, making stress for seniors another unique experience. In this chapter, we'll look at the way stress impacts women throughout their lives so that you can map out a strategy for dealing with the stressors unique to your gender and your current stage in life.

A Woman's World of Stress

It has been only in recent years that research organizations have begun to pay more intention to health issues in women, but women have known all along that being a woman can be stressful—biologically speaking and, certainly, culturally speaking as well.

Most of us have an easier time, physically, than our grandmothers and great grandmothers. For our grandmothers, taking care of a home, cleaning, cooking food, and washing clothes were incredibly labor-intensive. Of course, now, we've got automation to help us with many of the household chores. In addition, it has become socially acceptable as well as expected that men will help out at home. So, what are we stressed about?

Women may not have to do the laundry by hand anymore, but we've got plenty of other things to take up that saved time. We've got jobs, often impossibly demanding jobs. We've got financial pressure, relationship pressure, pressure to look good no matter what our age, pressure to be in shape, in charge, in control—pressure to be all that women have always been and more. Many of us are also juggling houses, spouses, and children. If we've left off any of the "requisite" parts—if we aren't married, didn't have children, decided not to work outside the home—we are bombarded with criticism. Sometimes, the criticism comes from within, in the form of worry, anxiety, panic, guilt, and fear. If the world doesn't expect us to do it all, we expect it of ourselves.

On top of everything else, women go through several intense hormonal changes during their lives and hormonal fluctuations each month. These hormonal fluctuations can compound the feeling of stress, and stress can, conversely, affect a woman's hormonal levels. So, what's a stressed-out woman to do? First, let's look at what we're dealing with.

Female Stress Mismanagement Syndrome

Studies show that, when under stress, women are more likely than men to communicate with others and talk through their concerns. This is a healthy reaction to stress—remember friend therapy from Chapter 9?—and a tendency women should be proud of. However, the reliance on others to be a source of advice and opinion can easily turn into something that actually becomes a source of additional stress.

Even in the twenty-first century, women tend (there are, of course, many exceptions) to be more concerned with how others perceive them than men are. Little girls are still encouraged (not necessarily by their parents but by others, including the television) to be passive, pleasing to others, helpful, polite, and a team player, and to learn the rules of socially acceptable behavior.

While little boys are also taught these things, in general, society as a whole tends to be more accepting of and make more excuses for boys who bend the rules a little or who aren't always quiet and polite. "Oh, boys will be boys. What are you going to do!" people are likely to imply with knowing smiles. Boys tend to get the message that independence, spirit, competitiveness, and even aggression are appropriate. Girls are rewarded for docility and social correctness.

Even if you encourage independence and assertiveness in your daughter, watch for signs that she is getting another message from her environment, including the media. Keep in touch and keep reminding her that she can excel at anything. Help foster her natural interests, whether they are traditional "girl interests" or not.

Because women learn at such an early age that how they look and how helpful and agreeable they are impact how they will be judged, women sometimes overemphasize appearance and socially acceptable behavior, perpetuating the stereotypes of which they are the victims. Society continues to reward us for doing so. The price is an unreasonable level of stress if we are seen looking bad; do something rude; work at a job that has traditionally been dominated by men; keep a messy house; attempt to supervise unruly children; are an assertive and take-charge boss, manager, or CEO of a company; or (believe it or not) are professionally successful at all! What will people *think?* What will people *say?*

To conquer female stress mismanagement syndrome, you don't have to start undermining your own good habits, but it is a good idea to practice doing things for yourself and the people you care about, rather than focusing on the judgments and opinions of people you hardly know. Whenever you are feeling stressed about what someone else thinks (or what you *think* someone else thinks), ask yourself these questions:

- Am I really bothered by what someone else thinks, or am I bothered because secretly I agree with them? (If this is true, reframe your worries from your own point of view.)
- Am I stressed about what others think out of habit? Do I really care?
- What is the worst thing that could happen if somebody doesn't approve of me?
- What do I really think is important in this situation, regardless of anybody else's opinion?

It's nice to know how to be polite and how to help others. It's nice to know how to keep your house neat and cook a satisfying dinner. But it's also nice to achieve career success, be independent and spirited, know how to get what you need in life, and not have to depend on anybody else to take care of you. People who don't see your positive qualities have narrow vision.

FACTS

Panic disorder is twice as common in women as in men. It most often begins in young adults and is characterized by repeated, unexpected panic attacks with both physical and emotional symptoms such as fear, chest pain, racing heart, shortness of breath, and abdominal distress. Nobody knows for sure what causes panic disorder; however, it is treatable.

The Estrogen Connection

One of the things that makes a woman a woman is the presence of the female sex organs and the particular hormone cocktail that is heavy on the estrogen and light on the testosterone. Estrogen and related hormones govern an amazing number of bodily functions, from ovulation to skin clarity. By menopause, estrogen levels in a woman's body have dropped by about 80 percent, causing many changes in the body, from hot flashes to osteoporosis.

Estrogen is the reason why women have a lower rate of cardiovascular disease than men. Estrogen has a protective effect on the heart. After menopause, men and women have about the same risk of heart attack, and women are more likely to die from their first heart attack than men.

But during periods of stress, estrogen levels drop temporarily because the adrenal glands are busy pumping out stress hormones instead of estrogen. These estrogen dips cause little windows of menopause-like cardiac vulnerability. Studies have shown that when subjected to stress, estrogen levels drop; during that period, the arteries in the heart immediately begin to build up plaque, leading to a higher risk of heart disease. Stress may actually cause damage to artery walls in addition to plaque buildup. Little nicks and tears from cortisol can speed up the accumulation of plaque on artery walls. Keeping estrogen levels constant by keeping stress in check is just one more reason to manage stress during your childbearing years.

Which Came First, Stress or PMS?

That time of the month. Our monthly friend. A visit from Aunt Flo. The lady in red. No matter what we call it, menstruation is a potential source of monthly stress for almost half a woman's life. Menstruation is often accompanied by discomfort. PMS, or premenstrual syndrome, can cause additional physical discomforts and emotional symptoms such as irritability, sadness, depression, anger, or exaggerated emotions of any kind.

Serious cases of PMS can be treated medically. If you get just a little emotional, a little bloated, a little achy, or gain a few pounds every month before or during menstruation, the best thing to do is step up your stress management efforts in a few specific ways that emphasize self-care. You might notice that many of these steps are basic stress management strategies you can do at any time to help relieve stress, but if you've been forgetting, this is the time to reinstate your good habits:

- Be sure to drink those eight glasses of water to combat bloating.
- Get plenty of sleep. Go to bed early.
- Avoid caffeine, sugar, and saturated fat.
- Eat plenty of fresh fruits, vegetables, and whole grains. You need the fiber and you'll feel more balanced.
- Drink extra milk and eat more yogurt. Studies show that calcium may be among the most effective treatments for the symptoms of PMS.
- Take it easy. If you really don't feel like staying out late or pushing yourself, don't.
- Relieve cramps by curling up in bed with a heating pad, a cup of herbal tea, and a really good book.
- Soak in a warm bath.
- Take ibuprofen (like in Advil or Motrin), which can help relieve cramps.
- Meditate, focusing on relaxing and warming your abdominal area.
- Get a massage.
- Research woman's history. What a good time to celebrate being a woman!
- One week after your period is over, do a monthly breast exam. Report any suspicious lumps, thickening, or changes to your doctor.

And don't forget that yearly pelvic exam! One of the best ways to stay healthy is to catch health problems early, when they can be treated much more easily.

ALERT

If you don't like taking pain relievers or prefer a more natural treatment for the discomfort of PMS and menstruation, try evening primrose oil, dong quai, blessed thistle, kelp, raspberry leaf tea, or Siberian ginseng. (If you are taking other medications, check with your doctor to make sure these herbs won't cause adverse interactions.)

Your Stress, Your Fertility

Deciding to become pregnant is thrilling, but the thrill can turn to confusion if your first few efforts don't result in pregnancy. Is stress the culprit?

Much research has been devoted to the link between fertility and stress, and although experts disagree, more and more doctors are recommending stress management therapies for their patients struggling with fertility issues. And recent research has helped to cement the connection between stress and fertility.

While some experts continue to assert that while infertility causes stress, stress doesn't cause infertility, the possible or probable connection between the two is certainly heartening. However, connecting stress and infertility could have a downside: People might blame themselves for their inability to conceive, causing more stress and exacerbating the problem. Certainly, there are many reasons why people aren't able to conceive immediately or ever, and people who are already having difficulty conceiving shouldn't blame themselves or their lack of coping skills for their fertility issues.

However, stress management techniques can help people feel better about themselves as they work on conceiving. And because mind and body are so inextricably linked, managing stressful feelings, especially those compounded by worry and anxiety at the inability to get pregnant right away, may give fertility a boost. If stress interferes with estrogen production (it does) and testosterone production (it does), it is certainly reasonable to suspect that deep relaxation, meditation, self-care, and other techniques that help to combat the stress response might help to balance your body and restore its equilibrium, which could help to promote fertility.

If you discover that you have a specific barrier to fertility, whether it can or can't be treated, practice stress management for any of the following: for speedier healing after surgery, to promote the effectiveness of your medication (through visualization—it's scientifically unproven in such cases, but who knows?), or to help you help your partner with whatever treatment he is receiving.

For centuries, women have used herbal remedies to enhance fertility. Try a tea made from any one or a combination of the following: alfalfa, nettle, raspberry leaf, red clover, and rose hips. Women over forty can take five to ten drops of dandelion root tincture before meals and add bitter greens such as dandelion and arugula to salads to aid the body's absorption of vitamins and minerals. Lady's mantle may strengthen the uterus, and chasteberry, false unicorn root, and partridgeberry may balance hormones.

Stress management can also help you deal with the feelings of loss you will experience if you are told you will not be able to conceive. Give yourself time, attention, and the permission to mourn. Take care of yourself, or let others do it, too. Then, let stress management help ease your search for other options such as adoption, or let it assist you in entering a new stage of life in which you construct a full and rewarding life as an autonomous adult.

Stress During Pregnancy, Childbirth, and Postpartum

Anyone who is pregnant can probably provide a long list of particular stressors, from first trimester morning sickness to third trimester swollen ankles. This is in addition to the emotional stress of preparing to add a new little person to the family and all the changes that brings about in the life of an individual, the life of a relationship, and the life of a family.

Childbirth is stressful in many ways. It hurts, for one thing! Your body is going through an amazing but highly stressful process. And your mind is adjusting to the drama of the situation in any number of ways.

The postpartum period is fraught with environmental as well as hormonal adjustments. Postpartum depression can make even the simple chores of daily life seem impossible.

Managing your stress is even more important during this intense transitional period of life because when you are pregnant, you are "stressing for two." While any of the techniques in this book are helpful during pregnancy, good health and self-care are crucial. When you are pregnant, it is essential to do the following:

- Drink eight glasses of water each day.
- Get enough sleep.
- Eat healthy, nutrient-dense food.
- Get some moderate exercise on most days of the week (unless your doctor recommends otherwise).
- Meditate or practice other relaxation techniques.
- Stop your bad health habits such as smoking and drinking. Get help if necessary.

Also important during pregnancy is to have support from your partner and/or friends and family. The worry and anxiety that comes with pregnancy will be much less intense if you know you have others to help you. Get support and don't be afraid to ask for what you need. After all, you are doing it for your baby.

If you don't have any support, find some and find some fast. You aren't without options. Most communities have organized support groups for single mothers, or other kinds of community activities through which you could make some friends. Some people who find themselves pregnant and without support decide to move closer to family or helpful friends.

Whatever your situation, don't try to do it alone. You might be able to do it, but the stress will be overwhelming, and that isn't good for your baby. Even if you feel able to deal with your situation now, you may feel different about it when the baby comes and you are overwhelmed with hormonal changes. Helping yourself helps your baby.

Having a birthing plan in place before you go into labor is also a great way to ease the laboring mother's mind. Write down how you would like things to go, including how you feel about pain medication (allow for a change of mind on this one, just in case), what you would like to be able to do during labor (listen to music, take a shower, have friends or family present), whether you approve the use of a video camera during delivery, and anything else you consider a priority.

ESSENTIALS

Managing the stress of childbirth can be an organized event. Classes in the Lamaze or Bradley methods and other techniques for easing childbirth are widely available. Midwives and doulas can ease the stress and fear of childbirth by being present at the birth to assist and offer a voice of calm and rationality. While the birthing partner should also be present to offer additional support, birthing partners often feel pretty stressed themselves and aren't always much help.

Birthing partners can help to ease the stress of the laboring mother with some specific strategies. Have your partner look at the following list, memorize it, and be ready to put it to use.

Ten Ways to Ease the Stress of a Laboring Mother

1. Follow her lead. If she wants you, be there. If she doesn't want you, take a break. Don't be offended.
2. Offer to massage her shoulders, neck, scalp, or feet. If she doesn't want it or suddenly wants you to stop, stop. Don't be offended.
3. Stay calm. Practice deep breathing along with her. It will help you both.
4. Tell her how great she is doing.
5. Don't act worried.
6. Hold her hand and try not to complain when she squeezes it really hard.
7. Redirect her to her point of focus during contractions, unless she tells you to stop.
8. Be her gofer. Get magazines. Change the music. Spoon out the ice chips. Keep the relatives informed.
9. Be her advocate. If doctors or nurses are being unreasonable or doing things that are upsetting her or that go against her birthing

plan, be assertive (not obnoxious) and insist that the mother's wishes be followed (unless it is a case of the mother's or baby's health, in which case the doctors know best!).

10. Stay mindful. You'll want to remember this experience, and chances are, there will be parts of the experience the mother doesn't remember. You can fill her in!

Postpartum

The postpartum period is marked by drastic hormonal fluctuations that can leave you feeling like an emotional wreck. Irritability, sadness, intense joy, intense anger, intense frustration, and sobbing at something as mundane as television commercials are par for the course.

In some cases, severe depression can occur, or even temporary psychosis. Make sure you have people around you to help deal with things when you can't handle them, and, if you have feelings of severe depression, feel unable to care for your new baby, or feel confused by irrational thoughts, please seek professional help. Postpartum depression and associated conditions are usually easy to treat.

Stress management techniques are important during this time, especially self-care techniques and relaxation techniques. You need support and you need to take care of yourself. Postpartum emotional upheavals can happen when you least expect them.

Oh, Baby!

So, you thought pregnancy was stressful. Well, now that you've got a baby, you know what real stress is! Parenthood has its own unique set of stressors. You aren't just responsible for your own life anymore. You are directly responsible for the care, nurturing, teaching, and protecting of another human being for approximately eighteen years.

That's a big responsibility, and the thought of it can be pretty daunting, and, yes, stressful. Parents of new babies are often unable to get enough sleep, and that makes everything else more difficult. But there are things new moms can do to manage the necessary stress of parenthood:

- Drink lots of water to stay well hydrated.
- Eat really healthy, soul-satisfying food.
- Take it easy. Let your body heal.
- Let people help you. You don't have to prove anything to anybody.
- Force yourself to make time for yourself, even if it's just ten minutes each day alone in the back bedroom breathing deeply.
- Sleep whenever the baby sleeps.
- Let yourself relish your time alone with your new baby.

Parents often have to make sacrifices, of time, of money, of autonomy. Sure it's worth it, but to parent well, you also have to manage your stress well. If you teach your children how to manage their stress as well, you'll be giving them a great gift. As children grow and encounter school, peer pressure, homework overload, and the expectations inherent in our society, they'll also encounter plenty of stress.

ALERT

Most teenagers probably experience at least as much stress as they cause their parents. If your family can learn how to manage stress together, you'll all have a stronger relationship. Teach your teens how to manage stress. You'll be giving them the gift of a lifetime.

Most important for a family life in which the stress is well managed is a sense of togetherness. It doesn't matter what elements make up your family. You don't have to have a husband, wife, 2.5 children, and a dog. As long as everyone knows they belong, feels loved, and spends time together, it's a family. A weekly family night may be all it takes. Play games. Talk about issues in the world. Watch movies. Take turns making dinner. Whatever you do, just being together will make the memories sweet.

Low-Stress Single Parenting

The fact that you don't have a life partner doesn't mean you can't be a good parent. Forget all those statistics (even if it's hard to forget them when people keep quoting them to you) about children in single parent families experiencing more problems and getting into more trouble.

Single parent families are still families. If the people in your single parent family share a sense of belonging, spend time together, have fun together, and are open about their love and mutual caring, they will be an excellent family.

ESSENTIALS

If your relationship is breaking up, you are probably experiencing many intense emotions; inflicting these emotions on your children can make the stress much greater for them. Being strong, calm, and happy with your children is important for them, but it can have a surprisingly positive effect on you, too. Acting calm and happy can actually make you feel calmer and happier. Don't bury your emotions, but compartmentalize them and deal with them when your children aren't around.

But life is pretty stressful for the single parent, who often has to fulfill the role of both parents on a daily basis. It isn't easy to have to cook the dinner, wash the dishes, sweep the floors, take out the garbage, and earn the money all by yourself—and then be cheerful and playful with the kids! But you can do it, and it's worth the effort. You can also put effort into stress management, which will make the rest of your life a little bit easier:

- Get enough sleep! You may think it isn't possible, but it's always possible to rearrange your schedule.
- Eat a healthy diet. Your kids will learn from your example.
- Sit down with your kids during meals and talk to them, even if you plan to eat later. Turn off the television!
- Don't let your entire life revolve around your kids. Go out as a grownup at least once each week.
- Pamper yourself. You certainly deserve it!
- Meditate every day.
- Remind yourself every day that although like any parent you are bound to make some mistakes here and there, overall you are doing an excellent job.
- Enjoy your time with your kids. You'll never have it back again.

- If you have to choose between cleaning and being with your kids, let the kids win out most of the time. Or, involve the kids in cleaning and make it a family affair. (My kids love to scrub the kitchen floor.)
- Try not to doubt yourself. But, if you find yourself doing so, consciously replace your doubt with a vote of confidence. Remember the little engine that could!
- Teach your kids to exercise. Learn a sport together, or do yoga together. Kids love yoga, and it's good for the whole family.
- Make it a family tradition to tell each other what you love about each other.
- Be silly!
- Be your own best friend. Nurture your inner confidence so that you'll have reserves when it seems like nobody is cheering for you.

Childless by Choice

Women who choose not to have children or who, for whatever reason, find themselves toward the end of their childbearing years without ever having had children are subject to enormous social pressure. Why? Because society still expects women to have children, and any woman who doesn't must be doing something wrong, right?

 **SSENTIALS**

If you feel the need to build up your stores of confidence and courage, learn the yoga warrior pose. Stand with your feet about four feet apart. Turn your right foot to face the right, keep your left foot facing straight ahead. Hold your arms out straight, one hand pointing right, one pointing left, then turn your torso so that you are looking straight out over your right arm. Your right arm, right foot, and face should all be pointing to the right. Bend your right knee and balance your weight between your two feet. Hold your arms out strongly and feel the power of the warrior! Repeat to the left.

Of course not! The world has plenty of people. We don't have any kind of civic duty to procreate. Yet, women who choose not to have children, whether or not they choose to marry, are often on the receiving end of constant commentary from well-meaning relatives and friends. "So, when are you going to settle down and have children?" These thoughtless comments can be painful to those who have tried and been unable to conceive, but they can also be painful to those who, even though they may sometimes grieve the path not taken, have decided that parenthood is not for them.

How do you handle the pressure? By staying calm and having ready answers. While you may be tempted to snap back with a similarly intrusive response to unwanted questions about your procreative status, you'll just add to the tension and make yourself feel worse. Instead, try these comments to end the conversation (if that's what you want to do):

- "Why do you ask?"
- "That's a personal matter."
- "Children aren't in my plan right now."
- "That path doesn't interest me."
- "I have other outlets for my maternal instinct."

Or, if you want a zippier response:

- "Oh, my goodness! I didn't realize there was a shortage!"
- "Well, you know, I didn't pass the test."
- "But it's the twenty-first century! Don't they have special equipment for that now?"
- "They don't encourage undercover agents to procreate."

Okay, maybe those answers don't all make complete sense—but you might at least confuse people into silence!

The point is this: Whether or not you choose to have children is nobody's business but your own. You aren't obligated to justify yourself to anyone (no, not even your parents). Don't let people make you feel guilty for your decision. Just breathe deeply, and let the comments go.

Stress and Menopause

Stress doesn't cause menopause. Aging causes menopause, and that's just the way it is. Remember that adage about changing the things you can change, accepting the things you can't change, and having the wisdom to know the difference? This is one of those things you can't change. If you are a woman, eventually you'll go through menopause.

If stress is often about change, then they don't call menopause "the change" for nothing. Menopause can be very stressful to both mind and body. Menopause is marked by plummeting estrogen levels, and the results can be hot flashes, depression, anxiety, a feeling of flatness or loss of emotion, wildly fluctuating emotions, vaginal dryness, loss of interest in sex, loss of bone mass, increased risk of cardiovascular disease and stroke, increased cancer risk . . . and the list goes on.

Could there possibly be a positive side to menopause?

Menopause is more than just a hormonal adjustment. Fortunately, many of the changes associated with menopause are temporary. While your risk of certain diseases will remain higher after menopause, the hot flashes, the depression, the mood fluctuations, even the loss of sex drive are all temporary.

Stress management techniques can help to alleviate or reduce many of the temporary side effects of menopause. Meditation and relaxation techniques coupled with regular moderate exercise including strength training are just the one-two punch your uncomfortable symptoms need. If you seek hormone replacement therapy (it's controversial, so talk to your doctor), you may be able to further alleviate many of the temporary symptoms of menopause, too. This will free you to focus on the good stuff: the new you!

You are still you after menopause, of course, but there is something liberating about moving to the next stage of life, postchildbearing. Even if you never had children, knowing you are past that stage in your life when people will ask you when you are *going* to have them is a freedom. You've also moved to a stage in life where you can be the center of your universe again. That doesn't mean that you need to become selfish. You can still devote time to helping family, friends, children, and grandchildren.

For many seniors, however, this isn't so easy. Just when your life was about to become your own again, you find yourself sandwiched: caring for elderly parents and primary baby-sitter to your grandchildren. Chances are increasing that your own adult children are even moving back in. Help! Maybe you love helping your family, but as you enter your post-childbearing stage of life, it is crucial for your own happiness and sense of well-being that you also devote some time to yourself. It isn't selfish. If you are happier, calmer, and more fulfilled, you'll also be more helpful to others in a productive (rather than a codependent) way. Make yourself a top priority, as you continue to love and support your parents and offspring. Don't let your life slip away without fully appreciating what you've accomplished. Keep your eye on the big picture.

The older you get, the more loved ones you will lose. With loss comes grief, and grief is extremely stressful. Keep in touch with your own feelings of loneliness and sadness when you lose people you love. If you've lost a partner, try not to let yourself become isolated. Finding companionship and others to love is one of the most important things you can do to help yourself.

Stress and the Senior Woman

Once you've passed the childbearing years, life begins to open up. You feel more secure, you know who you are, you have time to yourself. But the golden years can be stressful for women. Beloved children move out, and the house seems empty. Bodies get achier and less agile.

If you've worked most of your life and are now retiring, you may find yourself suffering from stress just when you thought you were taking a load off by leaving your job. Jobs are often a great source of self-esteem as well as money. Now, money may be tight after retirement, and the house may seem tight, too, when you and your partner are suddenly at home all day together. Even if you have plenty to do, you may feel like your work is less important because you aren't being paid for it or because you aren't getting direct feedback from a supervisor. You aren't used to being your own supervisor!

If you are far from relatives and friends, life may get lonely. Health problems are stressful, and depression is common in older women. What can a senior woman do to combat the negative effects of stress?

- *Stay engaged.* Participate in activities outside your home, whether volunteering, exercise classes, art classes, language classes, book groups, church, cooking classes, or social groups. You'll stay fired up about what's going on around you, and you'll keep your mind active, which helps to keep you feeling young.
- *Don't lose touch with friends.* Make an effort to stay connected. Maintain a mix of friends your own age—and younger friends, too.
- *Consider getting a pet.* Pets are proven to reduce stress and can provide you with a lasting and satisfying relationship. Small dogs and cats are easy to handle and give back tenfold what you give them. Birds can also be rewarding companions, and you can teach them to talk!
- *Stay active.* Take a walk or do some other kind of exercise every day. Walking alone or with friends is beneficial physically and emotionally.
- *Pay attention to what's going on in the world.* Talk about events with your friends and/or your partner. Work on being open-minded; make sure you can back up your opinions with good reasoning.
- *Try yoga* to help keep your body flexible and less prone to injury.
- *Eat nutrient-dense foods* with plenty of calcium, protein, and fiber. Soy foods may also help with the effects of menopause. Try vanilla or chocolate soymilk.
- *Lift weights* to keep your bones strong and to combat osteoporosis.
- *Keep drinking lots of water* and getting enough sleep.
- *Consider qualified holistic health care practitioners,* who may be inclined to put you on fewer medications and help you to adjust your whole lifestyle for better health.
- *Meditate daily* to explore the universe of the inner you. Get to know yourself all over again!

- *Keep your mind busy.* Take up a new hobby. Learn a new language. Read books in a different genre. Do word puzzles. Have intellectual discussions with your friends.
- *Do things for other people.* Service to others will make you feel good about yourself as well as help other people.
- *Start working on writing your life history.* You'll enjoy sorting through the memories, and your manuscript will be a valuable family treasure.
- *Value yourself.*

FACTS

A recent, widely publicized study described the differences in the way men and women handle stress. While men tend to react with aggression or by leaving the situation (a kind of "fight or flight" response), women are more likely to "tend and befriend," or protect their young and seek help from others. The hormone oxytocin, which helps to stimulate the maternal instinct in women, may be responsible.

CHAPTER 12
For Men Only

Like women, men also have a much easier time than their ancestors did. Machines make life easier, and computers make life more sedentary. Men live longer than ever before, but the fact that you aren't plowing your fields with a hand plow all day doesn't mean you aren't stressed. You *are* stressed, and it's no wonder. Men are expected to do more than ever before—be both provider and nurturer, strong and emotionally available, independent and supportive. Men may feel stress if they aren't always confident and strong, or if they aren't willing to share their emotions.

Male Stress Mismanagement Syndrome

Studies show that men and women tend to handle their stress differently. Women talk about their problems with others. Men don't. Instead, men tend to seek out the company of others, minus the sharing. Or, men turn to physical activity.

Both methods can work well, but men's stereotypical reluctance to express feelings can lead to increased negative effects of stress, including a sense of isolation, depression, low self-esteem, and substance abuse. Men are four times more likely than women to commit suicide, and men are more likely than women to abuse drugs and alcohol and commit violent acts.

How can you help yourself manage your own stress and combat your tendency to keep it all inside? Here are some tips for better male stress management:

- Don't feel like talking about it? Write about it. Keep a journal to vent. Even if you don't feel like writing about how you feel, once you get going, you may find it very therapeutic.
- Exercise is an excellent way to release pent-up anxiety, anger, or feelings of depression.
- Drink more water. It makes everything work better.
- Cut down on the caffeine. Caffeine can make you feel more anxious, and it can raise your blood pressure.
- Try meditation or other relaxation techniques.
- Use humor to diffuse tense situations.
- If you feel like your feelings are out of control, talk to a counselor or therapist. Sometimes it's easier to talk to somebody who isn't part of your personal life.

Real Men Do Feel Stress

Men are taught to be independent and strong, to deal with things rationally and logically. Sometimes, this approach can be an effective way to handle a crisis, to get things accomplished, or to let things go that aren't worth dwelling on. But sometimes, rationality and strength don't address the real problem, which doesn't go away. Some men turn to drugs, alcohol, or other addictions such as gambling or sex to numb the pain or sadness or anxiety that come from too much stress. Many men get depressed, but far fewer men than women are likely to admit it or seek help for their depression.

Sometimes, not feeling the stress makes it worse. Eventually, the stress will take over and force you to feel it. The best way to ensure you remain in control is to manage the stress as it comes. Let yourself recognize it so that you can deal with it.

Recognize that "manliness" and everything that word implies for you could be interfering with your ability to manage your stress. Life doesn't have to be a competition. Success isn't always measured in dollars and prestige. You don't have to get by on five hours of sleep or try to keep up with your buddies at happy hour after work.

And you don't have to deny that you are feeling stressed. You don't have to tell everybody you meet, but you don't have to deny your stress to yourself. You can manage your stress in many ways that can make your life easier, and you can do many of the techniques that relieve stress alone in your own home. It's your business.

ALERT

Men are most likely to have a heart attack in the morning. Some experts believe morning heart attacks could be related to typically higher blood pressure levels in the morning. Save your stressful moments—the meeting with that aggravating client, balancing your checkbook—for the afternoon.

Testosterone Connection

Studies have linked both physical and psychological stress to a drop in the level of testosterone, the hormone that gives men their masculine qualities such as facial hair growth, musculature, and deep voice. Testosterone is a hormone with a complex relationship to behavior: Testosterone levels can influence behavior, and behavior can influence testosterone levels. In ancient times, when some men were castrated (such as the eunuchs that served royalty in many different countries throughout history, or the Italian castrati with their beautiful, high voices), they would tend to be more docile, have a reduced sex drive, and develop more body fat.

Testosterone has been linked to dominant behavior in men. It is in part responsible for the male perspective and the feeling that control, rationality, and dominance are desirable traits in men. Countless studies that assert the differences between the genders in communication style, learning style, and even basic understanding of language are exploring the relationship between people who are driven more by testosterone and those driven more by estrogen.

Studies have shown that women tend to be attracted to men with more masculine features and more dominant behavior—not aggressive behavior, necessarily, but dominant behavior. While cultural factors certainly modify biological impulses and while there are many exceptions, masculine features and dominant behavior are biological signals of reproductive fitness.

Traditionally, in our culture, men went out to earn a living and support their families, fulfilling this urge to dominate. The estrogen- and oxytocin-driven females stayed at home, accomplishing the nurturing of children and caretaking of the home. But life today seems much more complex than it once was (although surely we oversimplify the past). As our society's needs evolve, its members don't like to be restricted to a certain role. Many women get enormous satisfaction from earning a living outside the home and supporting their families. Many men get immense satisfaction from staying home to raise their children, and they do an excellent job at being a caretaker. These so-called reverse roles aren't really reversed at all. Maintaining a household and raising children can fulfill a man's need to accomplish something important. A stay-at-home dad can be a dominant figure in a very positive way for his children. Household maintenance can be a matter of competition and pride.

Women, too, tend to excel in the working world by being communicative, empathetic, and nurturing. In other words, both men and women can do any kind of job, but they will tend to go about it in different ways. You may not run the house or care for the children in the same way as your partner, but that doesn't mean your way isn't just as good.

The point is that a man does not necessarily become frustrated or stressed just because he isn't doing the traditional "man" things. But, in fact, stress sets in when a man isn't allowed to be who he needs to be. The propensity toward dominance can result in feelings of stress when dominant individuals are placed in subordinate positions. If men are forced to act subordinate when it isn't in their nature—even if that means having to be subordinate to a controlling CEO—the result can be lots of stress. If left unchecked, that stress can turn into aggression or other forms of antisocial behavior. If men aren't able to fulfill their need to control their own situation, go out there and compete, and feel like they are making an important contribution, they may feel frustrated and unfulfilled.

What happens when stress depresses a man's testosterone level? A lowered level of testosterone could result in a drop in self-confidence and feelings of control, which can exacerbate an already stressful situation. This can be frustrating and can provoke anxiety in men who are used to feeling dominant. To maintain your health and confidence, it is crucial that you manage your stress. If you keep your testosterone level in balance, you'll feel better, and you'll be more confident and more in control of your feelings and actions. The best way to do this is to keep stress in check.

ALERT

Both men and women have some estrogen and some testosterone. In men, small amounts of estrogen are beneficial to the brain and other parts of the body, but if a man becomes obese or drinks too much alcohol, the body can start producing more estrogen than is healthy.

Your Stress, Your Reproductive Fitness

Stress can lower testosterone production. And lower testosterone levels result in a lower sperm count, which can drastically reduce a man's reproductive fitness. If you and your partner are trying to get pregnant, stress management is just as important for you as it is for her. How can you get back on the reproductive track? The same way your partner can. Do it together:

- Get daily moderate exercise.
- Eat healthy foods.
- Get sufficient sleep.
- Drink plenty of water.
- Meditate or practice relaxation techniques daily.
- Practice breathing deeply.
- Make a conscious effort to have a positive attitude.
- If you really aren't able to control something, let it go.

Anger, Depression, and Other Unmentionables

Stress can have some specific effects on men that, although often very treatable, can make men feel lost, frustrated, or hopeless. Anger management is an important skill for men. Your naturally higher testosterone level can make you more prone to anger and aggression than women (there are certainly exceptions). Suppressing anger can be just as dangerous as venting anger inappropriately. Both cause a surge in stress hormones that can be harmful to the body.

Frequent anger can also be a sign of depression. Depression is a very real problem for many men, who tend to be less likely to admit they are depressed or to seek treatment. Here are the signs of depression:

- Feeling out of control
- Excessive irritability or anger
- Loss of interest in things that you previously enjoyed
- Sudden change in appetite (much higher or lower)
- Sudden change in sleep patterns (insomnia or sleeping too much)
- Feelings of hopelessness and despair
- Feelings of being stuck in a situation with no way out
- Anxiety, panic

- Frequent crying
- Thoughts of suicide
- Sabotaging success (such as quitting a good job or ending a good relationship)
- Substance abuse
- Increase in addictive behaviors
- Decreased sex drive

If you are depressed, please seek treatment. Depression is easily treatable, through therapy, medication, or a combination of both. Once you are over the first hurdle, you will feel better about yourself and will be more able to implement lifestyle changes, such as daily exercise, that will help to further alleviate depression.

Pressures Everywhere

Men often feel that asking for help is a sign of weakness, but in the case of depression (and in many other cases, for that matter), asking for help is a sign of strength. The situation is never hopeless! Ask for help.

Another area of concern for many men, and something that can be a direct result of even minor and/or temporary stress, is erectile dysfunction (ED), or impotence. Isolated incidents of being unable to maintain an erection sufficient to complete sexual intercourse are normal. Being overly tired, drinking too much, having a bad day, or putting too much pressure on yourself to perform can all result in an incident. But if the condition persists—if you cannot maintain an erection at least half the time you try—then you could have erectile dysfunction, and erectile dysfunction can be caused by stress.

Other Causes

There are other causes. In men over fifty, the most common cause of ED is circulatory problems such as hardening of the arteries. It isn't just the arteries in your heart that can harden with age. The arteries to the penis can also get clogged, preventing sufficient blood flow for an erection. ED can also be a symptom of a serious disease such as diabetes, or kidney or liver failure. It can be caused by nerve damage to the area from disease or surgery, including spinal surgery, or surgery on the colon or prostate. ED can be a side effect of many different medications, including antidepressants (very common), medication for high blood pressure, and sedatives. Excessive alcohol consumption can also cause ED, and so can smoking.

FACTS

Do you need one more reason to quit smoking? Studies show that erectile dysfunction is more than twice as common in heavy smokers as it is in nonsmokers. Heavy smoking causes blood vessels in the body to shrink, which reduces blood flow all over the body, including to the penis . . . just when you need it most!

But, in many cases, ED has a psychological cause, and, in many cases, that cause is stress. Stress and ED do an insidious dance. You're stressed. You experience an incident of impotence. That makes you more stressed, increasing your chances of it happening again. It happens again. You get more stressed. How do you break the cycle?

In many cases, people who experience ED due to psychological causes will still have erections during sleep or in the morning. It's still a good idea to see a doctor to make sure there isn't an underlying physical condition. If it's clear that the cause is psychological, then you can focus on managing your stress.

See if you can pinpoint the cause. The stress that causes ED can come from any source. Overall life stress can certainly cause it, but other kinds of stress can, too, including the following:

- Stress in the relationship between sexual partners
- Stress caused by fear of poor performance
- Stress caused by a fear of intimacy or a sudden change in the nature of the relationship, such as an engagement
- Fear of disease
- Stress due to unresolved sexual issues including sexual orientation
- Depression and its accompanying loss of interest in sex

If you know or suspect where your stress is rooted, you can begin to work on that area. Practice meditation and relaxation tips. Get enough exercise. If you are afraid of something, talk about it, think about it, write about it, or seek help so that you can work it out and get past it. If you are depressed, seek treatment. If you are having relationship problems, confront them and work them out. Sometimes, all it takes is some open communication.

Or, maybe your ED is a signal that you are having sex with the wrong person. Think about that. Whatever the cause, most psychological causes of ED can be resolved, in which case, your function will return without any sign of having left you. When it comes to ED, "don't worry, be happy" may be easier said than done, but it's still pretty good advice.

QUESTIONS?

Should you try Viagra?
While some men reportedly use Viagra on occasion for greater stamina, the medication is not for people with normal sexual functioning. Men with erectile dysfunction may benefit from Viagra because it facilitates erection and can increase the desire for sex. However, all medications have side effects and risks, and Viagra shouldn't be used when it isn't needed. Talk to your doctor to help you decide if you should use Viagra. You need to be aware of the effects, the risks, and how to use it properly.

The Midlife Crisis: Myth, Reality, or Stress in Disguise?

While both men and women can experience a midlife crisis, the term is most often applied to men. The midlife crisis may or may not have a hormonal basis, but it is certainly a reality. During this time of life, typically in the late thirties to mid-forties, men begin to question the direction their lives have taken. They wonder if they've missed out on things. They are tired of their jobs, feel their relationships have stagnated, and fear that they have lost interest in life.

What a man does in response to his midlife crisis depends on the man and the intensity of the feelings, but you've all seen the stereotypes on television and in the movies: the divorce, the twenty-something girlfriend, the red sports car. Of course, it doesn't always work out this way. Sometimes, the response is depression, withdrawal, anxiety, or an increasing dissatisfaction with daily life. Sometimes, men change careers at this point in life and go for their dreams.

What does the midlife crisis have to do with stress? Years of chronic stress due to unresolved relationship issues or job dissatisfaction can build up to the final breakdown that is the midlife crisis. Additionally, the midlife crisis becomes a source of stress because of the changes it has effected in life.

ESSENTIALS

Who says you can't change your career? Just don't do it on a whim. Plan the change by researching the market in your field of choice, learning everything you can, getting any necessary degrees or certification, having a solid business plan, securing any necessary capital, then giving it everything you've got.

What can you do about it? First, before you get to your midlife crisis, learn to manage your stress. This can subvert a midlife crisis; after all, if your life is going just the way you want it to go, you won't have any reason for a crisis. If you're already heading full speed into yours, however, you can help to soften the blow by preparing for the stress-to-come:

- Make a list of all your unfulfilled dreams. Look at it and contemplate it. Which of the dreams are unrealistic, things you know you'll never do but just like to dream about? You can cross those off your list for now (or put them on a different list).
- Look at what's left. What have you really wanted to do, always intended to do, but haven't yet accomplished? Think hard about these items. Are they things you really want or things you just think you want? Relax, close your eyes, and visualize having these things. Sometimes we like the idea of something—getting a doctoral degree,

having a drop-dead-gorgeous partner, being extremely rich—but when we think about what it would take to get there, we realize it isn't really worth it. Which items do you think probably wouldn't really be worth the effort of getting there? Cross them off the list (or move them to a different list).

- Look at what's left. Why haven't you accomplished these dreams yet? What would you need to do to make them happen? Start thinking about what you could do to really make these dreams come true. Make a list of steps. If you have a partner, encourage her to make her own list, then talk about how you might both reach your dreams together while you are still young (*young* is a relative term, after all).

- If your dissatisfaction lies with your relationship, this is the time to do something about it, and that doesn't necessarily mean leaving the relationship behind. Take steps to revitalize your relationship. Break up your routine. Take a trip together. Change things around in the bedroom. Be romantic. Put some real attention and focus into your sex life. If you aren't both ready for these changes, discuss the reasons why. If you have past issues to work out, work them out. A professional therapist can be very helpful.

- Stop doing things you don't like and don't really have to do. If you really, truly can't stand your job, find a new one or start your own business. More and more opportunities exist for self-employment today, and more and more people prefer to stay close to home and redirect their energies to their homes and to living more in line with their dreams and desires. Can you get by on less money? Then, do it. If you cringe at the thought of that committee you are on, that group you joined, or that club you are in, then let it go. Don't waste your life doing things you don't like that aren't necessary.

- Give to others. All this self-examination can make you feel selfish. Balance it out with a conscious effort to give your time, energy, or money to people who really need it. You could devote some time to a charity that is meaningful to you or to a cause you believe in, or you could spend more time with your partner, talking to your kids, or playing with your grandchildren.

Stress and the Senior Man

It isn't easy when your body starts to betray you, and it can be hard to admit that you can't do all the things you could once do. Getting older is stressful for men and sometimes may seem to be fraught with loss: of muscle tone, stamina, sex drive, even hair. Women may say that men get better looking as they age, but men often don't feel better looking as they recognize they have gained weight and lost energy.

Retirement can also add stress in great heaps to your already full plate. The loss of a job, from which you've gained an identity and a sense of worth all these years, can be devastating for men—who suddenly don't know who they are or what to do with themselves. Of course, you aren't your job, and you probably know that, but after fifty years of working, you may feel like you've let go of a big part of yourself.

ALERT

Even though women typically live longer than men, men often lose their partners and are left living alone. It is difficult for many men to seek companionship elsewhere, and depression, loneliness, and isolation are common problems for men who have lost their partners, especially those living far from close relatives. Making the effort to maintain social contact is extremely important.

What can a senior man do to feel strong, confident, and stress-free? Manage that stress, of course! Try some of these tips (they're similar to the tips for senior women listed earlier in this chapter—we're all people!):

- *Stay engaged.* Participate in activities outside your home, whether volunteering, playing on a team, painting classes, writing classes, hobby groups, or church. Take up carpentry or cooking, fly fishing or ballroom dancing. Do whatever interests you. You finally have the time, so don't waste it! Maybe you always wanted to learn the law, or how to speak Italian, or how to be a bird watcher. Staying active will keep you fired up about what's going on around you. It'll also keep your mind active, which helps to keep you feeling young.

- *Don't lose touch with friends.* Make an effort to stay connected. Maintain a mix of friends your own age and younger friends. Plan to do your activities outside the home, along with friends. You might help someone else get out of the house who really needs it!
- *Consider getting a pet.* Pets are proven to reduce stress and can provide you with a lasting and satisfying relationship. Dogs and cats give back tenfold what you give them. Birds can also be rewarding companions.
- *Stay active.* Take a walk or do some other kind of exercise every day. Walking with friends is beneficial physically and emotionally.
- *Pay attention to what's going on in the world.* Talk about events with your friends and/or your partner. Work on being open-minded but on having opinions you can back up with good reasoning.
- *Try yoga* to help keep your body flexible and less prone to injury. More and more senior men are trying yoga and gaining great benefits.
- *Eat nutrient-dense foods* with plenty of calcium, protein, and fiber.
- *Consider taking a daily zinc supplement* to keep your prostate healthy. Pumpkin seeds are also rich in zinc. The herb saw palmetto may also be good for prostate health.
- *Lift weights* to keep your muscles and bones strong.
- *Keep drinking lots of water* and getting enough sleep.

FACTS

More white men over age eighty-five commit suicide than any other group. Even though women report attempting suicide twice as often as men, more than four times as many men than women commit suicide.

- *Consider qualified holistic health care practitioners,* who may be inclined to put you on fewer medications and help you to adjust your whole lifestyle for better health.
- *Meditate daily* to explore the universe of the inner you. Get to know yourself all over again!
- *Keep your mind busy.* Take up a new hobby. Learn a new language. Read books in a different genre than you normally do. Work out word puzzles. Have intellectual discussions with your friends. Build stuff.

- *Do things for other people.* Service to others will make you feel good about yourself as well as help other people.
- *Start writing your life history.* You'll enjoy sorting through the memories, and your manuscript will be a valuable family treasure.
- *Value yourself.*

Whether you are a man or a woman, in your twenties or in your nineties, stress can disrupt your health and functioning. But no matter your gender or age, you can do something to lessen the effects of stress in your life. Don't be a victim of your gender or your age. It's your body, your mind, and your life!

CHAPTER 13

Stress Management from Childhood to Forever

From the stress of being born to the stress of aging, encountering stress and dealing with it is a lifelong process. While you may be coming to the idea of stress management as an adult, kids today need stress management just as much as their parents. Teaching kids stress management techniques while they are still children will be giving them a gift that will last a lifetime. Learning how to commit to stress management as a lifestyle is a gift to yourself, too.

Junior Stress

Adults sometimes have the misconception (or the not-altogether-accurate memory) of childhood as one long parade of cotton candy and carousel rides. Perhaps it is the comparison with our adult lives that makes childhood seem so carefree. Yet, children today are falling victim to the negative effects of stress in greater numbers than ever before. The causes of stress in children tend to be primarily environmental (family, friends, school) until puberty sets in and adds those troublesome hormones to the mix.

Stress in children has been recognized and diagnosed only recently. Many children report having to deal with violence, peer pressure, underage drinking, drug use, and pressure to have sex, not to mention pressure to get good grades, be involved in back-to-back extracurricular activities, have a social life, and keep all the adults in their lives pacified.

ALERT

For kids dealing with learning disabilities such as dyslexia or barriers to success in traditional environments such as attention deficit hyperactivity disorder, school can be an unrelenting source of frustration and feelings of failure. If your child seems to be having problems succeeding in school, have him or her tested for learning or behavioral problems.

Even young kids can experience stress. They, too, are sometimes faced with difficult family situations and peer interactions, some of which may not seem difficult to adults but which can cause profound stress reactions in children.

Childhood experiences can impact the individual long after childhood. One study demonstrated that children who were poorly nurtured were less able to deal with stressful situations, were more likely to react in an extreme manner, and maintained high levels of stress hormones in their bodies long after stress subsided, compared to children who were well nurtured as children. The key to giving young children the future tools for handling stress is to provide a supportive, loving, nurturing environment. If you do so, you may be helping your child form the neural pathways necessary for healthy stress management.

High stress as a child, for example, that which would occur in situations of extreme neglect, may also actually destroy neural pathways already established. That could explain the higher incidence of learning disabilities in young children who have suffered from extremely high stress.

Chances are that your children don't experience the extreme stress of neglect, however. More likely it is the average stress that comes with childhood. Just as with adults, some stress is good for kids. It can enhance performance when it is most necessary (whether for getting out of a dangerous situation fast or performing well in a dance recital). It can also teach kids how to handle stress, since stress is an integral part of life.

FACTS

Suicide is the third leading cause of death in fifteen to twenty-four year olds and the fourth leading cause of death in ten to fourteen year olds.

Teaching Kids about Stress Management

If adults don't have to take stress lying down, why should kids? If kids learn that stress is a natural part of life and that they can do something about it, they won't have to wait until adulthood, when the negative effects of stress are already compounded, to start feeling better. Kids who understand stress management will be empowered to manage their own stress throughout their lives.

The first step to teaching kids about stress management is to be tuned in to the stress your kids are feeling. You may not always know all the details of the causes of stress for your kids, but if you live with your children and pay attention, you can probably tell when your child's equilibrium is disturbed.

Signs of stress in children are similar to signs of stress in adults. Suspect your child is suffering from stress if you notice any of the following:

- Sudden change in appetite that seems unrelated to growth
- Sudden weight loss or gain

- Development of an eating disorder
- Sudden change in sleep habits
- Chronic fatigue
- Insomnia
- Sudden drop in grades
- Sudden change in exercise habits (much more or stopping completely)
- Withdrawal, sudden refusal to communicate
- Signs of anxiety, panic
- Frequent headaches and/or stomach aches
- Frequent frustration
- Depression
- Loss of interest in activities
- Compulsion to overschedule
- Suddenly quitting many activities

Children of any age can learn stress management techniques. Teens may be interested in reading this book, and any of the techniques in this book will work for them as well. For younger kids, certain stress management techniques are more effective because kids enjoy them and are motivated to try them.

ESSENTIALS

Signs of stress in young children include increased whining, clinging, and crying; intense separation anxiety from parents or caregivers; aggressive behavior such as yelling, biting, kicking, and hitting; rashes and allergy symptoms; inability to concentrate, remember things, or pay attention; frequent forgetfulness and disorganization; impulsive or hyperactive behavior; zoning out; and sudden lack of creativity.

To help build a strong stress management foundation for your children and to teach them how to manage stress in healthy ways, consider the following strategies.

Soothing Infant Stress

For infants, try a daily infant massage. Gently and softly stroke your baby's legs, arms, and body to improve circulation and relax muscles. Talk softly and sweetly to your baby as you massage her, sing to her, and make eye contact.

New parents are often overwhelmed and find their energies scattered. Even so, make a commitment to set aside several fifteen-minute sessions each day during which you devote your full and total attention to your infant. Make eye contact, talk to her, play with her, and don't do anything else; turn off the television, the radio, put away the newspaper, and stop cleaning. Make it all about baby. He'll soon learn he is important and worth your attention. He'll learn that he is lovable, and a priority. Eventually, he'll learn to take care of himself as well as you took care of him.

SSENTIALS

If your child has a low stress tolerance, keep life moving at a slower pace, stay home more, and don't force your child to enroll in lots of activities. Studies show that kids with a lower tolerance for stress actually showed lower rates of illness and behavior problems when put into low stress settings than kids with higher stress tolerance levels. Just like adults, kids with low stress tolerance thrive when life is low in stress, and, as a parent, it's your job to help keep things leisurely and low pressure.

Toddler Time

For toddlers, life is a big exciting adventure to be explored. How mysterious the behavior of adults must be to a curious, enthusiastic toddler. The simplest efforts at fun can cause adults to yell, grab things away, or do other strange and frightening things. Even if your toddler can't always understand what you say, talking to her about what is and isn't allowed is much more effective than yelling. Firm but calm and ultimately consistent behavior is paramount to raising a toddler who has self-confidence and doesn't fear or mistrust adults.

Pay attention to your toddler's reaction to the world. Instead of forcing him to do something that makes him nervous, notice that he is nervous and take it slow or put off the activity until later. Some toddlers are always ready to jump into new activities. Others require more time to consider new activities before trying them. Respect your child's individual style. He'll learn that it's okay to be the way he is. He'll be less likely, later in life, to blame himself for his stress, and he'll be more likely to understand how to approach new things successfully.

Preschoolers and Kindergartners

Preschoolers and kindergartners love to learn, but children learn in different ways. Some parents tend to direct their children too much. Try stepping back and letting your child explore, learn, question, and discover on her own. Instead of constantly saying, "Did you see this? What do you think of that? How do you think this works? What might you do with this?" let your child take the lead. She just might teach you something, and you'll be reinforcing her confidence in her own learning style.

School Daze

Once children start school, it's easy for parents to overschedule them, especially kids with many interests. Music lessons, swimming lessons, soccer practice, baby-sitting, T-ball, homework, art class, gymnastics, scouting, socializing with friends, family time, dance class, chores—when do kids have a chance to relax and do nothing? Free time is actually empowering for children (that doesn't include watching television). During free time, children get to direct their own activities. Overscheduled children don't learn how to direct themselves. They spend years waiting for someone to tell them what to do. When they are suddenly expected to behave independently, they're at a loss . . . and that's pretty stressful. Plus, with too much to do, kids necessarily have bodies and brains that are working overtime. Learning how to relax as a child makes adult relaxation a much easier process.

Kids really enjoy yoga. Yoga classes for kids are becoming more widely available. Or, look for one of the many books about yoga for kids (you might start with those listed in Appendix B). Learning yoga as a child is a great way to form a lifelong habit of good health, strength, flexibility, and mind-body integration.

ALERT

Encourage your kids to take deep belly breaths when they are starting to get nervous, anxious, or fearful. Deep breaths directly combat the stress response in kids just as they do in grownups. They signal the body that everything is fine, returning heart rate, muscle tension, and blood flow back to normal.

Teens in Trouble

Being a teenager or a preteenager is always difficult because of the surge of hormonal changes teenagers experience with puberty. But some teens seem to handle the intense feelings of adolescence better than others. Why? Some theories suggest a genetic component, but chances are the answer is almost always at least partially due to external circumstances.

Many teenagers suffer from depression, self-doubt, anger, hopelessness, and other intense emotions, even in response to situations adults wouldn't necessary consider stressful. Many teens today also have to deal with extreme circumstances, from a nasty divorce at home to the threat or actual occurrence of violence in or after school.

If parents don't want to see that their teens are in trouble, they increase that distance that often exists between teenagers and adults—the generation gap, or whatever we choose to call it these days. If they try too forcefully to intervene in their children's lives, they may push their children away even further. It's a tricky job, parenting a teen, and many parents get by with their fingers crossed.

If you think your teen is perfectly fine, you may be perfectly right, but even the most well-adjusted teenager occasionally experiences overwhelming emotions. Even if your teen resists sharing her intense emotions with you, make sure she always knows she can. Keep the lines of communication open and pay attention so that you'll notice when your teen's stress level escalates. You'll be ready to do something about it, whether that means seeking counseling together, seeking medical treatment, or simply sitting down for a serious heart-to-heart.

Here are some important things you can do for your stressed-out teen:

- Be consistent.
- Don't lose your temper.
- Let your teen know you are always there; be a solid foundation.
- Let your teen know you love her, no matter what.
- Let your teen know he can always count on you to help him if he's in trouble.
- Make it clear what behaviors you think are wrong, and why.
- Set a good example by practicing stress management yourself.
- Provide opportunities for your teen to practice stress management techniques with you.
- Keep talking.
- Don't give up!

FACTS

One theory about why kids are more stressed than they once were is that they are overexposed to stimuli. In a media-intense culture, kids spend hours each day watching television, playing video games, surfing the Internet, and listening to music. Encourage your kids to spend some media-free time each day doing something relaxing, whether it's writing in a journal or taking a bike ride.

Stress Management Tips for Kids of All Ages

Healthy kids are more likely to handle the average stresses of life with ease. Lay the foundation for great health habits by teaching your kids how to take care of themselves. Set a good example by practicing good health habits yourself. You might also try these tips:

- Serve water instead of sugary drinks. Keep a pitcher full of good quality water in the refrigerator or buy bottled water that is as easy to grab and drink as a soda.
- Keep healthy snacks in the house instead of junk food. Prepared cheese cubes, carrot sticks, peanut butter, whole wheat bread, ready-to-eat fruit, whole-grain crackers, hummus, dried fruit, and whole-grain cereal with milk are all healthy, high-energy choices.
- Encourage daily activity. If kids aren't involved in school sports, look into other organized fitness opportunities such as gymnastics, dance classes, sports camps or clinics, or gym memberships.
- Make exercise a family affair. Walk, ride bicycles, jog, or run around on the playground together.
- Encourage self-expression. Many kids enjoy drawing, making things out of clay, building structures, or writing. These creative outlets can also be excellent outlets for stress because they build self-esteem and develop artistic talents.

ESSENTIALS

If your child is really stressed about an impending test, remind her to practice deep breathing, which will help to feed oxygen to the brain, making it work better. Taking a break during study time with a twenty-minute nap can also help your child to feel refreshed and able to get back to the books in a more effective state of mind. To work well, a power nap should be between twenty and thirty minutes—no shorter, no longer.

Making time for family or for just doing nothing is important for teaching kids that overachieving isn't always the answer. Reserve at least one evening each week as family night. Encourage a leisurely, relaxed evening together with no scheduled activities. Play games, make dinner together, talk, laugh, take a walk or a bike ride. Your kids will always remember this together time, and these evenings put a nice pause in busy schedules.

Perhaps most important, keep the lines of communication open. This sounds obvious, but keep reminding your kids they can talk to you, and keep talking to your kids. Let them know you are there to listen, and let them know what things are important to you. You know those commercials that tell you to talk to your kids about smoking, drinking, or drugs? Those are all important discussions, but you can also talk to your kids about other things that are potential stressors, like peer pressure, how they are enjoying or not enjoying different classes in school, how they feel about the various activities with which they are involved, who their friends are, and how they feel about themselves.

Last of all, try to never put your child in a position of responsibility for your stress. Make sure your child knows that you are the adult and that she doesn't have to take care of you. Taking care of you is your job. If you are suffering from severe stress, such as from a divorce or depression, it is essential to seek help from an outside source, not from your child. That kind of stress is too much for a child to bear. Do your best to keep your vulnerable moments to yourself. Set an example for your child by showing her you know how to manage your own stress in effective ways, including by asking other adults for help.

If your child does seem to be in trouble, take action. Take him to counseling, keep talking to him, and bring up topics, such as depression, that he may be afraid or embarrassed to mention. Be an ally and an advocate for your child. If he knows you are on his side, he'll feel he isn't bearing all his stress alone. That can be a monumental relief to a stressed-out child.

ALERT

Many teenagers engage in underage drinking, and the effects can be devastating. Underage drinking increases a child's risk of accidents, makes a child more vulnerable to dangerous situations, and puts physical stress on the body, especially in the case of binge drinking. Many teenagers have died from alcohol poisoning while trying to "have fun." Make sure your kids understand the dangers of alcohol.

The Seven Steps to Stress Management for Kids

Kids can also learn how to deal with stress on their own terms and in their own way. Memorizing a few stress management strategies can give kids access to help when they need it most—during a test, on a date, before a big performance. Show this list to your kids, post it on the refrigerator, or, better yet, e-mail it to them. They might just read it, and they might even use it (whether they tell you about it or not).

1. **Talk about it.** Feeling stressed? Tell a friend. Call it a vent, a rant, or a rage, but do it! Share your stress daily and you'll ease the burden. Listen to a friend venting stress and ease your friend's burden, too.

2. **Go with the flow.** Things aren't what you expected? That friend isn't who you thought? That class is way harder than you think you can handle? Go with the flow. Move along with changes in your life rather than resist them. Be like a river that finds the easiest way around obstacles and just keeps on flowing.

3. **Find a mentor.** Parents are great, but sometimes you feel more ready for advice from a nonparental adult. Teachers, counselors, coaches, bosses, aunts, uncles, ministers, priests, or other adult friends who have already been through what you are going through can make great mentors. Find a person that you can relate to and let him or her help you out when you need some advice or a good example.

4. **Get organized.** That test wouldn't be so stressful if you hadn't lost all your notes. You might be able to relax a little more easily in your room if you could get from the door to the bed without stepping on piles of junk. Work out a system that you can live with, and get organized. It's a good project, a great hobby, and a skill you'll value for the rest of your life.

5. **Establish good habits now.** You've probably seen adults who have obviously led a life of bad health habits and are paying for it now. This doesn't have to be you. If you start forming good health habits while you are still a kid, you'll have a healthier life ahead of you. Try to exercise for about thirty minutes on most days, and eat lots of

fresh, healthy foods such as vegetables, fruits, whole grains, and low-fat sources of protein such as lean meat, fish, beans, tofu, yogurt, and milk. Drink lots of water, and get enough sleep—enough so that you don't feel tired during the day.

6. **Adjust your attitude.** Sometimes it's easiest to be cynical or expect the worst, but studies show that people who have a positive attitude get sick less often, recover from sickness and injuries faster, and may even live longer. Life is a lot more fun when you look on the positive side. It's a habit you can learn.

7. **See the big picture.** Life may seem to revolve around that humiliating thing you said in front of the whole class last week or that failing grade or the team you didn't make. Whenever things seem horrible or hopeless, remind yourself to step back and look at the big picture. How will you feel about this in a year? In five years? When you are an adult with a satisfying career and a fulfilling personal life? If you learn to look at temporary setbacks with an "Oh well, moving right along" attitude, life will seem much less stressful.

Stress Management Forever

You've got the tools. You've got the knowledge. But the days go by, and, somehow, there never seems time to do anything about it. Can't you start your stress management tomorrow . . . later . . . when you have time?

No, because you won't ever have time. Tomorrow will become today, later will become yesterday, and you'll still be just as busy as you are today. If you don't start to de-stress now, it may never happen.

Maybe you can't join a gym today. But can you take a walk? Maybe you can't overhaul your junk-food diet today, but can you order the chicken Caesar salad instead of the double bacon cheeseburger? Maybe you aren't up for meditation tonight, but can you go to bed a little bit earlier?

Any major life change starts with little steps. You can weave stress management into your life one thread at a time. Luckily, you can work a daily antistress regimen into your routine with very little effort while enjoying a big payoff. Anything you do to help relax your body and calm your spirit is a positive step. To start establishing your new habits today, try doing just four little things every day. Only four, and they don't have to take very long. You can work them into your schedule in any way that works for you. You may already be doing some or all of them.

1. Do something good for your body.
2. Do something to calm your mind.
3. Do something to feed your spirit.
4. Do something to simplify your environment.

Doing one thing to maintain your sense of well-being in each of these categories each day is all it takes to begin a lifelong habit of stress management. What will you do? Any of the techniques listed in this book can be used to fit into these categories. You can even knock off two categories in one blow: Meditate for mental and spiritual maintenance. Then, add a brisk walk for physical maintenance and get rid of one stack of clutter you don't use or need.

Or, maybe you'll choose the body scan in the morning, yoga in the afternoon, twenty minutes of undisturbed quiet time listening to music in the evening, and dropping one of the activities in your life that you no longer enjoy.

Still too complicated? Eat a salad (body), turn off the television (mind), tell a friend how much you appreciate her (spirit), and throw away one thing you've been keeping around for no good reason (simplify).

ESSENTIALS

One of the best ways to feel less stressed is to help somebody else relieve his or her stress. Helping and nurturing other people helps you to feel better about yourself. It also helps you to regain a sense of purpose and direction, which makes it a great activity for people who have retired from a job that used to provide that purpose and direction. Most communities have many opportunities for volunteering in a variety of areas. Find something that interests you and start helping yourself by helping others.

You probably already have some ideas of how you can work these four antistress steps into your day. Don't feel like you have to keep them the same each day, either. Part of the fun is changing them from time to time, if you thrive on change. If you love your rituals, doing the same things each day is fine, too.

There are other ways to keep your body, mind, and spirit well fed that take only minutes. You can work in exercise time, meditation time, and time for any of the other techniques listed previously in this book. In addition, in the following sections, we'll look at some quick, easy, and practically effortless ways to boost your daily antistress regimen to new heights of effectiveness. You'll feel special implementing these small changes . . . and you are!

Open to Change

If you are change-resistant, this is a good one for you. For some people, no change is a good change, but change is inevitable in life and is almost always stressful, even if it's stress that feels good. Becoming more open to change is an attitude shift. Start spotting changes and then finding one good thing about every change you experience. Someone parked in your spot? You can get an extra few minutes of exercise by walking from a spot further away. It's good for your body! Your favorite restaurant is out of your favorite food? What a great opportunity to try something different. Your favorite television show is pre-empted? Another opportunity! Spend the evening reading a book or taking a walk or practicing a new stress management technique.

FACTS

A recent study showed that stress management programs could reduce the risk of cardiac events such as heart attacks up to 75 percent in people who already have heart disease. Another study demonstrated that stress management may be even more effective than exercise for reducing cardiac risk.

Major changes are even easier. Any change, no matter how disturbing to you, can have its positive side, even if you can't find it right away. But finding the positive side isn't even the most important thing. The most important thing is a willingness to accept that, yes, things change and, yes, that you can go with the flow.

Passive, Aggressive, or Passive-Aggressive?

Some people tend to deal with stress passively, letting things happen to them without trying to control the situation. Others tend to be aggressive, taking their stressful situations forcefully in hand. The passive-aggressive among us forcefully control stress in a seemingly passive manner, by inflicting guilty feelings upon people or by subtly implying what they want while acting as though they don't care either way.

Each of these habitual methods of dealing with stress has its damaging effects. For the passive stress manager, stress can begin to feel like an uncontrollable force. While maintaining a passive attitude is sometimes recommended (in this book as well as elsewhere) for effectively managing the stressful changes inherent in life, too much passivity can engender a feeling of hopelessness. If you give up, if you are not in control at all, then what good is it to try to live the way you want to live? If you are a hapless leaf being blown randomly about by the wind, what importance do you have? For the naturally passive, assertiveness training is in order. Chakra meditation (see Chapter 8) can be an effective way to regain control over the things you really can control. Meditation may also help to clarify the areas of your life over which you really are lord and master.

For the aggressive stress manager, stress can begin to feel like a formidable foe to be vanquished, and while a gung-ho attitude can certainly be helpful in some situations, eventually it is physically and mentally exhausting. It also puts you on the defensive. You begin to feel as though fate is conspiring against you, throwing you one challenge after another, and that if you don't sock them all out of the ballpark with your great big bat, you'll be a great big failure. For the naturally aggressive, meditation can be a healing tool as well as an enlightening experience into the nature of reality. A Zen approach may be particularly helpful. If things simply are what they are, if right now is the only reality, and if there is nothing to be improved upon, what is there to be aggressive about? Learning to accept rather than attack is a valuable stress management skill for aggressive types.

For the passive-aggressive stress manager, stress is something to subvert with trickery. Even if you don't fully realize it, you don't handle stress directly. You manipulate your circumstances underhandedly so that you can get what you need without feeling as though you've behaved inappropriately. This, too, can be an effective way to deal with certain kinds of stress. Sometimes the stress in life is best nuzzled into submission with flowers and candy. But sometimes, the passive-aggressive way is simply indirect and therefore wholly ineffective. Like the mother who struggles into the house with an armload of groceries calling out, "Oh, my goodness, these groceries certainly are heavy; if only someone would give me a hand," you don't ask for what you need. You just complain loudly and hope someone will step in unbidden and help you out. Like the stubborn teenager on the couch patently ignoring her mother's non-request, the stress in your life might just stay put. A direct acknowledgement of the stress you have and direct action to purge it from your life might be much simpler.

Only you can decide if you fall into any (or all) of these categories, and only you can begin to make the necessary changes to readjust your stress management approach. But, if you tend to be passive, aggressive, or passive-aggressive, you may not be handling your stress as well as you might.

QUESTIONS?

Do your feelings of stress go in cycles?
Some people are more easily stressed at some times and less easily stressed at other times, no matter what is going on around them. On your calendar, keep track of how much stress you are feeling each day. Just write *high, medium high, medium, medium low,* or *low* on your calendar. After three months, see if you can spot any patterns. If you know when you are more likely to be stressed, you can be prepared and take precautionary measures by paring down your schedule and stepping up your relaxation efforts.

Stay Inspired

When life is stressful, the stress always seems easier, more manageable, if the circumstances lift you to heights of positive feeling. Staying inspired is key to maintaining the necessary energy, enthusiasm, and motivation for keeping your life on track, your stress in check, and your goals in sight.

For you, staying inspired might mean a commitment to a beloved hobby, starting your own business, learning something new, taking up an art form, writing a novel, volunteering, or staying in touch with inspiring friends. Whatever keeps you excited about the day, glowing with anticipation, and happy to be alive should be a priority. If you make time for your source of inspiration, you'll be happier and better able to handle "the stumbles along the path."

The Daily De-clutter

Whether your house contains mountains of clutter or one messy surface in a back room out of view, clutter attracts stress. Just looking at clutter suggests clutter to the mind. While de-cluttering your entire garage, basement, or bedroom closet may be a monumental task to accomplish all at once, any big de-cluttering job can be accomplished in small steps. Every day, spend five or ten minutes—no more, unless you schedule ahead to spend a larger block of time—de-cluttering something. Maybe it will be that dump-it table by the front door, or the pile of laundry on top of the dryer, or one corner of your desk. Whatever it is, clear something out once each day and feel your mind let out a sigh of relief.

The Weekly Spa

Who says you have to go to a pricey spa at a resort? Sure, such a vacation is nice if you can manage it, but you can give yourself a mini spa every week in the privacy of your own bathroom. Give yourself a manicure, a pedicure, a facial, and a hair conditioning treatment. Soak in the bathtub with a splash of lavender oil, then moisturize from head to toe. While you relax in your weekly spa, play tranquil music, soak by candlelight, burn incense in a scent you love, and think about things you love, beautiful places, calming images. You'll feel pampered, your skin will look great, and you'll be both relaxed and energized.

Family Time

Nothing renews you like time with the people you love, even if that time can also be stressful. People with strong family ties have a much larger base on which to rely in times of stress. Start building that base with regular family gatherings. The family that spends time together grows stronger together. Let family time be an important component of your stress management plan.

Quiet Time

Family is good, but time spent alone with yourself is equally important for physical, mental, and spiritual renewal. Let yourself reflect on you—who you are, what you want, where you are headed. Spend at least ten minutes each day in quiet reflection, with nobody else in the room. This healthy habit is an incredibly powerful stress management tool.

ALERT

Loneliness is bad for your health! Loneliness and lack of social support trigger the release of stress hormones that suppress the immune system, and, according to some experts, a lack of social support is as bad for you as smoking, obesity, or not exercising. Lonely people are less able to fight off infections and may be more susceptible to serious diseases such as cancer.

Be Your Own Best Friend

Only you really know what you need. Only you can make it happen for yourself. Only you can decide what is good for you, what is bad for you, what can make your life better, or what will make it worse. Be an advocate for yourself. Stand up for what you need. If you don't manage your stress, who will? A best friend should know you like he knows himself. Be your own best friend, and that's exactly what you'll have.

Antistress Vacations

It's vacation time. Do you know where you are going? Another visit to see relatives? Another cross-country drive with six people in the minivan? Another trek from one tourist attraction to the next?

If your vacation stresses you out just thinking about it, you are missing the point of a vacation. Vacations are for relaxation and renewal, a purposefully fulfilling break from your regular routine. Make the most of your vacation weeks to super-power your stress management. Consider any of these antistress vacation ideas:

- **One man's cruise . . .** Some people live for their next cruise vacation. For others, being stuck on a boat with a bunch of strangers sounds anything but relaxing. But today's cruises come in all shapes and sizes. Check with your travel agent if you like the idea of hitting the open sea.
- **The spa.** If you want to be treated to a truly tranquil experience and you don't mind the price tag, visit one of the world's spas. Spa vacations are luxurious and offer everything from healthy cuisine and massages to meditation sessions, spirituality programs, yoga classes, and hikes to breathtaking vistas.
- **The nature experience.** If you are relaxed and renewed by nature, consider one of the many nature experience vacations. These vacations involve varying levels of physical activity in interesting natural places all over the world, from California to Tibet, from Colorado to the Alps.
- **The tropics.** If relaxing on the beach is your idea of a stress-free vacation, then go for it. Beaches rim the continent. You can even cross the ocean and vacation on a tropical island (Aruba, the Bahamas, Hawaii . . .). Let yourself bask.
- **The extreme vacation.** Basking's not your style? The extreme vacation is an increasingly popular concept involving the training in and

executing of some kind of extreme sport such as sky diving, parasailing, hang gliding, or mountain climbing. If that's your idea of a good time—and intense athletic activity is certainly an excellent way to learn mental focus—then go for it! (Just be careful!)

- **The don't-tell-anybody-but-we're-staying-home vacation.** Who says you have to leave the comfort of your own home just because you aren't going to work? Sometimes, the most relaxing vacation is the one that you *don't* take. Staying home means you can catch up on all those nagging, stress-inducing chores you need to finish; you can sleep in a little longer than usual; you don't have to spend the money associated with a vacation; and you won't have to deal with traveling, time changes, money exchanges, traveler's checks, or not being able to speak the language. If you don't tell anybody you're staying home, you'll have more freedom than ever. You can learn to appreciate your own home more than ever if you spend your vacation in it. It's not against the rules!

Stress Management for Life

You can change your life for the better simply by clearing out the stress that doesn't have to be there and managing the stress that does. You can feel better today, and you can feel even better in a few days, a few weeks, a few months, a few years. Stress management is for life, and with little changes here and there, with vigilance, with monitoring, and with a continued commitment to maximizing your individual potential by minimizing the things that are holding you back, things can only look up.

I'll leave you with ten final tips for managing the stress in your life for the rest of your life. You can do it! Stop wasting your time and letting the best part of you drain away from lack of energy. Let yourself be strong, energized, and in control of you.

1. **Know thyself, know thy stress.** You are worth your own time. The more you know about yourself, the more you'll understand about what stresses you out and what you can do about it.

2. **Stay tuned in.** Pay attention to how you feel. Write it down. Keep track, and you'll understand more about what needs to be done and why you do the things you do when life gets stressful.

3. **Keep building your stress management network.** Nobody can do it all alone. Let your friends and family help you, and be there to help them, too.

4. **Believe in yourself.** If you can break past the barriers, you can be that person you know you are inside. Trust in yourself and have confidence in yourself, even when it seems like nobody else does. Only you know your true potential.

5. **Keep your perspective.** When things seem out of control, step back to gain perspective. What will this mean in the scheme of things? What are your options? What are some alternate strategies? Is it worth letting go of this one?

6. **Don't worry, be happy!** Trite by now, perhaps, but it's a catchy song and even catchier advice. If you find yourself worrying, stop. Do something that makes you happy instead. It's good medicine.

7. **Accept what you can't control.** You have control over what you say, do, and, in some cases, feel. You don't have control over what other people say, do, or feel. You don't have control over many of the things that happen to you or affect you in life. If you can't control it, you might as well accept it. Anything else is just a waste of energy.

8. **Control what you can control.** You don't have to accept the negative effects of stress on your body, mind, and spirit. You don't have to agree to do everything you are asked. You don't have to be overwhelmed, overscheduled, or overworked. If you can control it, figure out a way to control it. It's your life. Nobody else is in charge but you. So, start being in charge!

9. **Live, love, laugh.** Those three things make it all worthwhile and put stress in its proper place.

10. **Always take care.** Take care of yourself. You are a person worth caring for. You deserve to love yourself and feel good about yourself, no matter what your imperfections. If you take care of yourself, you'll be in the best possible state to take care of others. It's all connected, after all.

Stress is just something that happens to us, that's all. It doesn't impact who you are inside, and its presence in your life says nothing about you, except, perhaps, that you are human. But if stress is hurting you, you can make it stop. Commit to yourself, commit to stress management, commit to being happy, and you'll find that it's looking like fair weather on the road ahead.

Good luck to you as you go along your way.

Appendix A

Stress Management Tools Reference Guide

H ere is your alphabetical listing of tools, techniques, and therapies for combating the stress in your life. Try a few, or try them all. You'll be managing your stress in no time!

Alexander technique: The Alexander technique is movement instruction in which clients are taught to move and hold their bodies with full consciousness and in a way that releases tension and uses the body to its best advantage. People say that practicing the Alexander technique makes them feel lighter and more in control of their bodies. The Alexander technique is popular with actors and other performing artists.

Applied kinesiology: This is a muscle testing technique that helps people determine where in the body they are experiencing an imbalance or problem. Then, massage as well as movement of certain joints, acupressure, and advice on diet, vitamins, and herbs are offered as treatment.

Art therapy: In art therapy, you can use any art form as an expression of creativity to help release stressful feelings.

Assertiveness training: Assertiveness training helps you to be direct and assertive rather than indirect. It helps to combat the tendency to internalize stress, anger, disappointment, fear, and pain by teaching techniques for acknowledging and expressing these feelings in effective and appropriate ways.

Attitude adjustment: Being negative is a habit, and adjusting your attitude to be more positive can be a habit, too. Just like any habit, the more you get used to halting your negative reactions and replacing them with neutral or positive reactions, the less you'll find yourself reacting negatively. Instead of "Oh NO," react with silence and take a wait-and-see attitude. Or react with an affirmation: "Oh . . . I can learn something positive from this!"

Autogenic training: Autogenic training, or autogenics, was designed to reap the benefits of hypnosis without the need for a hypnotist or the time typically involved in a hypnosis session. Autogenics uses a relaxed position and the verbal suggestion of warmth and heaviness in the limbs

to induce a state of deep relaxation and stress relief. Autogenics have been used to treat muscle tension, asthma, gastrointestinal problems, irregular heartbeat, high blood pressure, headaches, thyroid problems, anxiety, irritability, and fatigue. It can also increase your stress resistance.

Ayurveda: Ayurveda (pronounced I-YOUR-VAY-DA) is an ancient Indian science of living a long and healthy life, defying disease and aging, and promoting well-being and good health through a variety of practices. Ayurveda may be the oldest known health care system, probably over 5,000 years old! Amazingly, it is still widely practiced today.

Biofeedback: This high-tech relaxation technique, designed to teach the body how to directly and immediately reverse the stress response, puts you in control of the bodily functions once considered to be involuntary. A biofeedback session involves getting hooked up to equipment that measures certain bodily functions such as your skin temperature, heart rate, breathing rate, and muscle tension. A trained biofeedback counselor then guides the patient through relaxation techniques while the patient watches the machine monitors. When heart rate or breathing rate decreases, for example, you can see it on the monitor. You learn how your body feels when your heart and breathing rate decrease. Eventually, after a number of sessions, you learn to lower your heart rate, breath rate, muscle tension, temperature, and so forth, on your own.

Body scan: This is a relaxation technique involving a systematic scan of the body and conscious relaxation of tense areas.

Breathing exercises: These exercises involve any of various techniques for infusing the body with oxygen and energy, for the purposes of improved health and relaxation.

Breathing meditation: This meditation involves any of various techniques of measured, controlled breathing to relax the body and improve health.

Chakra meditation: This involves meditation on the seven chakras, or energy centers, in the body. Meditating to open and energize the chakras is an effective technique for freeing the body to do the work of extinguishing the negative effects of stress.

Conscious moderation: Conscious moderation involves making a conscious effort to consume food, drink, and other resources, including money, moderately for greater inner and outer balance.

Creativity therapy: In this therapy, you use creative expression, such as painting, writing, poetry, or playing music, as a way to release stressful feelings.

Dance: Whether you take an organized class—ballet, jazz, tap, ballroom dancing, swing dancing, country dancing, square dancing, Irish dancing, to name a few—or go out dancing with your friends every weekend, dancing is great cardiovascular exercise and also a lot of fun.

Dream journaling: Dream journaling is recording the dream images you remember every morning, then looking over them periodically to detect recurring themes.

Exercise: Exercise involves moving the body to improve health, mood, strength, flexibility, and cardiopulmonary function and to release excessive energy such as that generated by the stress response.

Feng shui: The ancient Chinese art of placement is used in the twenty-first century to help people enhance the flow of positive energy through their homes and properties.

Flower remedies: Flower remedies or flower essences are substances made from water and whole flowers, then preserved with alcohol. They contain no actual flower parts, but people who use and prescribe them believe they contain the flower's essence or energy and can promote emotional healing.

Friend therapy: Friend therapy is simple: Let your friends help you manage your stress! Research shows that people without social networks and friends often feel lonely but often won't admit it. Loneliness is stressful. Holding in your feelings is even more stressful. Sharing your feelings with your friends helps you to experience them and move on.

Gym/health club: This is a nice way to have lots of fitness options in one place.

Habit restructuring: Habit restructuring involves working to consciously eliminate or redirect habits that are having a negative effect on the body or mind.

Herbal medicine: Herbal remedies are taken for better health and stress resistance. Practice with caution or under the guidance of an experienced and qualified herbalist.

Homeopathy: Homeopathic remedies are taken for better health and stress resistance. They are highly diluted substances that counteract the symptoms of certain diseases.

Hypnosis: Hypnosis involves deep relaxation coupled with visualization and is achieved through a systematic process. When hypnotized, you retain your awareness, but your body becomes extremely relaxed and disinclined to move, your awareness becomes narrow, your thinking tends to become literal, and you become much more open to suggestion than you would be in a nonhypnotic state. This suggestibility allows for hypnosis to help relieve stress and correct undesirable behaviors.

Imagery meditation: This is a meditation technique that helps you imagine yourself in a different place or circumstance in order to induce relaxation.

Journaling: Writing in a journal is a way to release stressful feelings.

Lifestyle management techniques: These involve any techniques for improving and easing daily life, including techniques for simplicity, de-cluttering, organizing, time management, relationship management, family dynamics, and self-improvement.

Light therapy: This is a treatment for Seasonal Affective Disorder (SAD) that involves exposing the skin to full-spectrum light for extended periods of time to improve mood and symptoms of depression.

Mandala meditation: In mandala meditation, a significant kind of meditation in Tibetan culture, the focus of meditation is a mandala, or circular picture, sometimes very plain, sometimes highly ornate, containing designs that draw the eye to the center of the mandala, helping the mind to focus on that center point.

Mantra meditation: Any concentrated focusing while repeating a sound can be called a mantra meditation, whether it's Sufi chanting or the recitation of the rosary prayer. Some people believe that the sounds of a mantra actually contain certain powers; others believe that the key to mantra meditation is the repetition itself, and that any sound would do.

Massage therapy: In massage therapy, any of various massage techniques are used to relax the muscles and free blocked energy in the body.

Meditation: Meditation is focused concentration to gain control over the wayward mind and enhance relaxation.

Mindfulness meditation: This is a type of meditation in which the meditator maintains a mindful, highly observant state. Mindfulness

meditation is different from other meditations because it can be practiced anywhere, anytime, no matter what you are doing. It is simply focusing on total awareness of the present moment. Mindfulness meditation is inherent in many other forms of meditation, but it can also be practiced while walking, running, playing basketball, driving, studying, writing, reading, eating. Anything you are doing, you can do with mindfulness.

Nutrition: You should eat a variety of fresh, natural foods in moderate amounts to improve health and the body's ability to handle stress.

Optimism therapy: So, you think you are a confirmed pessimist? Optimism therapy is like an attitude adjustment but focused on the purposeful reframing responses as an optimist. Studies show that optimists enjoy better general health, a stronger immune system, faster surgical recovery, and longer life than pessimists.

Pain centering: This is a pain management technique that focuses on pain as an experience apart from the suffering and negative associations.

Passive attitude: Having a passive attitude can be a good way to manage stress. By having an "Oh well" attitude about stressful events you can't control, you can give yourself permission to let the stressful feelings go.

Pilates: This consists of specific core-strengthening exercises performed on a mat or on special machines that concentrate on the abdominal and back muscles.

Polarity therapy: Polarity therapy is a little like Reiki in that it is designed to free and balance the body's internal energy, but polarity therapy is more of a melding of Eastern and Western approaches, including massage, dietary counseling, certain yoga exercises, and psychological counseling for a full mind-body approach to energy balancing.

Pranayama: Pranayama consists of the specific breathing techniques of yoga.

Prayer: Prayer consists of focused, concentrated communication, a statement of intention, or the opening of the channel between you and divinity, whatever divinity is for you. A prayer can be a request, thanks, worship, or praise to God. It can be an intention of being thankful directed to the universe. It can be used to invoke divine power or an attempt to experience divine or universal energy directly. Many different traditions have many different modes and types of prayer. Prayer can mean whatever you want it to mean for you.

Reflexology: Reflexology is a little like acupressure, but in reflexology, all the pressure points are in the hands and feet. The theory goes that the entire body, including all the parts, organs, and glands, is represented in a "map" on the hands and feet, and that pressure applied to the right area of the "map" will help to balance the problem in the associated area of the body. Knowing the map allows people to work on themselves by rubbing their own hands or feet in the appropriate area.

Reiki: Reiki (pronounced RAY-KEY) is an energy healing technique based in ancient Tibetan practices. Practitioners of Reiki put their hands on or just above the body in order to balance energy by acting as a sort of conduit for life force energy. Reiki is used to treat physical problems as well as emotional and psychological problems, and it is, more positively, also used as a tool to support and facilitate positive changes.

Relaxation techniques: These include any of many techniques for relaxing the body and mind.

Reward-based self-training: This training involves choosing behaviors you want to establish, then rewarding yourself for your improvements and successes rather than punishing yourself for your slips and failures.

Rolfing: Rolfing is a deep type of massage designed to restructure the body's muscles and connective tissue to promote better alignment. If you like your massages hard, this one's for you. Some people claim that the deep tissue massage actually releases deeply buried emotions and that emotional outbursts are common during the course of the ten-session program.

Self-care: In self-care, you make a conscious regular effort to care for yourself and attend to your own physical, emotional, and spiritual needs.

Self-esteem maintenance: This requires working consciously to maintain and protect self-esteem for better physical and mental health and performance.

Self-hypnosis: This is a technique for hypnotizing oneself to achieve goals and stop negative behaviors.

Self-massage: If you learn about acupressure, Swedish massage, reflexology, and many other techniques, you can perform massage on yourself. You can massage your own neck, scalp, face, hands, feet, legs, arms, and torso. Many yoga postures also result in internal and external massage by bending the body in certain ways against itself or by using the pressure of the floor against certain parts of the body.

Shavasana: Shavasana, or corpse pose, is a yoga position that involves complete relaxation of the body.

Shiatsu and acupressure: *Shiatsu* is the Japanese word for "finger pressure" and is sometimes known as acupressure. Shiatsu is an ancient form of massage still widely practiced that involves the application of pressure through fingers, palms, elbows, or knees to pressure points in the body.

Sleep: Most adults need about eight hours of sleep each day, and some need even more. Getting enough sleep is an important step toward being able to manage stress.

Swedish massage: This common form of massage involves a massage therapist applying oil to the body and applying certain types of massage strokes—namely, *effleurage* (gliding), *petrissage* (kneading), *friction* (rubbing), and *tapotement* (tapping)—to increase circulation in muscles and connective tissue, help the body to flush out waste products, and heal injuries.

Swimming: Swimming is especially good for people who can't take much stress on joints, who are overweight and just beginning to exercise, or who enjoy being in the water.

Tai chi/chi kung: Tai chi and its precursor, chi kung (sometimes called Qigong), are ancient Chinese Taoist martial arts forms that have evolved into a series of slow, graceful movements, in concert with the breath, designed to free internal energy and keep it flowing through the body, uniting body and mind, promoting good health and relaxation. Tai chi is sometimes called a moving meditation. Chi kung involves specific movements and postures as well as other health-maintenance procedures such as massage and meditation to maintain and improve overall health and balance the body's internal energy (called "chi" in China).

Team sports: For people who like to play on a team and are motivated and energized by the energy of others, team sports can be an excellent way to get exercise and a social life at the same time.

Thought stopping: Thought stopping is the practice of noticing destructive or obsessive thoughts and consciously telling yourself to stop, then re-directing your thoughts in a more positive way.

Visualization: This is the technique of imagining something you want or a change you would like to see in yourself in order to mentally set your intention and help to effect the changes.

Vitamin/mineral therapy: This therapy involves taking vitamins and minerals to cover your nutritional bases and protect against deficiencies for better health and a more stress-resistant body.

Walking meditation: This is a form of meditation that is practiced while walking.

Walking: A versatile exercise choice for people of any fitness level, walking is excellent for boosting mood and reducing stressful feelings as well as improving physical fitness.

Water: To keep the body well hydrated and properly functioning, drink sixty-four to eighty ounces of water each day.

Weightlifting: Lifting weights is great for any adult. It builds bone mass and can reverse osteoporosis. It increases muscle tone and helps your body to burn more calories because the more muscle you have, the more calories you burn during the aerobic portion of your workout.

Worry control: Worry control involves learning to recognize obsessive worrying and re-direct that energy in more positive ways.

Yoga: Yoga is an ancient Indian method of exercise designed to "yoke" body and mind through specific postures, breathing exercises, and meditation.

Yoga meditation: This is a form of meditation designed to help the meditator recognize ultimate oneness with the universe; it can result in a state of pure, joyful bliss called samadhi.

Zazen: Zazen is the sitting meditation of Zen Buddhism, although many non-Buddhists practice zazen. It involves just sitting and is not necessarily affiliated with a religion or philosophy. When practiced regularly, just sitting becomes a mental discipline that results in a greater ability to manage stress.

APPENDIX B

Stress Management Resources for Easier Living

W hen it comes to stress management, knowledge is power. These resources will help you to further your knowledge about stress, good health, good nutrition, and yourself. I've also listed organizations you can contact for more information, therapy, or relaxation and Web sites for stress-free Web surfing. Happy explorations!

Note: Inclusion of resources in this book does not necessarily imply endorsement of these resources' health-related content, products, or services.

Organizations and Web Sites

American Academy of Experts in
Traumatic Stress
368 Veterans Memorial Highway
Commack, NY
631-543-2217
www.aaets.org

American Institute of Stress
124 Park Avenue
Yonkers, NY 10703
Phone 914-963-1200
Fax 914-965-6267
stress124@earthlink.net, *www.stress.org*

Ask Dr. Weil
Andrew Weil M.D.'s informative Web site on
integrative medicine and whole-self health care:
www.drweil.com

Center for Creativity
8360 Fenton Street
Silver Spring, MD 20910
301-589-6823
artstherapy@center4creativity.com
www.center4creativity.com

Center for Journal Therapy
12477 W. Cedar Drive #102
Lakewood, CO 80228
888-421-2298
info@journaltherapy.com
www.journaltherapy.com

Eating Disorder Referral and
Information Center:
www.edreferral.com

FlyLady, online help for the housework-
challenged:
www.flylady.net

Grief Net online grief support network:
www.griefnet.org

Healthjourneys, the Guided Imagery
Resource Center:
www.healthjourneys.com

National Association for Self-Esteem:
www.self-esteem-nase.org

National Center for Post Traumatic
Stress Disorder
802-296-5132
ncptsd@ncptsd.org
www.ncptsd.org

National Sleep Foundation:
www.sleepfoundation.org

Next Generation Yoga for Kids
200 West 72nd Street, Suite 58
New York, NY 10023
212-595-9306
jodibk@nextgenerationyoga.com,
www.nextgenerationyoga.com

Seeds of Simplicity: Organizing and Educating Voluntary Simplicity
P.O. Box 9955
Glendale, CA 91226
Phone & Fax: 818-247-4332, 1-877-UNSTUFF
www.seedsofsimplicity.org

Simple Joy e-zine: *www.simplejoy.org*

Stress Management Resources:
www.mentalhealth.about.com/health/ mentalhealth/cs/stressmanagement

Yoyoga with Joan: *www.yoyoga.com*

Books

Aslett, Don. *Is There Life after Housework?* Cincinnati, OH: Writer's Digest Books, 1992.

Beck, Mark F. *The Theory and Practice of Therapeutic Massage,* 2nd edition. Albany, NY: Milady Publishing Company, 1994.

Benson, Herbert, M.D. *The Relaxation Response,* Updated and Expanded Edition. New York: Avon Books, 2000.

Budilovsky, Joan, and Eve Adamson. *The Complete Idiot's Guide to Yoga,* 2nd edition. Indianapolis, IN: Alpha Books, 2001.

Budilovsky, Joan, and Eve Adamson. *The Complete Idiot's Guide to Meditation.* Indianapolis, IN: Alpha Books, 1999.

Budilovsky, Joan, and Eve Adamson. *The Complete Idiot's Guide to Massage.* Indianapolis, IN: Alpha Books, 1998.

Cameron, Julia. *The Artist's Way.* New York: Jeremy P. Tarcher/Putnam, 1992.

Carter, Karen Rauch. *Move Your Stuff, Change Your Life.* New York: Fireside, 2000.

Chopra, Deepak, M.D. *Ageless Body, Timeless Mind.* New York: Harmony Books, 1993.

Chopra, Deepak, M.D. *Creating Health,* Revised Edition. Boston: Houghton Mifflin Company, 1991.

Chopra, Deepak, M.D. *Perfect Health.* New York: Harmony Books, 1991.

Claire, Thomas. *Bodywork: What Type of Massage to Get and How to Make the Most of It.* New York: Quill, 1995.

Davich, Victor N. *The Best Guide to Meditation.* Los Angeles, CA: Renaissance Books, 1998.

David, Martha, Ph.D., Elizabeth Robbins Eshelman, M.S.W., and Matthew McKay, Ph.D. *The Relaxation & Stress Reduction Workbook,* 5th edition. Oakland, CA: New Harbinger Publications, 2000.

Dominguez, Joe, and Vicki Robin. *Your Money or Your Life,* New Edition. New York: Penguin Books, 1992.

Elgin, Duane. *Voluntary Simplicity,* Revised Edition. New York: Quill, 1993.

Epstein, Mark, M.D. *Going to Pieces Without Falling Apart.* New York: Broadway Books, 1998.

Farhi, Donna. *The Breathing Book.* New York: Henry Holt & Company, 1996.

Goleman, Daniel, Ph.D., and Joel Gurin (editors). *Mind-Body Medicine.* Yonkers, NY: Consumer Reports Books, 1993.

Goliszek, Andrew, Ph.D. *60 Second Stress Management.* Far Hills, NJ: New Horizon Press, 1992.

Hanh, Thich Nhat. *Peace Is Every Step*. New York: Bantam Books, 1992.

Harbin, Thomas. *Beyond Anger: A Guide for Men: How to Free Yourself from the Grip of Anger and Get More out of Life*. Marlowe & Company, 2000.

Harrar, Sari, and Sara Altshul O'Donnell. *The Woman's Book of Healing Herbs*. Emmaus, PA: Rodale Press, Inc., 1999.

Johnson, Don Hanlon (editor). *Bone, Breath, & Gesture*. Berkeley, CA: North Atlantic Books, 1995.

Kabat-Zinn, Jon, Ph.D. *Full Catastrophe Living: Using the Wisdom of Your Body and Mind to Face Stress, Pain, and Illness*. New York: Delta, 1990.

Kirsta, Alex. *The Book of Stress Survival*. New York, NY: Simon & Schuster, Inc., 1986.

Klauser, Henriette Anne. *Write It Down, Make It Happen*. New York: Scribner, 2000.

Lacroix, Nitya. *Relaxation: 101 Essential Tips*. New York: DK Publishing, 1998.

Linn, Denise. *Sacred Space: Clearing and Enhancing the Energy of Your Home*. New York: Ballantine Books, 1995.

Monro, Robin, R. Nagaranthna, and H. R. Nagendra. *Yoga for Common Ailments*. New York: Simon & Schuster, Inc., 1990.

Morgenstern, Julie. *Organizing from the Inside Out*. New York: Henry Holt and Company, 1998.

Northrup, Christiane, M.D. *The Wisdom of Menopause: Creating Physical and Emotional Health and Healing During the Change*. New York: Bantam Books, 2001.

Orman, Suze. *The 9 Steps to Financial Freedom*. New York: Crown Publishers, Inc., 1997.

Richardson, Cheryl. *Life Makeovers*. New York: Broadway Books, 2000.

Schiffman, Erich. *Yoga: The Spirit and Practice of Moving into Stillness*. New York: Pocket Books, 1996.

St. James, Elaine. *The Simplicity Reader*. New York: Smithmark, 1998.

Tirtha, Swami Sada Shiva. *The Ayurveda Encyclopedia*. Bayville, NY: Ayurveda Holistic Center Press, 1998.

Van de Castle, Robert L., Ph.D. *Our Dreaming Mind*. New York: Ballantine Books, 1994.

Weil, Andrew, M.D. *Eight Weeks to Optimum Health*. New York: Alfred A. Knopf, 1998.

Whitaker, Julian, M.D., and Carol Colman. *Shed 10 Years in 10 Weeks*. New York: Simon & Schuster, 1997.

Index

We Have EVERYTHING!

Everything® **After College Book**
$12.95, 1-55850-847-3

Everything® **American History Book**
$12.95, 1-58062-531-2

Everything® **Angels Book**
$12.95, 1-58062-398-0

Everything® **Anti-Aging Book**
$12.95, 1-58062-565-7

Everything® **Astrology Book**
$12.95, 1-58062-062-0

Everything® **Baby Names Book**
$12.95, 1-55850-655-1

Everything® **Baby Shower Book**
$12.95, 1-58062-305-0

Everything® **Baby's First Food Book**
$12.95, 1-58062-512-6

Everything® **Baby's First Year Book**
$12.95, 1-58062-581-9

Everything® **Barbeque Cookbook**
$12.95, 1-58062-316-6

Everything® **Bartender's Book**
$9.95, 1-55850-536-9

Everything® **Bedtime Story Book**
$12.95, 1-58062-147-3

Everything® **Bicycle Book**
$12.00, 1-55850-706-X

Everything® **Build Your Own Home Page**
$12.95, 1-58062-339-5

Everything® **Business Planning Book**
$12.95, 1-58062-491-X

Everything® **Casino Gambling Book**
$12.95, 1-55850-762-0

Everything® **Cat Book**
$12.95, 1-55850-710-8

Everything® **Chocolate Cookbook**
$12.95, 1-58062-405-7

Everything® **Christmas Book**
$15.00, 1-55850-697-7

Everything® **Civil War Book**
$12.95, 1-58062-366-2

Everything® **College Survival Book**
$12.95, 1-55850-720-5

Everything® **Computer Book**
$12.95, 1-58062-401-4

Everything® **Cookbook**
$14.95, 1-58062-400-6

Everything® **Cover Letter Book**
$12.95, 1-58062-312-3

Everything® **Crossword and Puzzle Book**
$12.95, 1-55850-764-7

Everything® **Dating Book**
$12.95, 1-58062-185-6

Everything® **Dessert Book**
$12.95, 1-55850-717-5

Everything® **Digital Photography Book**
$12.95, 1-58062-574-6

Everything® **Dog Book**
$12.95, 1-58062-144-9

Everything® **Dreams Book**
$12.95, 1-55850-806-6

Everything® **Etiquette Book**
$12.95, 1-55850-807-4

Everything® **Fairy Tales Book**
$12.95, 1-58062-546-0

Everything® **Family Tree Book**
$12.95, 1-55850-763-9

Everything® **Fly-Fishing Book**
$12.95, 1-58062-148-1

Everything® **Games Book**
$12.95, 1-55850-643-8

Everything® **Get-A-Job Book**
$12.95, 1-58062-223-2

Everything® **Get Published Book**
$12.95, 1-58062-315-8

Everything® **Get Ready for Baby Book**
$12.95, 1-55850-844-9

Everything® **Ghost Book**
$12.95, 1-58062-533-9

Everything® **Golf Book**
$12.95, 1-55850-814-7

Everything® **Grammar and Style Book**
$12.95, 1-58062-573-8

Everything® **Guide to Las Vegas**
$12.95, 1-58062-438-3

Everything® **Guide to New York City**
$12.95, 1-58062-314-X

Everything® **Guide to Walt Disney World®, Universal Studios®, and Greater Orlando, 2nd Edition**
$12.95, 1-58062-404-9

Everything® **Guide to Washington, D.C.**
$12.95, 1-58062-313-1

Everything® **Guitar Book**
$12.95, 1-58062-555-X

Everything® **Herbal Remedies Book**
$12.95, 1-58062-331-X

Everything® **Home-Based Business Book**
$12.95, 1-58062-364-6

Everything® **Homebuying Book**
$12.95, 1-58062-074-4

Everything® **Homeselling Book**
$12.95, 1-58062-304-2

For more information, or to order, call 800-872-5627 or visit everything.com

Adams Media Corporation, 57 Littlefield Street, Avon, MA 02322

Available wherever books are sold!
Visit us at everything.com

Everything® **Home Improvement Book**
$12.95, 1-55850-718-3

Everything® **Horse Book**
$12.95, 1-58062-564-9

Everything® **Hot Careers Book**
$12.95, 1-58062-486-3

Everything® **Internet Book**
$12.95, 1-58062-073-6

Everything® **Investing Book**
$12.95, 1-58062-149-X

Everything® **Jewish Wedding Book**
$12.95, 1-55850-801-5

Everything® **Job Interviews Book**
$12.95, 1-58062-493-6

Everything® **Lawn Care Book**
$12.95, 1-58062-487-1

Everything® **Leadership Book**
$12.95, 1-58062-513-4

Everything® **Learning Spanish Book**
$12.95, 1-58062-575-4

Everything® **Low-Fat High-Flavor Cookbook**
$12.95, 1-55850-802-3

Everything® **Magic Book**
$12.95, 1-58062-418-9

Everything® **Managing People Book**
$12.95, 1-58062-577-0

Everything® **Microsoft® Word 2000 Book**
$12.95, 1-58062-306-9

Everything® **Money Book**
$12.95, 1-58062-145-7

Everything® **Mother Goose Book**
$12.95, 1-58062-490-1

Everything® **Mutual Funds Book**
$12.95, 1-58062-419-7

Everything® **One-Pot Cookbook**
$12.95, 1-58062-186-4

Everything® **Online Business Book**
$12.95, 1-58062-320-4

Everything® **Online Genealogy Book**
$12.95, 1-58062-402-2

Everything® **Online Investing Book**
$12.95, 1-58062-338-7

Everything® **Online Job Search Book**
$12.95, 1-58062-365-4

Everything® **Pasta Book**
$12.95, 1-55850-719-1

Everything® **Pregnancy Book**
$12.95, 1-58062-146-5

Everything® **Pregnancy Organizer**
$15.00, 1-58062-336-0

Everything® **Project Management Book**
$12.95, 1-58062-583-5

Everything® **Puppy Book**
$12.95, 1-58062-576-2

Everything® **Quick Meals Cookbook**
$12.95, 1-58062-488-X

Everything® **Resume Book**
$12.95, 1-58062-311-5

Everything® **Romance Book**
$12.95, 1-58062-566-5

Everything® **Sailing Book**
$12.95, 1-58062-187-2

Everything® **Saints Book**
$12.95, 1-58062-534-7

Everything® **Selling Book**
$12.95, 1-58062-319-0

Everything® **Spells and Charms Book**
$12.95, 1-58062-532-0

Everything® **Stress Management Book**
$12.95, 1-58062-578-9

Everything® **Study Book**
$12.95, 1-55850-615-2

Everything® **Tall Tales, Legends, and Outrageous Lies Book**
$12.95, 1-58062-514-2

Everything® **Tarot Book**
$12.95, 1-58062-191-0

Everything® **Time Management Book**
$12.95, 1-58062-492-8

Everything® **Toasts Book**
$12.95, 1-58062-189-9

Everything® **Total Fitness Book**
$12.95, 1-58062-318-2

Everything® **Trivia Book**
$12.95, 1-58062-143-0

Everything® **Tropical Fish Book**
$12.95, 1-58062-343-3

Everything® **Vitamins, Minerals, and Nutritional Supplements Book**
$12.95, 1-58062-496-0

Everything® **Wedding Book, 2nd Edition**
$12.95, 1-58062-190-2

Everything® **Wedding Checklist**
$7.95, 1-58062-456-1

Everything® **Wedding Etiquette Book**
$7.95, 1-58062-454-5

Everything® **Wedding Organizer**
$15.00, 1-55850-828-7

Everything® **Wedding Shower Book**
$7.95, 1-58062-188-0

Everything® **Wedding Vows Book**
$7.95, 1-58062-455-3

Everything® **Wine Book**
$12.95, 1-55850-808-2

Everything® **World War II Book**
$12.95, 1-58062-572-X

Everything® is a registered trademark of Adams Media Corporation.

For more information, or to order, call 800-872-5627
or visit everything.com
Adams Media Corporation, 57 Littlefield Street, Avon, MA 02322

We Have

EVERYTHING® KIDS'®!

Everything® Kids' Baseball Book
$9.95, 1-58062-489-8

Everything® Kids' Joke Book
$9.95, 1-58062-495-2

Everything® Kids' Mazes Book
$6.95, 1-58062-558-4

Everything® Kids' Money Book
$9.95, 1-58062-322-0

Everything® Kids' Nature Book
$9.95, 1-58062-321-2

Everything® Kids' Online Book
$9.95, 1-58062-394-8

Everything® Kids' Puzzle Book
$9.95, 1-58062-323-9

Everything® Kids' Science Experiments Book
$6.95, 1-58062-557-6

Everything® Kids' Space Book
$9.95, 1-58062-395-6

Everything® Kids' Witches and Wizards Book
$9.95, 1-58062-396-4

Available wherever books are sold!

For more information, or to order,
call 800-872-5627 or visit everything.com

Adams Media Corporation, 57 Littlefield Street, Avon, MA 02322

Everything® is a registered trademark of Adams Media Corporation.